A WORKING COSTUME DESIGNER'S GUIDE TO FIT

T0347363

A Working Costume Designer's Guide to Fit explores the concept of fit in theatrical costumes – what it is, how to assess it, and how to achieve it.

Being able to assess whether a costume fits or not is a learned skill, which takes practice as well as information about what the fit standards are for different types of garments. Filled with detailed step-by-step illustrations, this book provides all the knowledge readers will need in order to achieve the perfect fit for their costumes, including:

- How costumes can support actors onstage when they fit correctly.
- How to take measurements and how to assess them.
- How to conduct a fitting and what materials are needed.
- How to resolve a number of issues that may arise during a fitting.
- How to fit a mockup test garment in preparation for building a costume from scratch.
- How to adjust a garment or mockup to fit better.

Chapters 8–14 also explore different categories of garments and discuss how to check them against the wearer's measurements before trying them on, what the standards of fit are for each category, and how to fit an existing garment.

This is an essential guide for students of Costume Design courses and professional costume designers of any experience level.

Jeanette deJong is an Associate Professor of Costume Design, History, and Technology at the University of Oregon. A member of United Scenic Artists, she has been designing costumes and teaching Costume Design since 1984. She is also the author of *A Working Costume Designer's Guide to Color* (Routledge, 2021). Her professional design credits include shows at Cincinnati

Playhouse in the Park, Indiana Repertory Theatre, Williamstown Theatre Festival, Actors Theatre of Louisville, Oregon Contemporary Theatre, Utah Shakespeare Festival, and Illinois Shakespeare Festival, amongst many other theatres. Her technical costume credits include shows at Glimmerglass Opera, Williamstown Theatre Festival, Seattle Repertory Theatre, Intiman Theatre, and Parsons-Meares Studio, New York.

A WORKING COSTUME DESIGNER'S GUIDE TO FIT

Jeanette deJong

Routledge
Taylor & Francis Group

NEW YORK AND LONDON

Designed cover image: © Jeanette deJong

First published 2023
by Routledge
605 Third Avenue, New York, NY 10158

and by Routledge
4 Park Square, Milton Park, Abingdon, Oxon, OX14 4RN

Routledge is an imprint of the Taylor & Francis Group, an informa business

© 2023 Jeanette deJong

Library of Congress Cataloging-in-Publication Data
Names: DeJong, Jeanette author.
Title: A working costume designer's guide to fit / Jeanette deJong.
Description: New York : Routledge, 2023. | Includes bibliographical
references and index.
Identifiers: LCCN 2022036823 (print) |
LCCN 2022036824 (ebook) | ISBN 9780815352181 (hardback) |
ISBN 9780815352174 (paperback) | ISBN 9781351131353 (ebook)
Subjects: LCSH: Costume design--Handbooks, manuals, etc. |
Tailoring--Handbooks, manuals, etc.
Classification: LCC PN2067 .D385 2023 (print) |
LCC PN2067 (ebook) | DDC 792.02/6--dc23/eng/20221107
LC record available at https://lccn.loc.gov/2022036823
LC ebook record available at https://lccn.loc.gov/2022036824

ISBN: 978-0-815-35218-1 (hbk)
ISBN: 978-0-815-35217-4 (pbk)
ISBN: 978-1-351-13135-3 (ebk)

DOI: 10.4324/9781351131353

Typeset in Bembo
by KnowledgeWorks Global Ltd.

CONTENTS

ACKNOWLEDGMENTS

A very heartfelt THANK YOU to the people who have helped me along the way to creating this book:

Owen Saffell and Charlie Saffell-deJong for their love and support;

Lucia Accorsi for her patience;

Heather Bair for her kindness;

And, especially, THANK YOU to all of the directors, costume shop managers, costume technicians, actors, and students who have shared their artistry with me.

INTRODUCTION

I have been a theater costume designer, technician, and educator for over 35 years. All three aspects of my background have informed and enriched the other two. As a teacher, I have found that there is a wonderful array of good costume books with terrific chapters, yet there can be missing pieces of practical information when one wants to complete a project. Focused on a specific subject and shaped by years of experience, this book is intended to be one of those "missing" practical chapters, a resource that can be turned to in order to solve a problem. Often, once designers or technicians are out of school and working, they find that there are gaps in what they need to know to successfully complete a project or assignment, no matter how excellent the program from which they graduated. My goal is to help answer questions that come up once a designer or technician is working and no longer has an instructor available to help them in person.

FITTING THE ACTOR is a reference for working designers and technicians. While fit is not as immediately noticeable as the color or texture of a garment, it will communicate information about the character to an audience. Understanding how to assess fit with confidence and how to improve the fit of a costume are learnable skills. I started my design life by being afraid of trying to fit an actor too closely and ended up with oversized, baggy costumes. Over time, I have learned about how garments **should** fit based on period and type of garment, and how to look closely at a garment in order to assess **whether** a costume fits a character appropriately.

In preparing this book, it became clear that the word "fit" has two separate but related meanings. The first is **FIT**, an adjective that describes how a garment rests on the wearer's body and the standards of how the garment relates to the outlines of the body. The second is **FITTING**, a verb that describes of

DOI: 10.4324/9781351131353-1

process of how to adjust a ready-made or mock-up garment during a meeting in which the wearer tries on the garment and adjustments are made in order to create garments that will correspond to the standards included in the idea of FIT. This book will cover both aspects of the word "fit" – what fit is, and how to achieve it during a fitting session.

This book is intended as a reference work. You may find it useful to read every chapter in order, as there is an intended accrual of information as the chapters follow one another. However, it may be more useful for a working designer to dip in and out of the book in order to find specific information. In that case, you will notice that important words and ideas are presented in **Boldface** or Capitalized, and that lists and subheadings are used so that information may be quickly accessed by the reader.

The opening chapters cover how to prepare for a fitting and the basics of how to conduct a fitting. Later chapters contain detailed descriptions of how to fit different types of garments, what to look for during a fitting, and how to adjust a garment in order to achieve good fit. An experienced designer or technician may wish to read some information once and then go on to use the specific directions for particular garments as needed.

Each set of fitting directions acts as a unit, meaning that some steps will be repeated in every section where they are pertinent. Within each chapter, there may be some information in the sections where fitting an existing garment is discussed that is repeated where fitting a mock-up is discussed. However, for brevity, there are some times where you may be referred to another chapter or section in order to avoid repeating large portions of the text. A variety of line drawings of localized fitting issues illustrate possible approaches to problems that the reader is trying to solve without being specific to particular costume silhouettes or characters.

There is a checklist reference in Chapter 4 that is valuable to review at the end of each fitting. Although an experienced person may not feel the need for such a list, I find it helpful as a way to check whether I have addressed all the issues before the actor leaves the fitting room. After all, if hospitals are now adopting checklists in the operating room, a designer or technician in a fitting can presumably make good use of a similar tool.

This book is for you. Please use it as you need in order to help you solve fitting problems that are getting in the way of your goal of creating elegant costumes.

1

"FIT" AND WHY IT MATTERS

Costume fit is explored in terms of the Communicative aspects, the Functional aspects, and the Practical aspects of fit. The Communicative aspects include showing the characters' taste, wealth, personality, modesty, age, and fashion. The Functional aspects of fit include the ability to move readily and comfortably to safely perform stage movements. The Practical aspect notes that a less expensive garment that fits well is a better choice than an expensive garment that fits poorly.

When does a garment truly "fit"? How can a designer assess whether a costume item fits correctly or not? What are the basic guideposts to whether something really fits correctly? When teaching students on this subject, my usual refrain is **"just because something buttons, zips up, or hooks together, that doesn't mean it FITS."** In other words, a garment may be able to be fastened on the wearer's body but may not fit correctly. Alternately, a garment may not be able to be closed during an initial try-on but can be readily altered to fit beautifully.

The **fit** of a garment is determined by whether it glides over and/or closely follows the wearer's body in specific areas, according to a customary sense of how a particular garment **should** fit. It is an assessment of how garments should hang on the body. In that case, **"fit" is a combination of traditions and current tastes as to how a garment should sit on the wearer** when the wearer is both moving and still.

There are standards of fit that can be applied when evaluating whether a garment should be chosen for a costume. If the costume designer knows how to alter a garment, and whether the work involved with the alterations is worth the time for a particular garment, they can make better decisions about how to proceed during fittings. At the same time, if a garment does not seem

DOI: 10.4324/9781351131353-2

to fit at first, it may be able to be altered to fit correctly, as long as the garment is of a quality to make it worth the time and labor involved. Looking at different types of garments and assessing how they should hang on the body is the key to being able to determine whether a garment can be considered to fit correctly. The goal of this book is to be a valuable guide in the fitting room to help a technician or designer judge whether a garment fits correctly or can be made to do so. REMEMBER: Just because a garment closes, it does not necessarily **fit**.

How well a costume seems to fit is an **interpretation** by the costume designer, the actor wearing it, and the audience viewing it. A young costume designer may interpret a garment as fitting if it is simply able to be put onto the body, without understanding the subtleties of correct fit for the garment. An actor, depending on how they prefer their own clothes to feel when they wear them, may pronounce a costume "too tight" or "too big" without being aware of how garments would fit in a particular time period or for specific character groups. The audience will combine their knowledge of the current fashion for the time in which they live with their own sense of what is right for the time period in which a play is set.

Does it matter whether a costume fits well or not? In a word, YES! Just as good fit is the hallmark of a well-dressed person, well-fit and well-constructed costumes are the hallmark of a good costume design. The actor wears an actual costume, not a costume rendering, and no matter how well a designer can draw, what is seen on the actor in motion on the stage in front of the audience is the real costume design. The costume rendering is a concept, but the actual costume is the reality. How the costumes fit can enhance the production by creating a sense of "rightness" on stage.

The ability to assess whether a garment fits correctly is a learnable skill. Chapter 3 covers the traditional assessments of how garments should fit. Chapters 4 and 5 cover how to conduct a fitting and how to interpret what you see. With practice, this information will become second nature.

Fit and Character – The Communicative Aspect

The garments that the audience sees onstage will be interpreted as being the result of deliberate choices by the characters. Audiences may notice that a garment seems too large, too long, or too tight for the actor wearing it and wonder why the garment does not fit and whether this is a character choice. A more knowledgeable audience may interpret the costumes as being made up of informed choices by the costume designer with the director and try to understand whether there are specific meanings being expressed or whether the choices are mistakes by the designer or director.

Whatever is placed on the stage will tend to be interpreted as a deliberate choice with a specific meaning. Take the time to learn the potential meanings of fitting choices, and the characters that you costume will be more accurately conveyed to the audience. How the costume fits the wearer affects how the character is interpreted because how a garment fits can express the character. This is especially true in terms of menswear. I cannot tell you how many times I have seen productions where the female characters' costumes are perfectly well fitted, whereas the male characters – often a much larger proportion of the characters onstage – are in ill-fitting coats and suits because the costume designer did not know or care about how to fit their garments correctly! Please do not let this mistake be part of your own work.

Fit can express a character's sense of taste and whether they care about the figure they cut, their wealth, their personality, their age, and whether the character is "modern" for the period and aware of the current styles. In addition, the difference between how well the garments fit on some characters relative to others can illuminate the relationships and differences between the characters.

Sense of Taste

How well garments fit will express the character's sense of taste and aesthetics. The sense of taste can be interpreted as being what the character feels is aesthetically pleasing, what feels comfortable to them, whether comfort is more or less important than current fashion, and what they feel flatters themselves.

Wealth

Fit can establish a character's wealth, because the elegance of how a garment fits and the beauty of the materials may be what delineates the clothing of the rich from everyone else in many time periods. Wealthy characters may wear garments that fit more closely to the body and that might restrict their movement, because they do not have to perform the same level of physical labor as do poorer characters and servants. For example, a wealthy woman may be able to wear a restrictive corset, longer skirts, and less comfortable clothing than her servants, because the servants need to be able to move more easily even if they are also wearing a fitted bodice and a long skirt. In this case, the servant's bodice may be loosened and the skirt may be adjusted by being slightly shorter or less heavily draped than their employer's garments. The servant's skirt may even be casually pulled up to allow for movement, as opposed to the formally arranged skirt on the employer. In addition, wealthy characters can be interpreted as being able to afford more exacting tailoring than their poorer counterparts and as having the taste to appreciate the subtleties of good fit. Less wealthy characters may be in clothing that is a bit too large, too snug, too long, or too short, to indicate that their garments were not made specifically for them, or that the garments are either hand-me-downs or are so old that they no longer fit a character who cannot afford to purchase new garments. In other words, a well-fitted garment will indicate that it was made specifically for the wearer, which suggests that the wearer has the wealth and taste to have the garment custom made for themselves by a skilled artisan.

Personality

Personality is expressed through garment fit. A conservative character may be costumed in garment styles and fits that are more covered and less body-conscious than other characters are wearing. An artistic or eccentric character might be in garments and combinations of clothing that don't follow the current fashion but reflects their sense of what is attractive, even if that is from an earlier time period or from a mix of places and times. A reclusive or shy person may be put in loose garments for the character to hide in, while a confident character could be dressed in garments that fit closely to the body without being too tight or that skim the body without needing to show it off.

Sense of Modesty and Display

Costumes can express the character's sense of modesty and comfort with displaying their body, especially as a means of sexual attraction. A character who is young and seeking a mate can wear close-fitting garments that accentuate the body's erogenous zones in a way that will communicate their display of sensuality, both for the character's time period and to the modern audience. A character who is trying to reclaim their lost youth or attempt to appeal to a much younger partner may be costumed in garments that are snug, short, and in a style that would be more appropriate for a younger character. A character who is modest would be more likely to wear garments that cover their body loosely within the standards of their time period and may wear hair and face coverings as well as garments.

Age and Sense of Modernity

The character's age as well as sense of modernity can be expressed through fit. A costume that is fit to the standards of a previous time period can indicate an older or more conservative character who is more comfortable in an earlier era. Older characters are often dressed in clothing that suggests an earlier time, presumably the era of their youth when they were in the prime of their lives. Such costumes are often longer and less revealing than the costumes of younger characters on stage. A character who appears to be the epitome of current fit for the fashions of the present day (within the period of the production) will seem to be more aware of current trends, events, and ideas. This sort of character is often a youthful adult, who is fully able to express themself, outside of their parents' clothing choices. A very fashion-conscious character, depending on the character's personality and function in the play, may be costumed in garments that show off the ridiculous or elegant aspects of their time period. A character who has apparently attempted to dress in the latest fashions but has gotten some of the aspects of the fit wrong, such as the wrong hem length, skirt or trouser shape, shoulder width, sleeve shape, or waistline placement, can appear to be in denial about their real age or out of touch with the aesthetics of their society. Children are often depicted in looser versions of the current fashion, with a shortened hem length to allow them to move around easily.

Fit and Actor Movement – The Functional Aspect

A well-fitted garment can allow the actors to move better. A costume is almost always in motion and needs to look correct despite this movement. In theatre, the actors may also be expected to dance, run, take part in stage combat, lounge on furniture or the floor, roll on the floor, drop to their knees, and move their bodies in a myriad of extreme poses. This tends to be very disconcerting the first time a designer goes to a run-through to see what an actor is doing in the beautiful costume that has been planned! **Be prepared for this by going to run-throughs early and often. Communicate with the stage manager so that they can keep you up to date on any stage movement that will have to be factored into the costume as it is being selected or constructed.**

Even on a production that is set during a decorous time period, there may be movement that a costume designer has not anticipated. The director works with the actor for hours at a time during rehearsal but meets with the designer for an hour or so a week for production or design meetings. So, the director will tend to be more concerned with accommodating actor comfort and making the production seem lively and fresh, than whether a movement is strictly "period" or not. In fact, I have seen a production where the stage action was consistent with the Italian Renaissance setting but, at the curtain call the director had the actors hold hands and raise them over their heads. The ladies' empire-seamed bodices suddenly pulled up and got caught above their bustlines for their final moments on stage! Therefore, keep in mind that actors in any production, despite the setting, can be expected to move in a modern, active manner on stage and allow for this when fitting their costumes.

If the production is set during a modern time period, if the characters need to sing and dance, or if stage combat or tumbling are a part of the staging, it is even more important for actors to be able to move comfortably than in a period production. The costume designer should expect that the actors in these productions will need to be able to gesture broadly, move quickly and easily in all different directions, and climb up or roll around the stage. In this case, during a fitting, each actor should be asked to perform their most athletic bits of stage movement while wearing their costumes and shoes so that adjustments can be made to the costumes to accommodate their actions while maintaining the desired garment appearance.

Fit and Availability of Garments – The Practical Aspect

Cheaper garments can look better than expensive garments, depending on how well they fit the wearer. A well-fitted but inexpensive garment can make a better impression than an expensive garment that hangs poorly on the actor, and thrift store items that are made of quality natural fibers can be successfully altered to fit beautifully, while new garments made of synthetic fibers can be difficult to alter successfully. This is true whether we are discussing clothing or costumes. The key is to know which garments are worth the time to alter, and which will not be successfully altered. More discussion of how to alter existing garments will be covered within the chapters on fitting. If you are building custom garments, there is also discussion on how to fit a mockup garment in the chapters on fitting.

In summary, the correct and careful fit of garments is important in creating an elegant costume design on stage. Fit can tell an audience about the characters, as well as allowing the actors to feel like they are inhabiting the characters. Good fit will also allow the actors to move easily and to perform their directed blocking.

The following chapters discuss the standards of good fit. Chapter 2 discusses measurements, how to take them, and what to look for when you are using them to create patterns or to check existing garments. In Chapter 3, we will look at the basic markers of "good fit" in general. In later chapters, we will explore specifics of fit for particular categories of garments, including which actor body measurements are needed to fit the garments, how to measure existing garments as compared to actor measurements, how to assess whether the garment fits correctly during a fitting, and how to fit both an existing garment and a mockup of the garment.

2

MEASUREMENTS

Measurements are the starting point for making a garment fit correctly. Even if it is possible to guess or approximate the range of measurements of a potential wearer, it is not efficient to start specific work before accurate, current measurements are available. While one may do some preliminary planning and work prior to getting measurements, there is only so much that can be done without obtaining concrete information. A draper cannot efficiently pattern, a shopper cannot efficiently pull or shop, and a designer cannot efficiently translate available period or style options for the project into concrete design choices without having accurate information. Actor measurements are the key to all of this.

Ideally, measurements are taken by the person creating the patterns, as each person will take, and each patternmaker will interpret, the measurements slightly differently. However, as long as careful measurements are available, slight adjustments to garments or a mockup can be made once the actor is in a fitting session. If an actor is not available for measurements for a current production, it is possible to use an older set of measurements as long as the measurements are obtained from a **reliable source** and they have been taken **fairly recently**.

In terms of reliable sources, it is possible to contact another costume shop that has measured the actor and get a copy of those measurements; this is common practice among regional, opera, and local theatre companies. If the actor lives in a city where you know a trusted person who could take the measurements for you that may be another option. Unless there is no other possible source available to you, do not depend on any measurements that may be listed on an actor's resume or offered by the actor's agent; these measurements are approximate, are intended as general size-range information for casting purposes, and may be more aspirational than accurate.

DOI: 10.4324/9781351131353-3

Recent measurements are the most preferable. For professional actors or singers, measurements that are taken within three years are usable. However, a person who has had a health challenge, a personal loss, or experienced stress since being last measured may have lost or gained enough weight that the width measurements are inaccurate. For student actors, measurements that are taken within one year are usable. For children or adolescents, it is very important to take measurements for each show – using older measurements or asking a parent about their child's garment sizes is not necessarily accurate in this case. (When you are taking measurements for actors below the age of 18, be sure to have their parents and/or another person with you at the appointment so that there is less possibility of the actor misinterpreting what you are doing.) Even if an actor has been measured within the time frames listed above, I prefer to check width measurements, if possible, at the start of each show's process.

Finally, for a modern-dress show, be sure the actor is wearing their usual chest support garments by requesting that they do so when you schedule the fitting, or by being willing to provide such garments for them to wear during the fitting. For a period show, it may be necessary to call the actor in for a second set of quick measurements once a corset and skirt shapers have been pulled.

Each costume shop or patternmaker has a preferred measurement sheet. For opera singers, the National Opera America measurement sheet is a good standard form that is used by many opera shops. Searching online for "Costume Measurement Sheets" brings up dozens of ready-made options that can be used as-is or adapted to a particular patternmaker's preferences. A patternmaker who prefers drafting from a specific set of directions in a book may prefer the measurement sheets contained in that book. Whichever measurement sheet(s) works best for your own purposes is the best choice for you.

In the rest of this book, I refer to measurements that should be taken on the actor to check ready-made garments or prepare patterns. The following measurements are those that I find are most important for checking garments, patterning, and evaluating size relationships on a body when I am designing a costume. Please note that the order listed below is not exactly the same as what is on the sample measurement sheet (Figure 2.5) because it can be more efficient to take all the horizontal measurements and then all the vertical measurements of an area of the body at one time, rather than switching back and forth. However, please feel free to change the order of measuring when you develop your own measurement sheet. The list below is grouped so that measurements that have an impact on each other are close to one another.

Taking Measurements

Height: Top of the head to the floor, in bare feet or in flat shoes. This is useful to confirm the lengths of body segments and to compare the lengths of body segments to determine body proportions, such as long legs or a long torso WITHIN the body frame of the actor.

Weight: Approximate weight is useful to compare with height for overall body proportion but knowing the actor's weight is not absolutely necessary. This can be a sensitive topic for people, so ask the actor for their approximate weight IF they are comfortable giving it.

Head length: The head length from the top of the head to the tip of the chin can be used when evaluating body proportions. This is most useful for the costume designer.

Commercial sizes, including shirt/blouse, trousers, jeans, jacket, and dress: The commercial clothing sizes that an actor wears are especially help-ful when shopping for a modern show. Be sure also to ask for their favorite brand names when asking about sizes – different manufactur-ers have different size categories, which can often be checked on the brand's websites against the actor's measurements. If possible, get the number sizes that an actor wears rather than S–M–L sizes. In some cases, different types of clothing will result in different numeric sizes. For example, the jeans size that someone wears is often smaller than the trouser size that they would wear because jeans often purposely fit snugger than dress trousers.

Allergies (to fabric, fur, and detergents), hair color and length, piercings, tattoos (including placement and size), and facial hair (see Figure 2.5): These are useful pieces of information to gather while taking measurements. Since they do not affect costume fittings, they will not be referred to after this point in this book. However, if you are designing costumes for film or television and the actor's tattoo(s) will be visible, some media may require a release from the tattoo artist.

Before starting the measurements, tie a ribbon or tape around the actor's nat-ural waistline and their armscye positions (the top of the armscye ribbon may need to be masking-taped at the top edge to their shirt or bare arms to stay in place) to act as consistent reference points for the measurements.

Drawings to illustrate the measurement positions follow in this chapter. Please note that these, and all the illustrations, are not precisely to scale and may be slightly asymmetrical.

Torso Measurements (1–25) (Figure 2.1)

1. *Base of neckline circumference*: Taken at the point where the neckline meets the shoulders and upper chest, this is the minimum neckline that can be worn.

2. *Neckline at top of collar band circumference*: This is usually 1–1 ¼" above the base of the neckline but can be 1 ½" or higher on a person with a long neck.

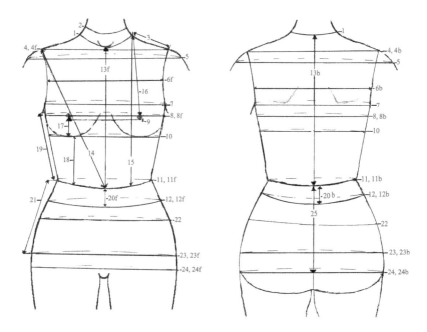

FIGURE 2.1   Drawing of the torso and trunk with measuring lines. Front (left) and back (right)

For a man, the higher measurement should be taken over the Adam's apple. Be sure to indicate **how far above the base of the neck** that this measurement has been taken. In the US, a man's shirt is sized by the measurement taken at the **base** of the neckline, which corresponds to the center of the band button and the center of the button hole. However, a measurement taken higher on the neck, such as over the Adam's apple on a man, should also be compared to the upper edge of the neckband of an existing shirt or used when drafting a neckband for a constructed shirt.

3. *Shoulder length from neck/shoulder point to shoulder tip:* From the base of the neckline at the side, measure to the point where the sharp shoulder bone ends and the curve of the arm begins. The end of the shoulder and start of the arm can be taken **interpreted differently by different people**, so it is most important to be **consistent** about where the shoulder length is ended on all the actors who are measured. I tend to take the end of the shoulder to **the outer edge of the pointy shoulder bone at the top of the shoulders, before reaching the fleshy arm**. If you have tied a narrow ribbon around the armscye, the outer edge of the ribbon at the top-most point will mark the end of the shoulder tip. For different period styles, the garment shoulder line may extend past or cut inward from this anatomical point.

4. *Shoulder tip to shoulder tip width*: Across the shoulders, between both shoulder tips at the point where the sharp pointy shoulder bones end and the top of the arms begins (not to the ends of the curve of the upper arms). Measure both the front and back of the body (4f and 4b).

5. *Around top of arms*: Measure the circumference around the ends of the visible span of the shoulder area, which INCLUDES the tops of the curved upper arms. Then, measure the front and back spans in this area. This measurement is useful for a wearer who has developed full upper arms but a narrow anatomical placement of their shoulder tips. I also use it when checking existing jackets.

5a. Some measurement sheets refer to this measurement as the *CAPE MEASUREMENT*, which is actually taken around the widest point of the curved upper arms, generally lower than 5.

6. *Armscye to armscye/upper chest width*: Across the upper chest, midway between the shoulder level and the chest level. This will meet the **most indented point of the armholes**. Measure both the front and back of the body (6f and 6b).

7. *Above the bust/chest circumference*: The full-body circumference, taken at the underarm level **above** the fullest part of the chest. If the actor will be wearing a corset, this is an especially useful measurement to take, **when they are wearing the corset**, in order to allow the costume to accommodate upper body curves. Then, measure the front and back spans in this area.

8. *Chest/bust circumference*: The widest part of the chest at the nipple line. While measuring, make sure the tape measure is level all the way around the body. When measuring a singer, take the chest measurement a second time while asking the person to expand their chest as much as possible – a standard 1″ or smaller expansion is accommodated by the normal ease in a garment, but a singer may have 2–3″ chest expansion that will need to be planned for in the garment. (People who are swimmers may also have a large chest expansion that needs to be allowed for.)

    Also record the front chest measurement from side seam to side seam and subtract that from the total chest/bust circumference to get the back chest measurement (8f and 8b).

9. *Bust point to bust point width*: Horizontal spacing between nipples. This measurement is helpful in establishing where vertical front darts should be placed. Ask the actor to indicate where the bust points are on their body.

10. *Underbust/empire line circumference*: The full-body circumference taken below the lower edge of the breast curves. This would correspond to placement of a bra's lower band. It is mostly useful for female-identified performer's costumes or for empire waist costumes. Measure both the front and back spans in this area.

11. *Natural waistline circumference*: The natural waistline is at the point where the body bends when a person bends from side to side. This may be at the smallest part of the mid-section, depending on how a person carries their body weight. It may also correspond to the person's navel, but this is not always the case. For the more detailed measurements needed for patterning purposes, also note the front waistline measurement from side seam to side seam and subtract that from the total waistline circumference to get the back waistline measurement (11f and 11b).

12. *Trouser/fashion waistline*: The fashion waistline level is fashion- and time-period driven and may be at the pelvic bones, at the natural waistline, above or below either of these two points, or the level at which the wearer commonly wears their trousers in their daily life. For modern men, the fashion waistline is often at the pelvic bone level and may be below the level of a rounded belly. **For a wearer with a very rounded stomach area, it is important to also take an additional measurement to record the Fullest Waistline circumference.**

     For the more detailed measurements needed for patterning purposes, also note the front waistline measurement from side seam to side seam, and subtract that amount from the total trouser waistline circumference to get the back waistline measurement (12f and 12b).

13f. *Base of neck to waist length/center front length*: In front, from the base of the throat down to the waistline. Note whether you are measuring from the neckline to the natural, fashion, or fullest waistline or any other point, as this will depend on the period style of the bodice or the type of garment you are measuring for.

13b. *Base of neck to waist length/center back length*: In back, from the nape of the neck down to the waistline. Note whether you are measuring from neckline to the natural, fashion, or fullest waistline, or any other point, as this will depend on the period style of the bodice or the type of garment you are measuring for.

14. *Shoulder tip to waist center*: This is a diagonal measurement, which will help determine the shoulder slope. Note where you are measuring to the natural, fashion, or fullest waistline or any other point. It should be taken both in front and back (14a and 14b).

15. *Neck/shoulder point (A.K.A. high point shoulder) to waistline*: This is a vertical measurement that starts at the point where the neck and shoulder intersect and goes over the curve of the chest/bust at the fullest point, near the bust point. Note whether you are measuring from the neckline to the natural, fashion, or fullest waistline or any other point, as this will depend on the period style of the bodice or the type of garment you are measuring for. Take this measurement both in front and back (15f and 15b).

16. *Neck/shoulder point (A.K.A. high point shoulder) to bust point*: This measurement helps establish the bustline level. Different patternmakers and

patterning directions prefer different reference points from which to take this measurement. Some patternmakers prefer to measure from the center of the shoulder to the bust point and then down to whichever waistline level being used for this set of measurements. The bustline support garment an actor will wear onstage with affect this measurement, so the measurement should be double-checked when the actor is in the correct support garment.

17. *Bust curve depth*: From the bust point down to the below the bust level. It is mostly useful for female-identified performers' costumes.

18. *Underbust to waist*: This is a vertical measurement, taken from the below the bust level down to the waistline. It may be taken at the center front, center back, side seams, and/or below the fullest part of the bust – just be consistent about where you take this for all actors you measure. It is mostly useful for female-identified performers' costumes.

19. *Side seam length*: Measured vertically along the side seam from the base of the armpit/underarm to the waistline. Some technicians have the actor hold a ruler horizontally under their arm on their dominant side and take the measurement from the top of the ruler to the waistline.

20. *Natural waistline to trouser/fashion waistline*: Because these two different levels may be important in different situations, it is helpful to know the **vertical space** between the levels in front and back (20f and 20b).

21. *Waistline to widest hip level*: From the desired waistline level (natural, fashion, or another point), measure down the side seam to the widest point of the hips/seat, where you have taken the hip circumference. Be sure to note **which** waistline level you are using as the starting reference point.

22. *Pelvic bone level circumference*: The circumference is at the level of the sharp bones at the side front of the body below the waistline. This is the point of a very low possible waistline on a garment, although some people use this measurement as the HIP measurement (which it is NOT, except in a vanity situation). This measurement is helpful to know if an actor has a rounded tummy.

23. *Widest hips circumference*: The **widest** point of the hips/seat area. This circumference may be at the top of the thighs, the widest part of the buttocks, or the fullest part of the hips, which can be below the crotch level. While measuring, make sure the tape measure is level all the way around the body. **This is the most important measurement for trousers and skirts and needs to be accurate**. If in doubt, take the measurement **twice** to confirm that the measurement is accurate. Do not be tempted, or pressured, to flatter the wearer by recording an inaccurate measurement for this point of the body.

For the more detailed measurements needed for patterning purposes, also note the front widest hip measurement from side seam to side seam and subtract that from the total widest hip circumference to get the back widest hip measurement (23f and 23b).

24. *Fullest seat circumference*: For an actor with a high, rounded seat, with wide hips or outer thighs that are at a very different level on the body than the seat, or a very low seat, it can be helpful to take a separate measurement of this area. This measurement may not be necessary for all actors.

    For the more detailed measurements needed for patterning purposes, also note the front fullest seat measurement from side seam to side seam and subtract that from the total fullest seat circumference to get the back fullest seat measurement (24f and 24b).

25. *Fullest seat depth*: Measure from the center back waistline at whichever level you are using as the standard in this set of measurements down to the level where you took the fullest seat circumference.

Crotch Curve Measurements (26–30) (Figure 2.2)

Crotch curve measurements can be invasive – I suggest telling the wearer what you are about to do and getting their consent before taking each measurement, so that they are comfortable with the process.

26. *Half girth*: This can be found by measuring **from the waistline level at center front, passing under the torso between the legs, to the waistline level at center back**. Be sure to note which waistline level you are using for the start and end points – natural, fashion, or another point.

27. *Front rise*: While measuring the half girth, note the measurement at which the tape measure reaches from the **front waistline level to the Crotch Point**, which is where trouser inseams would meet the curved crotch seam that passes under the torso. The front rise is approximately 33–40% of the half girth measurement.

28. *Back rise*: Subtract the front rise measurement from the total half girth to get this measurement.

29. *Deepest crotch length*: While measuring the half girth, note the point where the tape measure touches the **lowest point on the body**. This will tend to be at the lowest point of the buttocks curve. The crotch length is taken from the **lowest point on the body to the Back Waistline level**. Some measuring directions have you take the crotch length from the waistline level to the chair seat while the actor is sitting. However, I find that it is more accurate on many people to measure the **lowest point on the body's crotch curve while they are standing** rather than while sitting.

    On women, the deepest crotch length is usually *not* the same length as the back rise, as the fullest and lowest part of the seat on women is usually lower than the crotch point (where the front rise meets the back rise and where the inseams meet the curved crotch seam). On men, the deepest crotch length *may* be at the same level as the crotch point. See Chapter 14 for more discussion of this subject.

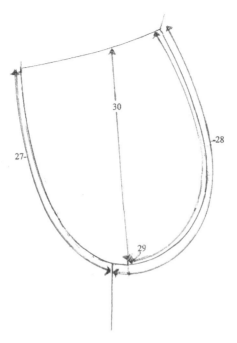

FIGURE 2.2   Cross-section of the crotch curve, with measuring lines and numbers

30. *Crotch level depth*: Measuring **vertically down the side seam**, measure from the **Waistline level** to the level that was previously established as the **Deepest Crotch Length**, which is the lowest point of the buttocks curve on the curved crotch seam. Be sure to note whether the crotch level depth measurement is taken from the natural waistline, fashion waistline, or some other point.

Leg Measurements (31–35) (Figure 2.3)

As with the trunk measurements, these can be invasive, so I suggest telling the wearer what you are about to do while taking each measurement, and getting their consent first.

31a–d. *Leg circumferences*: Depending on the style of the trousers, it may be necessary to take the upper thigh, bent knee, calf, and/or ankle circumference measurements to ensure the correct fit. Take these measurements on the dominant leg.

32. *Outseam*: From the waistline level down to the desired length of the trouser legs, which should be the **same point that is used as the endpoint for the Inseam measurement**. Be sure to note whether the measurement was taken from the natural waist, fashion waist, or some other point.

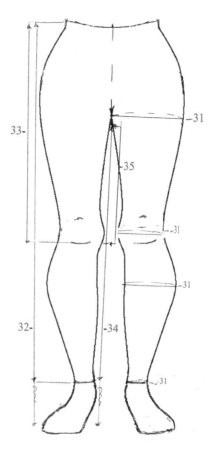

FIGURE 2.3 Drawing of the legs from the front view, with measuring lines and numbers

33. *Outseam to below the knee:* Take the outseam measurement to below the knee level if you wish to create a modern skirt.

34. *Inseam:* Have the wearer hold the top of the tape measure close to their body at the point where they feel comfortable having the top of the trousers inseams sit. Measure down from the top of the inner thigh **from the level of closeness to the body where the wearer would like to wear their trousers**, down to the desired length of the trouser legs. Women often prefer to wear their trousers close to their bodies at the top of the inseam for a more fitted look, while men often prefer ¾″ or more of clearance below their bodies at the top of the inseam for more comfort. For a sagged-trouser style, the inseam of the pants may be worn even further away from the body's anatomical crotch. Remember, however,

that the crotch level needs to be close to the body for better movement, particularly for dance. For full-length trousers, the inseam length can end anywhere from the ankle bone to the floor level. Be sure to note whatever level on the wearer's body you have used as the endpoint for this measurement.

35. *Inseam to below the knee:* Also take the inseam measurement to the below the knee level if you wish to create knee breeches or shorts.

Arm Measurements (36–47) (Figure 2.4)

Take the arm measurements on the dominant side of the wearer's body for better fit. For example, if the wearer is right-handed, it is likely that their right arm will be slightly more developed than their left arm. However, ask the actor about this issue before measuring, as some people write with one hand and use the other for everything else.

36. *Sleeve cap width:* Measure around the **fullest part of the upper arm** at the same level where you would take the armscye-to-armscye width (#6 in Figure 2.1) across the chest, which is often at the lowest level of the sleeve cap height, **the point where the arm separates from the chest area**. This measurement corresponds to the minimum width needed across the sleeve cap at the level of the cap notches. When drafting sleeves, one may sometimes end up with too high and narrow a

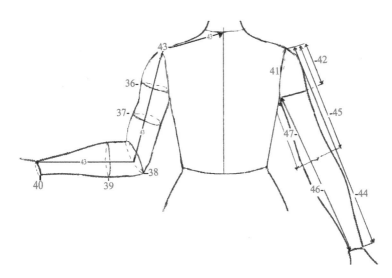

FIGURE 2.4 Drawing of the arms from the back view of the body, with measuring lines

sleeve cap to fit the wearer, even if the sleeve cap measurement is technically correct to fit the armhole with the correct ease. The sleeve cap width measurement is very useful when creating sleeves for someone with full upper arms.

37. *Bicep circumference*: The fullest part of the upper arm **below** the point where the arm separates from the chest area. This is best taken on the actor's dominant side, with the biceps muscle flexed.

38. *Elbow circumference*: Taken around the bent elbow on the actor's dominant side.

39. *Forearm circumference*: Taken around the widest point of the arm below the elbow on the actor's dominant side.

40. *Wrist circumference*: Taken around the wrist bones on the actor's dominant side.

41. *Armscye circumference*: Taken around the armhole, starting and ending where it meets the shoulder bones, this is the **minimum armhole space** that the actor will be comfortable in wearing. For different period style garments, the armscye position may be slightly extended wider onto the upper arm area or be slightly lowered from the actor's armpit.

42. *Sleeve cap height*: The distance from the tip of the shoulder bones down to the level on the arm where it separates from the chest area. This measurement can be checked by subtracting the underarm sleeve length from the sleeve length.

43. *Shirt sleeve/center back to wrist length*: From the bone at the center back of the top of the spine, measure horizontally to the tip of the shoulder on the wearer's dominant side (i.e. on the wearer's right side if they are right-handed), to the tip of the elbow when the elbow is bent, down to below the wrist bone. This measurement is used for the shirt sleeve length on a purchased garment.

44. *Sleeve length*: From the tip of the shoulder, measure down to below the wrist bone, when the elbow is ben. This measurement is used to draft a sleeve.

45. *Half sleeve*: The underarm measurement to the elbow point.

46. *Underarm sleeve length:* From the base of the armpit, measure to below the wrist bone. This measurement is useful when drafting a sleeve.

47. *Half underarm seam:* Underarm measurement to the inner elbow level.

Head Measurements (48–51)

If the actor will be wigged and/or wear a hat, these measurements are useful. An illustration for these measurements has not been included.

48. *Head circumference*: Taken around the widest part of the head, usually right above the tops of the ears, parallel to floor.

49. *Hairline circumference:* Taken on an angle that curves around the head following the edge of the hairline.
50. *Forehead to base of the hairline/poll:* Over the top of the head.
51. *Ear to ear:* Taken from the tops of the ears, over the top of the head.

A Sample Measurement Sheet (Figure 2.5)

There are many different measurement sheets available to use. Figure 2.5 is based on the measurements discussed in this chapter and will be referred to elsewhere in this book.

Interpreting Measurements

Once you have taken the measurements needed to create a pattern or check an existing garment, it is also possible to look at the **relationship** between some sets of measurements to get a sense of the actor's posture and overall shape.

Numerous drawing guides use the idea of "heads" as a way to set up the lengthwise proportions of the figure, based on the length of a person's head. The "fashion figure" is based on proportions that range from 8, 9, or 10 heads that make a drawing look exciting but has little relation to how a garment will look on most real people. An 8-head figure is a tall person and is unusual in the real world. An average-sized man may range between 6 ½ and 7 ½ heads, and an average-sized woman may range from 6 to 7 heads. Within a figure, vertical divisions are made in proportion to the actual size of the person's head. The top of the head to the end of the chin is the first division, end of the chin to near the chest/bust level is approximately the second division, and the midpoint of the body is roughly at the top of the Inseam, whether that is 3 or 4 heads down on a particular person. The top of the legs to the bottom of the feet will be divided between the number of head-lengths that are taken up by the upper body IF the figure is balanced from top to bottom.

Of course, people are all different and few people will line up precisely with a geometric scale of exact proportions. However, comparing measurements within a person's own measurement sheet can be useful. The shoulder tip to shoulder tip width measurements in the front versus the back can tell you whether the person tends to round their shoulders inward or carry them squarely. The center front neck to waist measurement, which is often approximately 2″ shorter as compared to the center back neck to waist measurement, can tell you whether the person hunches their posture over or stands up straight. The height measurement versus the inseam to floor measurement will tell you whether the person's legs are shorter or longer than the standard ½ of their overall height. Different periods in fashion compare the shoulder tip to shoulder tip measurements, the bust circumference, waistline circumference, and hip level circumference in different proportional relationships for their

MEASUREMENTS

NAME_____ HEIGHT_____ ALLERGIES (Costume Materials)
_____

PRONOUNS_____ WEIGHT (approx.) _____ HAIR COLOR_____

DATE_____ HEAD LENGTH (top to chin)____ HAIR LENGTH_____

PRODUCTION_____ SHIRT/BLOUSE_____ PIERCINGS_____

ROLE(S)_____ TROUSERS_____ TATTOOS_____

_____ JEANS: Waist_____ Inseam_____ FACIAL HAIR_____

CONTACT INFORMATION JACKET_____ BRA: Band_____Cup_____

_____ DRESS_____ Notes: _____

TORSO AND TRUNK

1., 2. NECK Circumference
Base_____ top of collar _____ (How far above____)

3. SHOULDER LENGTH FROM NECK/SHOULDER
POINT TO SHOULDER TIP _____

4. SHOULDER TIP TO SHOULDER TIP (Sharp
Bones) F_____ B_____

5. AROUND TOP OF ARMS (Outer Ends of Deltoids)
Full circumference _____ F_____ B_____

5a. Cape: Torso and Around The Widest Part Of Arms
Full circum _____ F_____ B_____

6. ARMSCYE TO ARMSCYE
F_____ B_____

7. ABOVE BUST/CHEST Full circum _____
F_____ B_____

8. CHEST/BUST Full circumference_____
F_____ B_____

9. BUST POINT TO BUST POINT _____

10. UNDERBUST Full circumference_____
F_____ B_____

11. NATURAL WAISTLINE Full circum _____
F_____ B_____

12. TROUSER/FASHION WAIST circum _____
F_____ B_____

13. BASE OF NECK TO WAIST LENGTHS (Note
whether Natural or Fashion Waist) F_____ B_____

14. SHOULDER TIP TO WAIST CENTER
F_____ B_____

15. NECK/SHOULDER POINT TO WAISTLINE
F_____ B_____

16. NECK/SHOULDER POINT TO BUST POINT
(Bust Point Level Depth, Front only) _____

17. BUST CURVE DEPTH (Bust point to under-bust)
_____

18. UNDERBUST TO WAIST (Note whether Natural
or Fashion Waist) F_____ B_____

19. SIDE SEAM LENGTH (Armpit to Waistline)
(Note Whether Natural or Fashion Waist) _____

20. NATURAL WAISTLINE TO TROUSER/
FASHION WAISTLINE F_____ B_____

21. WAISTLINE TO WIDEST HIPS/HIP LEVEL
(Note whether Natural or Fashion Waist)
Side _____ F_____ B_____

22. PELVIC BONE LEVEL circumference _____
F_____ B_____

23. WIDEST HIPS circumference _____
F_____ B_____

FIGURE 2.5 A sample measurement sheet, based on the measurements discussed in this chapter *(Continued)*

24. FULLEST SEAT circumference_____
F_____   B_____

25. FULLEST SEAT DEPTH from CB waistline (Note whether from Natural or Fashion Waist)_____

26. HALF GIRTH (CF waist to CB waist along crotch seam)_____

27. FRONT RISE (CF waist to crotch cross-seam)
_____

28. BACK RISE (CB waist to crotch cross-seam, or Half Girth minus Front Rise. (Note from Natural or Fashion Waist)_____

29. DEEPEST CROTCH DEPTH (CB waist to lowest point **on the wearer's body along the curved crotch seam**)_____

30. CROTCH LEVEL DEPTH (Side seam, from waistline to Deepest Crotch Depth)_____

LEGS
Note whether the vertical measurements are taken from the Natural, Trouser, or Other waistline)

31a. FULLEST THIGH circumference_____

31b. ABOVE KNEE circumference_____

31c. FLEXED KNEE circumference_____

31d. CALF circumference_____

31e. ANKLE circumference_____

32. OUTSEAM (waistline to floor)
Side_____ F_____ B_____

33. WAISTLINE TO BELOW KNEE
Side_____ F_____ B_____

34. INSEAM (actor holds tape at preferred top point)
To Ankle_____ To Floor_____

35. INSEAM (actor holds tape at preferred top point)
To Below the Knee_____

ARMS
Measure on Dominant Arm

36. SLEEVE CAP WIDTH (fullest upper arm, taken from Armscye to Armscye Across Upper Arm)_____

37. BICEP circumference_____

38. ELBOW (bent) circumference_____

39. FOREARM circumference_____

40. WRIST circumference._____

41. ARMSCYE (Minimum Armhole)_____

42. SLEEVE CAP HEIGHT (Shoulder tip down to Base of the Underarm_____

43. SHIRT SLEEVE (Center back neck to shoulder to bent elbow and below wrist bone_____

44. SLEEVE (Shoulder Tip downwards)
To Below Wrist Bone_____

45. HALF SLEEVE (Shoulder Tip downwards)
To Below Elbow_____

46. UNDERARM SEAM (Armpit downwards)
To Below Wrist_____

47. HALF UNDERARM SEAM (Armpit downwards)
To Elbow_____

HEAD

48. HEAD circumference, parallel to floor_____

49. HAIRLINE circumference_____

50. FOREHEAD TO BASE OF HAIRLINE_____

51. EAR TO EAR Over Top of Head_____

FIGURE 2.5 *(Continued)*

idealized fashion figure. However, despite the time period being depicted onstage, we should fit garments carefully on all wearers, to celebrate the different figure types that may not be the fashion standard in a certain situation but are still beautiful and worthy of being seen at their best.

As a designer, I will look at an actor's measurements to see whether there are garments that I can pull from stock for them or will use the measurements to check a mockup garment. I will also use the relationships of measurements to check whether design choices about seam placement or garment fullness on my part will enhance the actor's appearance in terms of the time period or the character they are portraying. For example, the placement and length of a shoulder seam or the height of a waistline seam can be an important part of creating a period impression, and a shift of ½–1″ may make a huge difference in whether a costume looks correct or not.

When one is fitting transgender actors, as long as the garments fit the widest points of their bodies so that they can move smoothly onstage, the placement of the armscye seams or fullness of trousers or skirts can be adjusted to create the desired look. Full upper sleeves and generous armscyes that are placed slightly closer to the vertical centers of a bodice can be a good choice for visually narrowing the shoulder line on a trans woman while accommodating their shoulders, and a skirt with a gathered waistline and petticoats will add more fullness to the lower body; a jacket with added shoulder pads and armscyes placed slightly wider across the chest will visually broaden the upper body of a trans man, while trousers with pleats may fit better through the thighs. Paying attention to body measurements and their relationships will be the first step in choosing garments that can fit an actor well.

3

OBTAINING GARMENTS FOR COSTUME USE

The first step in fitting costumes is obtaining items to fit. Unless the production is blessed with at least three of the following resources – a very large budget; a large, excellent, and talented costume staff; an unlimited time frame; and access to a variety of glorious materials and costume stock – it is likely the costumes for a production will be assembled from a combination of sources rather than being completely created for that particular production. Creating costumes for a specific design concept is a great luxury. Most theatres do not have the resources to completely build entire productions for each one of their shows. Fortunately, there are many costume sources available aside from building costumes, such as pulling items from stock, purchasing items, borrowing or renting from other theatres or costume rental houses, or borrowing from the actors' closets.

Pulling Items from Stock

Many theatres will have a costume stock that is the result of what was obtained or created for past productions. Ideally, these items will be able to be re-trimmed, re-dyed if needed, and re-fit. The most useful garments are made from natural fibers which are easier to alter or re-dye. It is also helpful if garments are constructed and linings are put in in such a way that they allow for easy alterations. This would include leaving 1–2″ or more in seam allowances at the side seams, center fronts, and center backs, adding side seams in waistbands that line up with the garment side seams, putting shoulder seams and center seams into neckline facings, and individually piping each section of a bodice at the neckline and lower edges rather than using a continuous piece of piping that is not easily adjusted.

DOI: 10.4324/9781351131353-4

Non-profit theatres often receive clothing donations from people who are cleaning out their own or their family members' storage areas or homes. Community donations can sometimes yield treasures but can also be the remains of someone's parents' estates, which means that the items are 30–60 years old and are from the 1960s to the 1980s. A few choice examples of garments from these periods are handy to maintain if the theatre tends to produce scripts from those eras. Otherwise, donations should be assessed for their value in terms of being able to be reworked for likely future productions. Fabric content and garment sizes should be factors in deciding what to keep and what to pass along to other worthy organizations.

Whether the costume storage area is large or small, filled or sparse, ORGANIZATION is important in ensuring that the stock is really useful. Having a clearly organized stock can save time and money. It will also save the shop from repeatedly building or purchasing essentially the same costumes because earlier versions are too hard to find in a disorganized space. Regular cleaning and organizing sessions in the storage area will help preserve what the theatre owns and make it more useable. Different theatres may organize the stock by time periods, types of garments, or group entire productions together. Howsoever the stock is organized, grouped items should be stored together or clearly noted whenever they are stored apart.

Hanging items should have enough room between them so that they can hang vertically and not twist behind each other. Any boxes or bins should be clearly labeled and placed in an accessible area so that nothing is "lost" due to stacks of boxes being hidden behind jammed racks of hanging garments. Be sure that storage containers are watertight, closed to pests, and structurally sound to protect the garments inside, as costume storage areas can be located in sub-optimal locations such as basements, attics, and converted storage buildings due to how much space is required to house the costume stock. If the storage space is less than idea, dehumidifiers (both chemical and mechanical) and lavender sachets can help mitigate dampness and insects.

What to Avoid

Some garments are not worth keeping from a donation, pulling for a costume, or taking the time to fit or alter. Sometimes it takes putting a garment on a dress form or an actor to see the flaws, but often the issues are clear right away. Avoid garments that are in poor condition, made of poor-quality materials, or are the wrong size unless you have absolutely NO other option available.

Garments that are stretched out, clearly frayed, torn, smashed and unfixable, faded, or stained can be useful if a distressed effect is what you need. Otherwise, they will appear sad and tired. If it is useful to have a distressed stock of items, box them together and label them.

Harsh colors will be difficult to mix with other colors or patterns unless the garment can be overdyed or you need a gaudy effect.

Certain materials will be difficult to make look attractive onstage. Static-prone fabric such as nylon or thin silk will stick to the wearer, especially during a static-prone time of year such as the winter or for a production where the wearer will be crawling, climbing, and performing other static-producing actions. Garments in which the fabric is so thin that the understructure, interfacing, facings, and raw seams show through will look cheap. Fabrics with a high proportion of synthetic fibers are difficult to successfully alter or modify the color and will retain body odors or stains. They also will not breathe, so they will be hot for the actor to wear.

Finally, measure garments as you pull them and look at the seam allowances available inside in order to avoid pulling garments that have no hope of fitting the actors. If measuring indicates the items will definitely be too tight, markedly too short for the wearer's body in the pant rise, or much too short or too long in the bodice, sleeves, or skirt, leave them on the rack.

Purchasing Garments

Modern garments can often be obtained more easily and inexpensively by purchasing than by building them in the costume shop. Purchasing items will free up time for the shop to build and alter other costumes that cannot be easily purchased. It is also possible to alter, modify, re-dye, and re-style purchased garments to get a more customized result.

Checking for Quality

Price is an indication but not an absolute guarantee of quality in purchased clothing. No matter where you shop, be sure to check a potential purchase carefully before you buy it. Once you have selected a garment and have ascertained that it will fit the actor, character, color scheme, and budget, look at it critically before you purchase it. Pay attention to the fiber content, construction quality, and whether there is sufficient fabric in the seam allowances and hems to allow for alterations.

New garments should be labeled inside for fiber content(s) and care requirements. Quality fabrics contain 100% or a very high percentage of natural fibers, so that the fabric breathes well and is comfortable to wear. The fabric should be supple rather than stiff, unless the garment is intended to be crisp or boxy. The colors should look good in the sunlight as well as the lights in the store; check the color by a store window and/or with a flashlight if possible. (Less expensive fabrics will look better in black or white.) If you are shopping for expensive garments, look for items made of quality fabrics that are worth keeping in stock after the production is over, thus turning expensive items into smart investments. Good quality fabrics tend to be made completely or primarily of natural fibers (cotton, flax/hemp/ramie/bamboo, silk, wool/mohair/cashmere), and/or some types of human-made fibers from natural sources (rayon/viscose/Tencel).

Look at the garment inside and out to check on the construction. Surface patterns should match at seamlines such as side seams, center fronts, center backs, shoulders, collars, lapels, plackets, and pockets. Seams and topstitching should not pucker or pull. Sleeves should be sewn smoothly into the armholes without puckering or pulling. Collars and lapels should have firm but supple interfacing to maintain their shapes. Pockets should lie neatly within the body of the garment and be symmetrical. Buttonholes should be cleanly bound, not fraying, be evenly sized and spaced, and lie accurately on the vertical (shirt front plackets and sleeve plackets) or horizontal lines (cuffs, jacket and waistcoat fronts, waistbands, and most other areas) of the garment. Zippers should be applied to lie flat and straight so that they will not gape or bow on the wearer. Jacket lining should not pull or bunch at the hem, sleeves hems, and armscyes. Darts, tucks, and hems should be smoothly pressed, and exposed seams should be pressed and cleanly finished with binding or serged edges. Finally, hems should be put up neatly, pressed appropriately, and have enough fabric depth to hang correctly.

If you would like the option of altering the garment, check that there is enough fabric in the seam allowances to allow for this. On an unlined garment, it will be easy to see the seam allowances, but on a lined garment, the seam allowance depth can be ascertained by running your thumbnail over the fabric near the seamlines to feel how far out the edge of the seam allowances extends. Many modern garments are made with very narrow serged-together seams that will not allow alterations, and with darts that are marked with punch holes that will not allow the dart placement to be adjusted.

Retail Sources

Costumes can be purchased new from retailers or used from thrift shops, in person or online. The merchandise available and price points offered at each vendor should be balanced against their return policies.

Retailers include large national department stores that carry a wide array of garments that have large stock in the stores and available to order and great return policies; national or international fast-fashion chains which have rapidly changing stock at low prices but limited return or no-return policies; large-box retailers with a limited clothing section, with low prices and different return policies; overstock retailers with discounted prices and short-term return deadlines; local stores that offer more varied merchandise at different price points but may only allow returns for in-store credit; and thrift stores that offer donated items from a variety of sources, merchandise that is unique and is offered at low prices, but that usually cannot be returned or only returned for in-store credit within a week (so that you will have to shop strategically and schedule fittings closely).

Whether or not one purchases costume options at a specific retailer will often depend on the return policy. Low prices on un-returnable items can quickly add up to be more expensive than purchasing full-priced garments that can be returned if they don't work. Check on the return policies before you purchase, and if you are interested in un-returnable options, you can take photos of items in the store and compare them to items that CAN be purchased and tried on before being returned. Finally, look at similar garments in different price ranges, including at the most expensive retailers, to accustom your eye to quality fabric and workmanship. I often purchase a range of returnable items to see what styles work best on an actor, with the knowledge that most of the garments will be returned.

Online Sources

Online shopping has expanded the variety of what is available, even if one lives in a remote location. Online retailers can offer interesting, hard-to-find, specialty, and/or inexpensive items that are delivered quickly to your door, which is very convenient during a busy project. However, a purchase that may be straightforward in person in a store can be more complex online, where one doesn't ever meet the vendor or examine the product in real life.

It is very important to be clear about the retailer's return policy and timeline, because while it is convenient to receive packages quickly, it is easy to miss a return deadline when one is busy on a production or if the return process is cumbersome. If an item is not returnable, it carries the same risk as purchasing items in person that are not returnable PLUS the risk that a garment that looks good in a photo may be disappointing once it is received and examined.

Before making an online purchase, check it for quality as much as you are able, keeping in mind the list in the "Checking for Quality" section. Look at online comments and reviews for the item and for the vendor. Examine the item carefully in photos from all available angles, look for the fabric fiber contents, and look up the item description and dimensions.

Be very careful about the garment sizes. Manufacturers have their own size charts, which can be seen on their websites if you look for a garment to put in the shopping basket and then click on the Size Chart for that type of garment. In all cases, be sure that the sizes are translated into a scale that you understand, such as in metric versus imperial measurements. I suggest using the exact measurements shown on the pertinent size chart as a guide to selecting what size to order, rather than depending on the sizes that might be chosen from other vendors. Check what is meant on the site by European sizes versus British sizes versus S–M–XL sizes versus US numeric sizes versus denim sizes. Add in the additional aspects of body shape expectations for SIZE

RANGES such as Junior or Young Men's sizes versus Misses or Men's sizes versus Women's Plus or Big and Tall sizes versus Petite or Tall sizes. Finally, consider the size range that is usual to the area where a garment is manufactured versus the size range when you are located when you are deciding on S–M–XL sizes. Because sizes differ between vendors and retail location, take size numbers with a grain of salt, and be ready to adjust the garment in some manner once it is received and tried on the actor.

Once you have decided on a garment that is offered online, be aware of the retailer's location, the shipping method, shipping costs, and expected arrival time for the purchases. Products shipped from across the country, across the continent, or from another continent will usually take longer to receive than from a local vendor (and likely have a larger carbon footprint in the process). To save time, one may pay for a speedier shipping method, which can get quite expensive to save a few days or weeks. Of course, if the vendor does not process the order or deliver it to the shipper in a timely manner, the expedited shipping costs may not be worthwhile. If a purchase is made during a time of the year that is traditionally very busy for shippers or occurs during extreme weather, natural disaster, epidemic, international embargo, a time of regional lack of shipping capacity, or requires a customs inspection, shipping will take longer than one has planned. Give yourself several days extra between the expected arrival date and when you need to try the garment on the actor prior to first dress rehearsal.

The ordering and purchasing process can be different on each website, and a poorly designed site can freeze up repeatedly, lose the order midway through the process, or be confusing enough that one ends up ordering more or less of the garments than one believes they had. A well-designed purchasing website is wonderful to use, encouraging customers to return in the future. The customer service department should be easily available and responsive when one has questions about the order or if items are lost or delayed (which may not be clear until there is a problem AFTER the purchase has been made); check vendor ratings if they are available; and consider how well the purchasing process has been designed. The type of currency accepted, whether it is only the vendor's local currency, a range of international currency options, cryptocurrency, or a third-party online payment system can be a bar to purchasing merchandise. A good vendor should also send an itemized email receipt after the purchase is finalized, which is less automatic than one would wish. And, of course, be careful to check that the website indicates that it is secure, although this cannot always be confirmed.

Borrowing and Renting

Borrowing and renting are great methods for obtaining costumes, especially if you are looking for period costumes or specialty items that cannot be purchased from a fashion retailer. The difference between borrowing and renting, obviously, is whether there is a charge to obtain the garments themselves. However, in most cases, the garments will need to be washed or dry-cleaned before being returned, there may be transportation costs to travel to the theatre or company from which the costume will be obtained, there may be a pulling cost if the costume staff cannot travel to pull in person, and any shipping costs to and from the costume source will be charged to the borrower or renter. Even if one is borrowing costumes without a rental charge, there will still be some costs.

Groups of theatres in a local area may create a borrowing group in which they can pull from one another's stock at no charge for use in productions. The group may include universities, colleges, high schools, community theatres, regional theatres, and/or opera companies but is not open to the wider community. This is a terrific asset, sharing resources, saving time and money, and reducing waste. Treat anything borrowed with the greatest care in order not to lose borrowing privileges.

In some situations, the actor may own a garment or shoes that would be perfect for a production. They may allow you to borrow the items and may even prefer to wear their own shoes to be more comfortable. Equity actors may also ask the theatre to RENT their garments if they are used for their costumes. Equity rental charges are relatively small and are well worth it to be able to use garments that fit well and which would not be affordable to purchase with the production budget. If one is using borrowed costumes, treat them very carefully, have them cleaned, and return them in their original condition.

When pulling costumes, have the actors' measurements with you and compare them to the garment measurements to focus your borrowing or rental choices. If you are ordering rental costumes from a website and cannot take garment measurements in person, **verify what the website measurements mean**. For example, some websites measure the chest/bust circumference of a garment such as a jacket and list THAT number, but a person with the same chest/bust circumference as the number listed for the garment will need an additional 3–4″ in the garment to allow for wearing ease. In other words, a US size 42 jacket should fit a person with a 42″ chest, but the garment itself will actually measure 45–46″ at the chest level. This type of confusion is more common than one would suppose, and if the measurements on the site do not include the usual wearing ease, you will need to add the correct ease amounts to the wearer's body measurements to get the right measurement for what will fit your wearer. The discussions for How to Measure an Existing Garment in each chapter on how to fit garments will include the standard **wearing ease** that a garment should include in addition to the wearer's body measurements. Take size numbers on ready-made garments with a grain of salt. If you are able to pull costumes in person, be sure to measure everything you are interested in before you take them with you, to save having to pay rental fees and shipping costs on garments that have no chance of being used.

It is more cost-effective to rent a FEW extra options when you are select-ing costumes, to avoid paying for additional shipping or pulling fees. While a rental house may not charge the full rental fee for costumes returned before the production opening date, there is usually a Re-Stocking Fee along with the shipping costs incurred to return the unused garments before the show opens. Be sure to get the unneeded items into the mail on time to avoid paying the full rental fee.

Most rental agreements list what you can and cannot do to the garments while they are in your possession. However, even if this is not spelled out, you **cannot alter the garments permanently**, which means no dyeing, cutting, gluing, or permanent alterations such as adding cut-out buttonholes or cutting down a neckline or armscye. You are also usually expected to restore the cos-tume to its original size and appearance if you adjust it, alter the hem lengths, or add trim. Be sure to budget the time and labor to restore the costumes. You will need to dry-clean the garments before they are sent back, usually within a week of the show closing.

If you have received rented garments that do not fit perfectly, there are some reversible alterations that can help. If the neckline of a garment is too high, one may be able to slightly open up the shoulder seams and center seams (if they exist) to fold down the neckline to a wider circumference. The waist-band on a skirt or trousers can be extended and dropped slightly if the side seams are slightly opened up, to create a larger circumference. Armscyes that are too snug may be opened up by opening up the side seams of a garment and reinserting the sleeves along with an underarm gusset made of fabric that is similar to the garment body. I have also cut new sleeves for dresses out of coordinating fabric to the garment and added more of the coordinating fabric on the garment as trim to make the alteration look intentional.

If you are working on a large production with garments gathered from a variety of sources, it is very important to keep complete records about what comes from what source so that you know where the costumes need to be returned. Take photos when you borrow each item, and good notes about any changes that have been made for your production that you will have to reverse.

4

PREPARING TO CONDUCT A FITTING

A costume fitting appointment brings together garments, an actor, a cutter/draper/patternmaker, and a designer to evaluate how the garment fits the actor's body, expresses the character, supports the concept of the production, and furthers the designer's vision.

I have conducted thousands of fittings with individual actors or with groups of performers being fit at the same time, and in a wide variety of standard and non-standard locations. However, despite the fact that a fitting appointment may be taking place in an odd location, the essence of the event remains the same. This chapter examines **What** should be in the fitting space, **Who** might be in the fitting room, and **How to call the actor** to a fitting appointment. How to conduct the fitting itself is covered in later chapters.

Items in the Fitting Room

A fitting space needs a place with **privacy** for the actor to change out of their clothes and into the costume pieces. Even if the actor is not shy or is used to changing garments in front of others, there should be a private space available for the actor to change if they would like to. This is especially important for someone trying on a corset or other support garments, or when fitting actors under age 18. If the fitting room is a separate space from the costume shop, there should still be an area for the actor to be able to change clothes in private. This may mean having an inner curtained area within the room, or having everyone besides the actor leave the room until the actor is ready for the other people to come back into the room.

The fitting area should have a **chair** for actors to use when putting on shoes, and a place for them to put their own clothes after they have changed

DOI: 10.4324/9781351131353-5

into the costume. If the actor is being fit barefoot, they will appreciate standing on a square of carpet or on a folded towel. A full-length mirror will allow the actor to see their final appearance. This can be an inexpensive **mirror** propped up against the wall, but be careful of the mirror's angle as it can distort the reflected body proportions and make the actor unhappy with their appearance. **Good lighting** will help the designer see color and garment shape clearly.

An actor will often be assigned to wear a washable garment such as a T-shirt or camisole under their costumes as a "**skin layer**" to absorb sweat during a performance. Have these undergarments near to the fitting area if you have not chosen them beforehand and try them during the fitting appointment.

Appropriate undergarments such as corsets, petticoats, skirt shapers, slips, body smoothers or shapers, body padding, or period bras should be available to put on at the start of the fitting. The actor may need help getting these items on. Be sure that the undergarments fit securely and comfortably before you proceed. Add shoes and hosiery if you have them at hand.

There will need to be a **hanging rack or flat areas to stack garments.** Costumes being tried during the fitting appointment should be arranged in the room prior to the actor's arrival. **Sort the garments in order of preference with the best options first.** Not all garments need to be tried on but it is helpful to have some options available so that you have somewhere to turn if your first choices do not work. Be sure also to have a place to put items that are discarded so that you are not confused later – I like spaces to put items that are clearly **Good** options, **Maybes**, and **Nos** during a fitting. If you find items that will work, pin a label to the garments with information about the character, scene, and actor.

Renderings and research materials should be brought to each fitting appointment. The designer will want to bring in their show binder, and there should be note-taking materials in the room for whoever is assigned to keep records.

You need to have access to a **variety of tools** during a fitting appointment. If the fitting room is dedicated to this purpose, the items can be stored in the room in clearly labeled drawers or rolling storage carts. If the fitting room is a found space, you may need to bring the tools with you. The types of tools you will need include:

1. *Measuring tools* include a tape measure, and an L-square and or hem marker/floor ruler to mark hem levels from the floor.
2. *Marking tools* such as a fade-able fabric marker, water-soluble marker, chalk pencil, or dressmaker's/tailor's chalk to write on a mockup garment. It is helpful to use different colors of chalk or marking pens for different rounds of fittings or final alteration lines. For existing garments, I suggest using **large safety pins** to indicate where to adjust the garments. Some

people prefer using straight pins, but they tend to fall out after the fitting appointment or can poke the actor or person conducting the fitting.

3. *Adjusting tools* – Small shears (known as tailor's points), a seam ripper, 8–9″ shears.

4. *Useful items* – I also like to have some scrap muslin handy if I need to piece in more fabric during a mockup fitting or drape a detail, and I use ½–1″ elastic to create suspenders or gather in a garment area as needed. Shoulder pads are useful for fitting jackets, and also for simulating body padding if needed. Hair elastics and hair clips will keep the actors' hair out of the way when you are fitting the neckline. Wig caps and bobby pins are useful for fitting wigs.

Persons in the Fitting Room

The essential relationship during a fitting appointment is between the actor and the person who is adjusting the costume. The person adjusting the costume may be the patternmaker, the costume designer, or someone who is functioning as both the designer and draper in the production. In most cases, there is an actor, designer, and draper present. Anyone else in the room should be there to assist the process – be sure to clarify that any first hands or assistants in the room should NOT be interjecting their impressions or opinions during the fitting. For an actor who is under 18, it is important to give them privacy while they are dressing, and there should always be a second adult in the room, which may be the actor's parent(s) or other costume personnel, while one is adjusting their costume. Otherwise, try to avoid the actor's friends, partners, children, and/or pets joining the fitting.

Some directors like to be part of a fitting, but this can be distracting and tip the balance of the relationships in the room. I try to avoid the situation by taking photos of each look that is being considered and sharing them with the director, or by having the costumed actor step out of the fitting room to show the director in person once I am happy with the costume. It is difficult to absolutely refuse the director's admittance to the fitting room, but one can mitigate the situation by keeping them informed of the best options after the session is over so that they are not tempted to attend.

The relationships between the designer and actor, and the designer and draper, must be cooperative. The actor must feel trust in the designer, that is they will make the actor look attractive and appropriate as well as listen to the actor's concerns. The designer must be able to communicate clearly and efficiently with the draper and vice versa. The draper must be sensitive to how the actor feels in the garment, careful not to poke the actor with a pin or nip them with shears, and make the actor feel secure about their body.

Issues can arise if any of these three people feel that their role in the process is being usurped or if they do not respond well to commentary from the other persons. For example, the designer may want to touch the garments during the fitting, but the draper may feel pushed out of the way if the designer gets up and touches the garment to adjust the fit in some way. How technical can the designer's requests be to the draper? Some drapers have strong artistic opinions, but the designer may feel that their design is being impinged upon if the draper makes comments. How artistic and design-oriented can the draper's suggestions to the designer be? These are issues to clarify prior to the actual fitting so that the process does not become a battle of wills in front of an actor. In addition, the actor may feel that because they are playing the role, their personal taste and ideas are most important. Consider how the designer can support the actor's work while making strong design choices.

In a professional costume shop, there are usually additional people in the fitting room. They may include the costume shop manager, who needs to keep abreast of the overall shop workload; the assistant shop manager or shopper, who needs to keep track of what needs to be purchased or pulled; the first hand, who takes notes and hands safety pins to the draper; and, potentially, an assistant costume designer who may help keep the designer focused, the research materials at hand, and help locate items that are needed during the fitting. Once the garments are fit, a wig person may bring in the wigs for the costume, and a craftsperson may bring in hats or accessories or be called in if garment colors need to be adjusted.

In an academic costume fitting session, one can expect the costume shop manager; the draper, whether they are a student or a staff member; the costume designer as well as a costume design faculty member if the designer is a student; and a person taking notes and handing safety pins to the draper. If students who have worked on the costume that is being fit are in the costume shop during the fitting appointment, it is nice to call them in to see their work at the end of the session.

Getting the Actors in for a Fitting

Different theatres will have different methods for calling in actors for fittings. Professional theatres will tend to coordinate fittings through the stage manager, academic theatres will call actors through the stage manager or by contacting actors directly, while small theatres may expect the designer who is also working as the key technician to contact the actors directly.

With the designer's availability in mind, the standard protocol is for the costume shop manager to make a request for specific actors to come to the fitting area for a set amount of time within a particular future time frame. In professional theatre, the fitting might be set up for as soon as the day after the fitting request is made, while in smaller or academic theatres, the fitting may be scheduled within the next week. For a Broadway production, the costume shop is often a separate business in the New York City area and not associated with the theatre company producing the show, so the producing organization will have to arrange for actor transportation from the rehearsal site to the costume company during the rehearsal day. Logistics in this case are tricky, and appointments may need to be adjusted multiple times for days before the actor actually arrives for the fitting.

In an Equity theatre with the rehearsal area and costume shop in the same building or complex, the actors will generally be scheduled for a time adjacent to their rehearsal call for that day, or for a time in the midst of their rehearsal day. Since their rehearsal times are during the work day, this means having fittings during regular business hours. If actors are coming from the rehearsal hall, expect that they will be a bit late. They will likely have been excused right at the scheduled fitting time, have to travel to the fitting area, and need to stop by the restroom before they arrive. In addition, if they are expected to return to rehearsal, they are often expected to be back there at the exact time of the end of their appointment. The stage manager will often call the costume shop before the end of the appointment to check that the actor is heading back to the rehearsal. This means that a fitting that is called for 2:00–3:00 in an Equity theatre will really take place from 2:10 to 2:50, at most.

For an academic theatre, fittings are conducted during regular shop hours. The actor should be expected to arrive and leave right on time. Student actors are often coming from class or work and need to get to their next class or job, so the fitting must be wound down so that they can get back into their street clothes on time at the end. Due to the process of calling in student actors, the actor may have been scheduled up to a week prior to the appointment and may forget the appointment, so an email or text reminder from the costume shop or the stage manager is helpful. If available, a digital scheduling system can allow the actors to sign up for fittings and receive reminders online.

For small theatres where rehearsals take place during the evenings, actors often try to get their fitting appointments adjacent to their rehearsal calls.

Be sure to request enough time to comfortably complete the fitting tasks planned for that session. Trying on ready-made garments takes more time than may be expected; fitting muslin mockups takes at least 30 minutes per costume look. A fitting of 90 minutes is the maximum you can expect to request, and for anything past 60 minutes, it becomes difficult to maintain focus. Don't go past the set appointment time without first asking the actor whether they are willing to do so. In an Equity theatre, there may be a financial penalty to the costume shop for going overtime, and the actor may be expected to return to rehearsal right after the scheduled fitting. In an academic theatre, the student actor is likely to have a class to rush off to but may feel constrained to stay if the designer is a faculty member. In all cases, respect the actor's time and be ready to use time efficiently. Multiple fitting sessions may need to be scheduled if an actor has multiple costumes to look at.

Number of Fittings

It is expected to have an average of **three** fitting appointments per actor after the measurements have been taken, even if the garments are all purchased items. Factor in whether an actor moves quickly or slowly through the process of changing clothes, and this may mean additional fitting appointments to get everything done. For an Equity actor, there may be a contractual limit to how many fitting appointments they may be called for and when during the work day they can occur. Be organized before the fitting starts in order to maximize your limited time with the actor.

For constructed costumes, you can expect to have AT LEAST:

1. A mockup fitting. If the initial test garment has a lot of corrections, a second mockup fitting may be necessary and should be welcomed. Intended closure placements and an approximate hem level should be marked at this time.
2. A first fabric fitting, in which the shell of the garment will be sewn, sleeves may be basted in or available to pin in (either in fabric or in muslin), and collars, waistbands, and/or lining may be assembled but might not be attached. If the lining layers are not available, be sure not to over-fit the garment shell during this fitting or the final garment could be too snug.
3. A final fabric fitting, in which the lining is inserted (either sewn in or basted in), collars and cuffs are attached, and some closures (zippers, hooks, snaps) are added. Buttons and buttonholes are generally NOT put in for this fitting as they are not readily changed. The goal for this fitting is to confirm the final look of the garment, check closure placement, and set hem levels. It is helpful to double-check that all accessories and garments are available for this fitting, so that the fitting can also be used as a review of the entire costume look with the actor prior to first dress rehearsal.

For pulled and purchased costumes, you can expect to have AT LEAST:

1. An initial try-on of your best guesses for the character and their costumes. This is a good opportunity to discuss the character with the actor and to get their take on your approach (within reason). You will see how their measurements translate into their actual figures, and what will look good on them and what may need to be adjusted. I consider this the "broad strokes" of finding the character. Try to have the base undergarments available if they will affect the costume fit.
2. A second fitting with additional choices to refine or re-establish the character's look. If shoes were not obtained for the first fitting, have them for this fitting, and be willing to send them to rehearsal after the fitting.

3. A final fitting to check that all items are present, including all accessories and details. This is a good chance for the actor and designer to discuss all of the changes and to be sure that each is clear about what is worn at what point in the play. I also talk through any quick changes with the actors at this time. I use a summary of this meeting as the basis of the dressing lists that I give to each actor at the first dress rehearsal.

5

STANDARDS OF GOOD FIT

Knowing how a garment **should** fit will allow a designer to make informed choices. Garments look better if they fit well and are made of quality materials that will allow alterations. It makes sense to spend money on skilled labor to alter good quality garments made of natural fibers rather than purchasing expensive garments that may not fit perfectly and/or are made of synthetic fibers. It is often a matter of learning which garments are worth altering.

This chapter will cover the general standards of GOOD FIT that can be applied to most garments. While there are more specific elements of fit that are applied to various types of garments, the list in this chapter is a good starting point. Consider this information when trying on garments to assess whether the garments will be worth using. Please note that when trying on garments, the assumption is that the person is wearing **the same type of support garments** that they will wear with the garment in the future, and that **all the layers of an intended ensemble are being tried on together**.

Before the fitting, be sure to measure the garments you are fitting at key points (chest/bust, shoulder width, waistline, back waist length, hip, neckline, and sleeve lengths) and check against the actor's measurements. Better to have the garment a little too large or long than to have it very snug on the actor. The specific measurements to take for each category of garments are included in the chapter on that type of garment.

General Standards of Fit

In assessing whether the garment fits the wearer, there are guidelines to keep in mind. After you have had the chance to fit a number of actors, the guidelines will become second nature. **Until you are comfortable assessing**

DOI: 10.4324/9781351131353-6

how garments should fit on an actor, I suggest reviewing this chapter and the next before each fitting appointment. Current fashions or the time period in which the design is set may change how the guidelines are interpreted. However, for most time periods, garment styles, and wearer figures, a well-fitting garment can be assessed on the following guidelines:

1. The center lengthwise grainline of the fabric making up a bodice, sleeves, skirt, trousers, or jacket will USUALLY be **perpendicular to the floor.** This will keep the lengthwise, or warp, grain running up and down the length of the figure. In most cases, the lengthwise grain should be run precisely up and down the center of the torso, arms, and legs. This allows the fabric to hang vertically, as well as making the front edges of a jacket or shirt hang plumb without pulling or stretching. Because the lengthwise grainline is the least-stretchy and most stable direction of the fabric, using a lengthwise vertical grainline will allow a center garment closure to lie smoothly without twisting and will prevent the garment from "growing" in length over time.

   There are certain situations where the lengthwise grain is used **across** the body so that the crosswise, or weft, grain is perpendicular to the floor, such as in a full gathered skirt that needs to stand out away from the body. In other situations, the bias or diagonal grain, which has a softer and stretchy-er quality than the lengthwise or crosswise grains, is used on a garment to create a figure-hugging silhouette that flows outward at the lower edges. However, unless the garment is cut on the bias or has specifically angled seams, **all vertical seams**, including side seams, are usually perpendicular to the floor.

2. The garment should hang smoothly when the wearer is standing straight. However, remember that the actor's natural posture may not be perfectly straight up-and-down or balanced side-to-side. Some people have a distinct tilt to one side, roll their shoulders forward, push their abdomen out, or slouch in some manner. Actors often carry their typical posture with them onto the stage, so it makes sense to fit their garments as they are standing relaxed in the fitting room. Therefore, be sure to allow the wearer a few minutes to relax into their natural posture or the posture that they will adopt on stage as you start the fitting session, as the costume will be seen on a wearer as they stand and move on stage. I generally ask them about their rehearsals so far or make other conversation as the fitting begins so that the actor will loosen up.

   One can ask an actor who tends to slouch to stand up straight in the fitting room, but they will commonly return to their typical posture after a few minutes on stage. Keep this in mind so you will not be disappointed when you see them in the costume during dress rehearsals, and accept the actor as they tend to naturally stand or move.

3. The garment should be comfortable when the wearer walks, bends, and sits, and it should return to its original position on the body when the wearer stands up. The garment should fall back into place after the wearer raises and lowers their arms. It should not catch on the body or crawl up the figure, which indicates that the garment is too snug or made of a fabric that may need to be lined in order to fall smoothly.

When fitting a period garment, the concept of **comfort** is relative, so the garment must allow the wearer to perform their stage actions as needed, even if they may feel more restriction than they are used to when wearing their own clothing. Discuss how the costume should feel when worn, and how the actor should move in the garments to create a period impression, such as hitching the front of trousers legs before sitting, buttoning a jacket when standing up, or adjusting a skirt neatly while sitting. If the costumes will inhibit movement, it is very important to make rehearsal garments or the garment mockups available for rehearsals. In this case, enlist the stage manager to make sure that the actors actually wear the rehearsal garments and shoes for each rehearsal. That way, if there are truly any issues with movement, there is a greater possibility for them to be addressed well before the show garments are completed.

4. The garment should be neither too tight, too loose, too wide, or too narrow. It should not strain, collapse, crawl up, or sag over the figure. No diagonal or horizontal strain wrinkles should appear within the body of the garment. These wrinkles will point to a fit problem, which is usually a **too tight** area of the garment. Armholes, sleeves, and necklines should not pull, sag, or wrinkle across the upper sleeve or chest, particularly when the wearer moves. **Horizontal pulling wrinkles indicate that a garment is too tight,** while **vertical conical sags indicate that a garment is too large**. Both conditions may be present in a single garment or ensemble, in different areas.

A garment that fits well is flattering. It will have enough fabric to glide over the body and fall vertically. A too tight garment adds visual weight because the garment will have horizontal wrinkles that point right to the area that is too tight. A too loose garment adds bulk to the figure by creating a loose, boxy, overly large silhouette.

Ease

EASE is the extra amount of room that is added to the body measurements when measuring or patterning a garment. **It is the difference in size between the body and the garment in order to allow for comfort and movement.** There are two different types of ease with two different purposes: wearing ease and style ease.

Wearing Ease is the amount of room built into every garment so that the wearer can move comfortably, even in slim-fitting garments. This is extra room above the body measurements. The standard range for wearing ease in woven fabrics in fitted or semi-fitted garments are: chest – 1–4″, waistline – ½–1.5″, and fullest hip – 1–4″. These ranges differ by specific garments, discussed in later chapters.

The exception to this is for garments made of woven fabrics with Spandex added, or knits where the fabric is expected to stretch over the body curves. For stretch woven fabrics, the exact blend and percentage of Lycra/Spandex in the fabric will determine how stretchy the fabric will be. However, a good **starting point is to expect to have half the amount of ease as would be needed for a non-stretch fabric** for that type of garment. The ease ranges would thus be: chest – ½–2″, waistline – ¼–3/4″, and fullest hip ½–2″. For knit fabrics, wearing ease amounts depend on the amount of stretch in the fabric, determined by the stretch and recovery when the fabric is grasped and pulled. The ease may range from the same as needed for the stretch woven fabrics listed above to **.85% to .95%** of the body measurements (i.e. the garment will measure LESS than the body measurements, rather than adding ease amounts to the body measurements for woven garments). Look carefully at knit garments during a fitting; even though they may be able to stretch around the actor they may also be so tight that the garments will have unwanted horizontal wrinkles.

Style or design ease is the **added fabric used to create the design silhouette**. The amount of added fullness is part of the style and cannot be completely removed in the fitting without changing the overall design. The placement and amount of added fullness is often a marker of a time period and is best evaluated by having both the costume renderings and some clear research images available to consult during the fitting. Keep your research materials at hand so that you can keep the correct silhouette in mind when you evaluate whether the garment is too wide or narrow according to the period that you are trying to represent. The actor may be unfamiliar with the period style, and having clear research available will illustrate the style to the actor while helping the fitting team make informed decisions. At the same time, seeing the effect of the style fullness in a muslin mockup is a good way to determine whether the drawn design is what the designer really wants to see on stage and whether it is in proportion to the stage space.

If style fullness is markedly altered during one costume fitting, be sure to evaluate whether this procedure needs to be repeated with all other similar garments in the production to create a unified impression.

5. The neckline should fit smoothly on the body without gapping or pulling. Check the exact neckline shape and size AFTER the garment bodice has

been completely fit. However, at the start of the fitting time, be sure to get the neckline at least large enough for the actor to feel un-constricted, by either un-fastening some of the closures on an existing garment or by carefully clipping slightly into the neckline seam allowance on a mockup at several spots, until the fabric lies smoothly over the wearer's upper chest.

6. Shoulder seams should lie straight across, and smoothly against, the top of the wearer's shoulders unless the style has purposely dropped shoulder seams. The shoulder seams should be centered on the shoulders from neck to armscye unless the style has a dropped shoulder line and should not gap at the neckline or shoulder ends.

7. All darts and shaping seams should point to the fullest part of the body curves, not above or below. Dart tips should **end within 1 inch of the bust points** and angle toward shoulder blades, stomach, seat, elbow tips, and other rounded areas on the wearer's body.

8. The bodice length should be correct and the waistline seam or waistline shaping should fit comfortably at the natural waistline of the wearer. The exception to this is if the style is purposely designed with a raised or dropped waistline, or with extra length to create a blouson or puffed effect at the lower edge.

9. Side seams should lie halfway between front and back of the figure, perpendicular to the floor, unless the desired style has specifically angled or off-set side seams.

10. Closures should fasten smoothly and easily, without horizontal pulling, creating gaps between closures, or repeatedly coming undone. If the garment is intended to be snug, there may be tension on the closures. However, be careful that the garment is not so snug that the closures are too difficult to fasten. This is especially true of a snug bodice with an invisible zipper closure – while the bodice may technically be large enough to fit the wearer, it is difficult to zip an invisible zipper on a snug garment (particularly at the point where the skirt zipper reaches the waistline and needs to continue up into the bodice), and the zipper will tend to un-zip during wearing. As invisible zippers can break more easily than conventional zippers and can get caught on seam allowances, they should be used sparingly on costumes, particularly those that are involved with quick changes.

11. The back view of all garments should be checked, especially as the wearer walks. Jackets, skirts, and pants should fit smoothly over the hips and seat without binding or flapping loose in back. Have the wearer sit, to check for comfort and to ascertain that the garment returns to the correct body position when standing. If the garment binds on the body or does not fall back into place when standing, it is too snug.

12. Full-length sleeves should hit below the wrist bones. For most sleeves, the grainline falls down the length of the arm, which means that it slightly angles toward the front of the body from the shoulder line to the wrist.

If the vertical grainline is off, the cap area of the sleeve will appear to twist slightly. To correct this, the sleeve should be rotated in the armhole until the grainline falls smoothly toward the sleeve hem when worn. To allow for comfortable movement, the armscyes (i.e. armholes) should be neither baggy nor tight, and the sleeve cap should have some ease by being larger than the armscye in which it is sewn. Maximum movement will be gained with a shorter and wider sleeve cap, sewn close to the body armpit.

Shirt cuffs should fit neatly, without binding at the closures or hanging slack. A very slight extra vertical length (approximately 3/8″) in the sleeve just above the cuff will allow the cuffs to stay in place during movement. If the shirt is worn with a suit jacket, the sleeve length may need to be ½–1″ longer than the actor's center back to wrist measurement to keep the sleeve from riding up under the jacket. If a ready-made shirt cuff is slightly too long, buttoning the cuff at the inner of the two cuff buttons will keep the cuff from falling over the hand.

13. Neckline shape and collar can be perfected once the garment is completely fit. The neckline should fit smoothly over the body when the fabric is cut to the desired depth. If the neckline gaps during a mockup fitting, a small dart can be pinned out in the neckline area which can be adjusted in the garment pattern in bust area darts or shaping seams. If the neckline gaps in a finished garment, it may be at least partially addressed by a narrow dart in the shoulder seam at the neckline intersection to tighten the vertical drop of the neckline. If the theatre owns the garment, a gaping neckline on an existing garment can have piping added to the neckline, and the cording inside can be pulled up to snug in this area.

    Collars should be fit **after** the neckline is determined. The back of a shirt or jacket collar should fit smoothly across the shoulders without pulling. A shirt collar should fit close to the back of the neck without gaping or straining, while a jacket upper collar should fit smoothly around a shirt collar. When folded down in place, the lower edge of a shirt or jacket collar should cover the seam on the garment neckline.

    A collar intended to stand at the neck should neither bind nor gape and should rise to a flattering level on the wearer's neck.

14. Hemlines should be level to the floor unless the style specifically calls for a different hemline shape. Mark the hemline up from the floor rather than down from the waistline to account for posture and body curves. Be sure that the actor is in their intended shoes and remind them not to look downward at you while you are marking the hem, or the hem will end up too short in the front.

15. Finally, pay attention to the finishing touches on each garment such as jacket lapels, pant or skirt waistlines, pockets, and pleats, as these details will help create a well-fitted impression. Always fit the garment body first and then move on to the detail areas.

Once you are comfortable with the markers of good fit, you will be prepared to have the actor try on the garments that you have selected for them. In essence, most fittings will be either of ready-made garments or of mockups, or some variation in between. Therefore, the following chapters will deal with both possibilities within the categories of different garments. We will begin by looking at the general outline for a fitting and then examine the details of good fit for different types of garments.

6

GENERAL METHOD FOR A GARMENT OR MOCKUP FITTING

The fitting time you have with actors is limited and should be utilized efficiently. Start each fitting appointment with a clear sense of what you need to accomplish, and have all the needed supplies in place. Deliver the garments to the fitting area by the night before the fitting appointment. Whether you are a designer or draper or both, give yourself time to get to the space prior to the appointment and see the set-up of the room, especially if you are not in your own studio. Do not arrive at the fitting at the last minute, or rush in after a morning of shopping, pulling, or other responsibilities. Instead, schedule the event so the entire fitting staff (if any) will have a chance to catch their breaths and can focus on the event.

Have the fitting area prepared with all needed tools, copies of renderings, and research pictures. An actor/scene chart is helpful to check for costume changes, and be sure to assemble all garments needed, including undergarments, support garments, hosiery, and shoes. Even in a professional theatre, as a designer, I prefer to set up my own fitting room by arranging the garments by type and in order of preference for the actor to try on. Know where all your garment options are placed so you can locate them immediately. The time allotted for a fitting is always limited, and you should not go over the allotted appointment; when working with Equity actors you should not keep them over the appointment time. More discussion of the fitting room set-up is contained in Chapter 4.

For a mockup or built garment fitting, be sure that the technicians who are building the items are aware of the fitting appointment time well in advance so that the garment is ready. Keeping the actor waiting in the fitting room for a technician to finish a garment is a waste of their time. If you are working in an academic shop, be sure to have tasks clearly laid out for the less-skilled workers

DOI: 10.4324/9781351131353-7

to do out in the shop during the fitting time. This will save the faculty or staff from having to field student questions in the midst of a fitting appointment.

Before the fitting appointment, be sure to measure any existing garments you are trying on at key points and check against the actor's measurements; the measurements to check are included at the start of each of the following chapters for fitting specific garments. If garments that you are trying to fit have been altered for a previous production, remove the alterations before the appointment time if the alterations will not fit the actor. Better to have the garments a little too large or long than to have them too snug on the actor. Actors are as sensitive as anyone else about their bodies, and it is important that they feel that they are being treated with sensitivity during a fitting. After all, they may be in their underwear with one or more people staring at them, trying to get a garment to fit on them. In this case, it is easy for the actor to feel that their own body is the problem, but the garment itself is always the problem, not the actor's body. If, despite your preparation, you have a garment that proves to be too snug during a fitting appointment, move on to the next choice on the rack. Meanwhile, the too-snug garment can be handed off to a technician in the costume shop IF it is possible to let out a seam quickly in order to make the garment usable to be re-tried.

When you are fitting costumes that are composed of purchased garments, remember that commercial garments are fit on models with particular combinations of measurements that the brand feels are closest to their Target Customer, which are then graded up and down to make different sizes. If the wearer doesn't have the same type of proportions as the fit model for the brand, or if they are several sizes smaller or larger than the size of the fit model, the garments from a brand may not automatically fit. Make the actor feel taken care of, and pre-screen garments prior to the fitting so that they are not faced with a large assortment of garments that do not fit them.

If you are fitting mockup garments, be sure to baste the garment together using long stitches so that the garment can be easily adjusted during the fitting session.

Actors and directors will want shoes and period undergarments as soon as possible for rehearsal purposes, so it may be necessary to have fittings for these items during a separate appointment prior to fitting any mockups or garments.

Finally, until you are comfortable with this process, I suggest re-reading this chapter before each fitting as you gain experience.

The Fitting Process

1. Before trying on the garments or mockups, the actor should be fit in **all the layers that will be worn with the final garment on stage, including support garments, padding, skirt shapers, shaping hosiery, and the other layers in the costume.** For example, if the

fitting is for a jacket that is to be worn over a shirt and vest, have a shirt and vest in the room to fit under the jacket.

If the actor needs to wear a support garment, such as a specific style of bra or a body shaper, be sure that they come to the fitting wearing this garment if they will be providing it for the performances. If the theatre is providing these garments, be sure to have the support garments ready for the actor to try on with the garments you are fitting. For example, if the actor is supposed to wear an underwire bra with the costume but does not wear this type of bra in daily life or own such a garment, **it is the responsibility of the costume shop to obtain the bra for purposes of the production and for fittings**. If the actor will wear a "skin layer" such as a T-shirt or camisole under the final costume, have them try this on as well.

2. Be sure the actor is wearing the **shoes** they will wear onstage if at all possible. If you can try on potential shoes during an earlier measurement session, you will save yourself work later. If you don't have shoes chosen, have a range to try in order to get a sense of the height and shape of the final shoes, as they will affect actor posture and movement as well as the hang of garments and where the garments will end on the body.

3. If you have a range of existing garments from which to choose, separate the garments after you try each one on into groups of "Good," "Bad," and "Maybe." The "Good" items should look good and fit well with little or no alteration needed, and be of a fabric quality that is worth pursuing if alterations will be needed. The "Maybes" may be re-tried later during the appointment to see if they can be altered, especially if there are no "Good" options at the end of the session. The "Nos" simply are not fixable, are not flattering, or are not usable as compared with other, better choices.

4. Put on the garment(s). **Try to close the garment, but if the garment does not fit, assess whether it can be made to fit with a reasonable amount of time and skill**. For existing garments, quickly assess whether it is worth trying to make them fit or whether you have other options on hand to try, then move on to the other options to determine which of these will give the best result. You may have to go back to the best option available from the group once you have tried on all of the items available. Determine whether it is necessary to pull or purchase more garments for a second round of fittings.

   If you are fitting a muslin mockup, it can be easier to fit the garment if parts of the garment are stitched with the seamlines sewn on the outside or to try on the mockup inside out so that the adjustments can be pinned more easily. Pin the garment closed at the correct points along the marked seamlines. If the mockup cannot close completely, assess how to adjust the muslin within the fitting appointment, or take notes on how to alter the pattern after the fitting. It may be necessary to create a second mockup if the adjustments are extensive and complex.

5. Be sure to fit **both sides of the garment equally** – the best result will be an averaging of the two sides of the fit garment rather than depending on fitting one side of the garment and hoping that you have accurately kept the center line of the garment on the center line of the wearer's body.

   The exception to this is if the wearer has a markedly unbalanced posture, such as having had scoliosis. In this case, it will be necessary to adjust each side of the garment as needed so that the overall result hangs smoothly on the wearer. Be sure to clearly indicate the vertical center lines of the garment where it falls on the wearer for later reference, and to clearly label the wearer's right and left sides of the pattern so that it will be accurately cut from the final fabric.

6. **Assess the accuracy of the fit,** whether you are choosing options from existing garments or when fitting a mockup. If there are fastenings on existing garments, fasten them. Do the closures lie flat, do they gape because the garment is snug, or do they hang looser than planned? For a mockup, can you close the garment at the planned center lines?

   If the closures do not close, or they close but gape, this is because the garment is too snug. Check whether the closures can be moved slightly without altering the visual balance of the garment, or whether there is enough fabric in side seams/pleats/seams to let out the garment at the area that is snug. These alterations will be most successful if an existing garment has not been dyed after construction and is made of natural fabrics. On dyed garments, the old stitch lines may be visible after the alteration. With synthetic fabrics, the alterations may not be able to be smoothly pressed into the desired new shape.

   If the garment is hanging looser than the desired effect, move on to other areas of the fitting for now. The best method of addressing the fullness according to the desired period or style effect for the garment usually becomes clearer as you work.

   If you are fitting a mockup with a high neckline that is too small on the wearer, you will need to **clip the neck to the extent needed to make the wearer feel comfortable at this point**. Ask them if you may touch them, explain what you are about to do and that this is to protect them from your shears, and get their consent to place your hand between the ends of your shears and their neck when clipping. If you nip someone during a fitting, it is difficult to get them to relax and trust you after that moment. Once the garment can fit comfortably enough at the neckline to continue, proceed with the fitting.

7. Start with the **widest body curves** of the garment area, such as the chest/bust level of an upper body garment or the hip/seat level of the lower body garments. You may have to work back and forth between the support point level (the shoulders for the bodice and the waistline for

a skirt or trousers) and the widest body curve level (chest/bust or stomach level for the bodice, and hip/seat level for a skirt or trousers) to get the garment to hang smoothly. In most cases, the horizontal grainline of the garment, whether perceived in an existing garment or drawn onto a mockup, should lie parallel to the floor at the fullest part of the body curves, and the center lines of the garment should be on the lengthwise vertical grain in order to hang perpendicular to the floor.

8. Be sure that the **darts and shaping seams** point toward the fullest points of the body. If they do not, they may need to be lengthened, or the existing darts or seams may need to be un-picked and reshaped so that they fit smoothly over the body curves. Success for this step depends on whether the seam allowances are wide enough to be adjusted, or whether the darts have not been slashed. For commercial garments, seam allowances are usually miniscule and serged together, and blouse darts often have a punch hole approximately ¼″ from the sewn tip to act as a marker for the factory technician assembling the garment. Both of these facts will prevent the chest seams or dart tip placement from being adjusted very much on a commercially made modern garment.

9. Once the widest point of the body in a garment area is accommodated, work from the upper-most edges of the garment and fit the **support points**, such as shoulders, neckline, or waistline before moving **down the garment with the flow of gravity**. For example, AFTER the bust and hip levels are determined to accommodate the wearer's body, attend to the shoulders of upper body garments and the waistline of lower body garments. The shoulder or waistline levels may need to be raised or lowered to make the rest of the garment lie smoothly, or the shoulder or waistline widths may need to be made looser or narrower.

10. Once the garment is hanging smoothly from its support points, re-check that the fullest area of the body fits smoothly within that segment of the garment. Then, assess whether the garment needs to be taken in or let out to **fit smoothly down to the lower edge of the waistline and/ or hemline**.

11. Determine whether **more or less fullness should be added** to the garment at certain points or throughout to achieve the desired look. Carefully look at the design renderings and your research images to check this. Be very sure to look at the back and side views of the garment so that the garment looks good in totality. Adjusting fullness is easier to ask for with a mockup; with a finished garment, you may need to let out or add panels of fabric to achieve the desired fullness. If you are constructing a garment and have the budget for extra fabric, try to build in a deep hem, wide seam allowances for later adjustments, and decorative "opera tucks" that incorporate extra fabric in the body of the garment that can be increased or decreased for later wearers.

12. Check whether the **sleeves** of the garment fit comfortably on the wearer so that they can move comfortably. For a mockup fitting, sleeves should be hand-basted into armscyes, as they often need to be adjusted in order to hang smoothly on the wearer, and may even need to have more fabric added or subtracted across the upper arm to fit well. It is important to have both sleeves inserted in the garment to get an accurate picture of what the final garment will look like, even if you expect that they will need to be adjusted during the fitting appointment.

13. Have the **actor move around** the fitting room: sitting, walking, and doing any types of movement they are being asked to do onstage. This may result in the costumes needing to be let out in strategic spots in order to allow for movement as well as allowing the garments to fall back into place after the movement has ended.

    If actors are performing stage combat or dancing, they should go through their routines during the fitting – you may find that the actor needs more width across the bodice back at the mid-armhole level in order to fully extend their arms. Also, have the actor walk up and down stairs, particularly if the skirt or trousers are narrow. Even if the stage set has no stairs, there may be escape stairs or a stairway between the dressing rooms and the stage that the actors must negotiate in costume.

14. Once the body fits correctly, make sure that the **neckline fits** accurately for the design and does not reveal more than is planned. If the neckline needs to be lowered or reshaped, **draw in the desired neckline before clipping**. Any collars for the garment can then be added to the corrected neckline of a mockup or can be moved on the corrected neckline of an existing garment.

15. Mark the hem clearly if the existing garment will be hemmed after the fitting, or set a rough **hemline** if you are fitting a mockup.

16. Be sure the garment is **perfect**. An existing garment should be made of quality fabrics, in a flattering color, and be the correct length. Each garment should fit well when standing, sitting, and moving; allow for stage movement; look good at all angles, including the back, and coordinate with the other garments in the costume and on other characters.

    Be sure to check the fit of the garment against your research material if you are trying to reproduce a period effect or a specific style. If you are a working designer but are not quite sure of the results, it is a good practice to ask the draper their opinion of the garment's fit in order to enlist their expertise in your work and to train your own eye in what to look for in future. If you are a student conducting a fitting in a classroom situation, be sure to get your instructor to sign off on your results before you have the wearer remove the garments. If you are a costume technician in a fitting, be sure to get the costume designer to approve the results and agree to any adjustments before the actor removes the costume.

17. Record the fitting with clear written notes for later reference. Clearly designate the garments you will and will not be using for the actor to avoid discarding useful items, inadvertently assigning the same garment to multiple actors, or doing alterations on the wrong garment. Be sure that you have **clear notes** for any alterations, either on a hang tag on the garment or on a master "To Do" list.

18. **Take photos** from the front, back, and side views of the actor in costume. These are valuable to consult if there are questions about fitting notes, and to share with the director. If you send the photos to the director, be sure to clarify which costume the photos represent and whether the photos contain garments or items that are NOT part of the intended costume. As a designer, use the photos to consider whether the level of fit on this costume is appropriately similar to other costumes in this production.

Checklist for Each Garment Fitting

The list below is a handy guide to check for each fitting and summarizes the basic steps:

1. Be sure to have measured the garments you are fitting at key points and check against the actor's measurements.
2. Prepare the fitting room:

   All needed tools for fitting, as noted in Chapter 4
   Renderings and research materials, and actor/scene chart and/or the script
   Undergarments, shoes, and support garments
   Garments to be fit, arranged in order of preference

3. Review the correct standards for the garment you are fitting, keeping in mind the wearing ease and design ease that are appropriate for the final result.
4. Have the actor put on all the layers that will be worn with the final garment on stage, including support garments, padding, garment layers, and the actual shoes they will wear on-stage or a close facsimile in terms of heel height.
5. Put on the garment(s) and try to close. For ready-made garments, assess whether they can be made to fit with a reasonable amount of time and skill or whether you have other better options on hand to try on. If you have other options, determine which of these will give the best result or whether it is necessary to pull or purchase more garments for a second round of fittings. If a mockup does not close completely, assess how to adjust the muslin within the fitting,

or how to alter the pattern. It may be necessary to create a second mockup.

6. Be sure to fit BOTH sides of the garment for the best result.

7. Assess the accuracy of the garment fit once the wearer has enough room in the neckline to breathe. First attend to the widest body points of the garment, then work from the support points of the garment (shoulders, above the bustline for a strapless garment, or the waist-line) back down to the widest body points. Proceed in the direction of gravity to create a smooth fit that allows the wearer to move while the garment hangs smoothly.

8. Mark clearly where alterations need to be made. If working with a finished garment, a line of safety pins is a marking device that will remain in place until the alterations can be completed. If working with a mockup, you may prefer to write on the garment itself.

9. Check the fit of the garment in relation to the rest of the garments and the shoes to be worn with the costume. If possible, set a hemline level.

10. Be sure the garment is perfect. It should fit well, be comfortable, look good at all angles, be the correct length, and coordinate with other garments to be worn together.

11. Record the fitting with clear written notes and/or photographs for later reference. Clearly designate the garments you will and will not be using for the actor, to avoid discarding useful items or inadvertently assigning the same garment to multiple actors.

12. Consider whether the level of fit on this costume is appropriately sim-ilar to other costumes in this production.

With the basic techniques for conducting a fitting in mind, in the following chapters, we will move on to how to interpret the categories of folds and wrinkles you may see and the finer points of fit for specific categories of garments.

7

INTERPRETING WHAT YOU SEE DURING A FITTING

While conducting a fitting, you should start to see a commonality in how fabrics fold and pull when the garment does not fit perfectly. With the caveat that assessing fit has to be seen in terms of the period style or fashion that you are trying to reproduce, here are the broad categories of what you will see, with the standard adjustments that each issue will need to correct it.

1. Fabric pulling in **thin horizontal "draw-lines"** across parts of the body indicates that the garment is **too snug** for the wearer (Figures 8.3, 9.3, 11.2, 13.2, and 14.3, among others). The draw-lines often radiate out from the area that is too snug, and from rounded body areas, such as the bust points; across the hips, seat, tummy, or thighs; and across arms or from armscyes or crotch seams. The space across the too snug area needs to be increased.

On an existing garment, let out any vertical seamlines in the area with the draw-lines. Since commercial garments often do not have much seam allowances inside, you may only gain a small amount of fabric, but this may be enough if the alteration is made on several seamlines. If your theatre owns the garment, you may also split the garment vertically and add a piece of decorative trim, matching or coordinating fabric as available, or a gusset of fabric at the side seams to add more width to the garment.

DOI: 10.4324/9781351131353-8

On a mockup, let out the seams by un-stitching the seamlines in the affected area, and re-pinning the garment together with narrower seam allowances. A mockup should be cut with generous seam allowances and basted together, so that adjustments can be easily made during a fitting appointment. If the seam allowances are still too small to fit the wearer, one can pin in extra wedges or strips of muslin to adjust the garment to fit. Try to avoid cutting into the middle of a mockup garment while an actor is wearing it, as it can be jarring for the actor. Better to take good notes, and to cut and fit a second mockup. The garment pattern will need to be expanded wider, at the vertical seams and/or by adding wedges of additional room in the body of the pattern piece (Figure 13.2).

Be sure to clearly mark the new seamlines, and cross out any seamlines that are no longer accurate. You will also need to consider how these adjustments will affect any sleeve, collar, or garment pieces that are sewn to the altered seamline.

2. Fabric hanging in **soft, somewhat triangular folds**, tapering downward and outward from a support point on the body, such as the shoulders, bustline, neckline, waistline, or top of the sleeve, indicates that the area is **too loose** for the wearer's body (Figures 8.4, 9.6, 10.3 right, 11.3, 13.3, and 14.5, among others). While some of these folds may be desirable for a particular style, such as a soft blouse, dress, or flared skirt or trousers, if the folds are more pronounced than you prefer for the garment, you have several options:

On an existing garment, you may be able to taper in the existing seamlines, take out part or all of a panel of a loose skirt, or add decorative shaping details, such as gathers, tucks, pleats, or smocking to take in some of the excess fabric. You may also add what is known as an "Opera Tuck," a decorative vertical tuck that is taken in a garment to make it smaller in an area while allowing the garment to be let out again for a later use.

On a mockup garment, you may make the same adjustments as noted above for an existing garment. However, **if the garment itself is too flared**, the extra wedges of fabric on the garment may be pinned out of the mockup in several places, which will reduce the flare of the pattern piece more evenly and gracefully throughout the garment area than by just taking it out of one or two seams (Figure 13.3). The pinned-in mockup pieces would then be traced as a corrected pattern, or the original garment pattern can have wedges of paper folded out of it and eliminated to match what was pinned out of the mockup.

If the folds taper downward and outward from a position on a seamline, from the bust points or below a curved tummy or seat, the area below a rounded body area is hanging too loose. This may be an issue of the garment being **too flat** for the wearer's curves; refer to item 6 in this chapter for a fuller discussion of this issue. However, the solution may also be as simple as slightly increasing the intake on an existing dart, or tapering in a seamline.

3. If the fabric settles in **rounded, horizontal folds**, the garment is **too long** in that area. This particularly happens within a fitted garment that does not fall freely on the lower edge such as a bodice sewn to a skirt, an upper sleeve that is sewn to an armscye, or the rise in a pair of trousers. The solution is the shorten the area.

On an existing garment, increase the seam allowances on the support seams at the top of the wrinkled area to shorten it by lowering the placement of the seamline. On a bodice with horizontal folds settling above the bustline, lower the shoulder seamline position to shorten the upper chest length (Figure 8.7, left). On a bodice with horizontal folds settling above the waistline, raise the waistline seamline on the lower edge of the bodice ONLY to shorten the chest-waistline length (Figure 8.14, left). You will also need to adjust any vertical darts in this area to fit the garment waistline.

On a sleeve with horizontal folds settling across the sleeve at the level where the base of the armscye is located, shorten the upper sleeve length at the top of the sleeve curve (Figure 9.3, left). Be sure also to check whether this adjustment will affect the amount of ease in the upper sleeve – there should be approximately 1 ½" more length on the sleeve cap seamline as compared to the armscye circumference.

On trousers with horizontal folds of loose fabric across the front of the curved crotch seam or under the base of the seat, the rise is too long in the front and/or back (Figure 14.9). This may be adjusted by removing the waistband, pulling the upper area(s) of the trousers upward and increasing the seam allowances. Any darts will need to be increased to fit the waistband, or slight easing may be added to the upper edge of the trousers before the waistband is replaced. Re-stitch the waistband onto the lowered seamline position, which may be slightly dipped toward the front if the back of the garment fits but the front is too long – a common occurrence on women's trousers (Figure 14.12).

An alternative method of shortening the trouser rise is from the inseam seamline (Figure 14.7). While this is not the standard, the advantage is that the waistband and pockets will not be affected. In this case, take in the upper ends of the inseams through the lower crotch area to shorten the overall length. As this alteration will change the lengths of the inseam front versus the back, you may be left with slight easing on the front inseam as it is re-sewn to the back inseam. However, the result is usually not visible to the observer.

On a mockup, lower the position of the seamline on the upper edge of the too long area to shorten it, while addressing the issues raised in the previous section on altering a too long existing garment. You may also pin out a horizontal fold of fabric out of the mockup and transfer that alteration to the paper pattern to shorten the too long area (Figures 14.7 right and 14.9 right).

If you prefer to adjust the rise on mockup trousers by adjusting from the inseam rather than from the waistline, you can redraw the front and back crotch curves by reworking the pattern inseams and/or crotch curve shape (Figure 14.9, center).

---

4. If the fabric pulls in **tight, vertical "draw–lines,"** the garment is **too short** in that area. This particularly happens within a fitted garment that does not fall freely on the lower edge such as a bodice sewn to a skirt (Figures 8.7 right and 8.14 right), an upper sleeve that is sewn to an armscye, or the rise in a pair of trousers (Figure 14.8). The solution is the lengthen the area.

On an existing garment, let out the seam allowances on the support seams at the top of the wrinkled area to lengthen it. On a bodice with horizontal folds settling above the bustline, decrease the shoulder seam allowances to increase the upper chest length. On a bodice with vertical drawn-lines through the waistline, decrease the waistline seam allowances on the lower edge of the bodice ONLY to increase the chest-waistline length (you will also need to adjust any vertical darts in this area to fit the garment waistline).

On sleeves with vertical tight lines radiating from the upper edge or the lower 1/3 of the armscye, the sleeve cap may be too short to fit the wearer. In this case, let out the armscye seam as much as possible to gain more length in the upper sleeve. You may also need to lower the underarm position on the bodice and sleeve. This is a tricky alteration and is a sign that it may be better to choose a different garment

On trousers with somewhat vertical "pulls" of fabric from the front of the curved crotch seam or under the base of the seat, the rise is too short in the front and/or back. This may be adjusted by removing the waistband, lowering the upper area(s) of the trousers to "drop" this area, and reducing the seam allowances. Any darts will need to be adjusted to fit the new waistband position, or slight stretching may be needed on the upper edge of the trousers before the waistband is replaced. Re-stitch the waistband onto the raised seamline position (Figure 14.8).

An alternative method of lengthening the trouser rise is from the curved crotch seamline. While this is not the standard, the advantage is that the waistband and pockets will not be affected. In this case, let out the upper ends of the inseams through the lower crotch area to increase the overall length. As this alteration will change the lengths of the inseam front versus the back, you may be left with slight easing on the back inseam as it is re-sewn to the back inseam. However, the result is usually not visible to the observer.

On a mockup, raise the position of the seamline on the upper edge of the too short area to lengthen it, while addressing the issues raised in the previous section on altering a too short existing garment. You may also note on the mockup how much to lengthen a specific area of the garment and then add a horizontal wedge of paper to lengthen that area of the pattern (Figure 14.8, right).

If you prefer to adjust the rise on mockup trousers by adjusting from the inseam rather than from the waistline, you can redraw the front and back crotch curves by reworking the pattern inseams and/or crotch curve shape (Figure 14.8, left).

5. If the garment seems to **billow loosely in the center** of the garment but fits well around the edges, the garment is **too rounded** for the wearer. It may appear that there are loose, un-darted areas over the body curves, such as the bustline (Figure 8.10, left) or trouser seat (Figure 14.7, right). The solution is to flatten the area, by reducing the dart angles and curves on any shaped seams.

On an existing garment, this requires a complex set of alterations, which may never result in a well-fitted garment. Unless there is no possible other garment available, you have the time and expertise to correct this issue, and the garment is made of quality fabric that will allow alterations to be made smoothly, **choose another garment**.

On a mockup, double-check the wearer's cup size, or the difference between their waistline and hips, while patterning or draping to avoid creating a garment that is too rounded.

The garment will need to have a horizontal double-ended wedge pinned out of it over the too loose area, tapering to zero at the vertical seamlines (Figure 8.11). Then, a vertical double-ended will need to be pinned out, tapering to zero at the upper and lower edges of the garment. In essence, FOUR RADIATING WEDGES OF FABRIC NEED TO BE REMOVED FROM THE GARMENT, with most of the excess taken out over the middle of the garment and little or none taken out where the wedges intersect with the seamlines.

On the pattern, make the alterations by CUTTING OUTWARDS FROM THE CENTER of the pattern piece, such as over the bust point or the fullest part of the seam or upper arm, while NOT cutting through the outer edges of the pattern piece. OVERLAP the center area of the pattern BY THE AMOUNT THAT WAS PINNED OUT during the fitting appointment. Tape the paper pieces together. Once this is complete, redraw any darts that were affected by the adjustments just described. You will likely need to redraw a dart tip, approximately 1″ from the bust point or other body curve, and draw the dart legs to connect to their original starting points on the seamlines. You will also need to smooth out the outer seamlines on the pattern, being sure to retain a straight line for the center front and center back of the garment.

6. If the garment seems to **strain slightly over the rounded body areas** and the garment has radiating folds around the edges, the garment is **too flat** for the wearer (Figures 8.10 right and 14.6 left). The solution is to add more curve to the area, by increasing the dart angles and the curves on any shaped seams (Figure 8.11).

On an existing garment, this is a sign to choose another garment, perhaps of a larger size and from a different manufacturer. Otherwise, the garment will need to be partially taken apart, dart angles increased, and seamlines adjusted before being re-sewn.

On a mockup, double-check the wearer's cup size when drafting, and drape over a form that has had padding added to reflect the wearer's body curves.

A garment that is too flat will need to have horizontal wedges, and then vertical wedges pinned out of it at the outer edge seamlines, radiating to zero near the high point of the body curves. In essence, four wedges of fabric need to be taken out of the edges of the garment where the wedges intersect with the seamlines, with none taken over the body curves. In essence, the amount of extra fullness removed from the edges of the garment will resemble the cut-out wedges at the edges of a flat map of the rounded Earth. Theses cut-out wedges would affect the lengths of seamlines (which would need to be corrected to fit the rest of the garment pieces), as well as the total dart intakes on the pattern. To avoid all of these darts or seam adjustments, it makes more sense to add more fullness within the seamlines of the pattern piece.

On the pattern, make the alterations by CUTTING INWARDS FROM THE HIGH POINT POSITION in the center of the pattern piece, such as over the bust point or fullest part of the seat (Figure 14.6, right) TOWARDS THE EDGES OF THE PATTERN PIECE. Open up the center of the pattern by rotating each of the cut areas. Apart to get the pattern to lie smoothly, it may be necessary to cut past the tips of the overlapped pattern areas, to open up additional room over the body curve. Tape the pieces together, adding paper in the center of the pattern over the body curve.

Once this is complete, redraw any darts that were affected by the adjustments just described. You will likely need to redraw a dart tip, approximately 1″ from the bust point or other body curve, and draw the dart legs to connect to their original starting points on the seam lines. Because the existing darts will have greatly increased angles after this alteration, consider splitting the new dart intake into multiple darts. Adding more darts to distribute the angle of the revised dart will result in a more graceful fit over the wearer's curves. The alteration may result in a side seam that flares outward from the vertical side seam at its upper edge; the seam may be redrawn as a straight vertical line and the amount that is thus reduced at the side seam can be reduced from the dart intake(s). Be sure also to confirm that the outer edges of the pattern match the lengths of adjoining pattern pieces.

With an understanding of the common types of fitting issues you may encounter, we can now begin to fit actual garments. Each of the following chapters will focus on a different category of garments or garment areas. Some of the chapters will give more specific details on how to make alterations than others. For example, the chapters on bodices, sleeves, skirts, and trousers provide some detailed alteration directions, while the chapters on shirts and jackets focus more on what you should look for in assessing whether the garment actually fits or not. This is because it is often easier to select a different shirt than to alter an existing shirt, or because it is so difficult to alter an existing jacket successfully that it should only be attempted in limited situations such as adjusting a sleeve length or very slightly moving the front button placement in or out. The chapter on garments without a waistline seam discusses why a waistline seam is important on a fitted garment and suggests NOT creating a fitted garment without a waistline seam if you can avoid it.

You are now ready to conduct a fitting appointment, understand what you see during the fitting, and make adjustments to improve the fit of garments on a wearer.

8

BODICES

A bodice is a fitted upper body garment that follows the lines of the wearer's figure. It may fit very closely or have added style ease, depending on the designer's preferences or the style of a particular time period. For women, a bodice is the basic unit of the upper part of a dress or gown, extending from either the shoulders or above the bustline down to the waistline level as defined for the period. For men, a bodice is the basis of a fitted doublet or can be developed into a fitted waistcoat or even into a fitted jacket with the addition of more ease, length, collars, and sleeves. When patterning or draping a costume, the bodice is often the starting point. Much of the style of a specific time period is created by the length, width, shoulder line shape and width, waistline placement and shape, and method of controlling fullness that is contained within a bodice. While sleeves, skirts, or trouser shapes are also important, the bodice is a very important way of establishing a costume's period style.

Parts of a Bodice

Figure 8.1 shows the parts of a standard bodice.

Body Measurements Needed to Fit a Bodice

The measurements below are the base measurements needed to check a ready-made garment. When patterning a bodice, one will need more measurements than those listed here. Please refer to the directions in your patterning book, or your preferred list of measurements, for choosing and padding a dress form. The measurements below are listed in order of importance

DOI: 10.4324/9781351131353-9

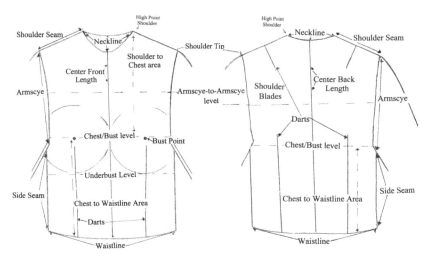

FIGURE 8.1 Bodice front (left) and back (right)

for bodices; the numbers refer to the measurement sheet and discussion in Chapter 2 (Figures 2.1 and 2.5).

The **wearer**'s measurements needed are as follows: chest/bust circumference (8), waistline circumference (11), center front length (13f), center back length (13b), side seam length (19), shoulder tip to shoulder tip (4), and neckline circumference (1). If the bodice will have sleeves, you will also need armscye (41), sleeve cap width (36, this is a non-standard measurement), and sleeve length (44).

Checking an Existing Garment before a Fitting

After taking the wearer's body measurements, use them to check a pulled or purchased garment to assess the potential fit on a specific wearer. The measurements are discussed in order of importance for bodices; the numbers refer to the measurement sheet and discussion in Chapter 2 (Figures 2.1 and 2.5).

> *Chest/bust circumference (8)*: A bodice with sleeves should usually be at least 2″ wider, and up to 4″ wider than the wearer's chest measurement. A sleeveless bodice will have 1″ ease at the base of the armholes because it does not need as much ease to allow for the constriction that sleeves create. If the bodice is strapless or otherwise very tightly fitted at the bust, the garment can be the same measurement as the wearer's chest, or even 1″ smaller than the wearer's body.
>
> *Waistline circumference (11)*: The bodice should be at least 1″ wider than the wearer's waistline measurement to allow room for breathing and

for the thickness of a skirt or peplum that may be sewn to the lower edge of the bodice. For a bodice made of heavy fabric or joined to a thickly pleated skirt, it may be necessary to allow up to 2″ ease in the waistline to allow for the thickness of the waistline seam.

Center front neckline to waistline level (13f): The bodice front is often worn at the natural waistline level or ½″ below the natural waistline at the center front but may be longer if the style calls for a "V"-shaped waistline at center front, or longer or shorter if the period style calls for it.

Center back neckline to waistline level (13b): The bodice back is generally worn at the natural waistline level but may be longer or shorter.

Side seam length (19): The bodice may fit exactly to the wearer's measurement in this area or be ¼″ longer to allow for movement. If the design includes a blousing effect, the side seams should be at least 1″ longer than the wearer's body and the center front and/or back lengths may be longer as well.

Shoulder tip to shoulder tip (4): The bodice may fit across to the tips of the wearer's shoulders, can be somewhat smaller than that width, or can extend 1–2″ past the shoulder tips or to the curve of the upper arms. Confirm the research for a particular time period when checking this measurement on a garment, as compared to the actor's measurements.

Neckline circumference (1,2) at the neckline seam. For a neckline that fits right at the base of the wearer's neck, there should be ½″ ease beyond the wearer's measurement. For a neckline that extends up the neckline, check the higher neckline measurement, especially on a man's garment.

If the bodice will have sleeves, you will need additional garment measurements:

Armscye around the armhole position on the garment. This is generally more comfortable for the wearer if the garment has at least ½″ more room than the person's body measurement, especially if the garment armscye is dropped down onto upper arm for a particular design effect (41).

Sleeve cap width (36), across the sleeve, right above the point where it joins the garment at the base of the armhole. The sleeve will be more comfortable if there is 1″ ease in the upper sleeve. This is a non-standard measurement for many measurement sheets but is very helpful when checking existing garments or creating sleeve patterns. This measurement will assure the sleeve will fit the arm at its widest part.

Sleeve length (44), from the top of the sleeve to the desired garment sleeve length. For a garment with an added cuff, the entire sleeve should have ½″ or more additional length to allow the wearer to move easily without the cuff binding on their arm

Check Measurements and Adjust if Possible

Measure any possible existing garments carefully to be sure that they fit the wearer's measurements with the correct ease, as described above, or are somewhat **larger and/or longer, in order to allow for adjustments**. If you are working with a rental garment, a garment that you do not want to permanently reshape, or a modern purchased garment, it is likely that you can only **take in and/or shorten** the garment from its existing outlines.

After checking the measurements, if a garment appears to be a possible choice for fitting on an actor **be sure to adjust any seams in advance that you would need to in order to allow the actor to try it on during an upcoming fitting appointment**. Be kind to the actors and prepare the garments that they will try on in advance. It is very dispiriting to an actor not to be able to put a garment on if it appears that the costume team expects that it should fit. It will also save you valuable time during the fitting appointment if you do not have to un-stitch a garment while the actor is waiting.

Differences between Fitting Existing Garments versus Mockups

Fitting a mockup bodice differs from fitting an existing garment because a mockup can be readily cut into and adjusted; seamlines can be moved by redrawing their placement and crossing out the incorrect seams; panels of fullness and length can be added to the garment shape, and excessive length or width can be pinned out during a fitting and then folded out of the pattern before cutting the final garment fabric. There are also several caveats that should be kept in mind while fitting the mockup:

1. The mockup might not be constructed with interfacing and linings, so it is not as thick as the finished garment will be. Therefore, be careful not to over-fit a muslin mockup and make the corrected pattern too small for construction in the final fabric.
2. A mockup constructed of muslin may not fall exactly the same way as the final fabric may fall. If available, it is helpful to use an inexpensive fabric that hangs similarly to the intended final fabric to create an accurate facsimile of the final garment shape.

Mockup seam allowances should be 1″ or more on most seams to allow for flexibility during the fitting session.

Mark all the stitch-lines for future reference, either with a hand running stitch, machine basting, or in contrasting color lines of marking pencil or stitching. Mark the center front of the bodice if it has been cut on the fold (a bodice will usually be cut with a center back closure). Mark the horizontal line at the chest/bust level. Mark the waistline, neckline stitch-line, and the armhole stitch-line because these makings will greatly help you during the fitting process. Before trying on the garment, be sure that the seams and darts are sewn accurately, using the longest stitch on the sewing machine (or by hand basting) so that the seams and darts can be easily changed or removed if needed during the fitting appointment.

Some drapers choose to fit the garment without the sleeves sewn in, but be sure to have mockup sleeves sewn and available so that they can be pinned in once the bodice has been fit. I suggest that the sleeves should be hand-basted into the armhole so that they can be easily adjusted during the fitting. In all cases, be sure you have marked the stitch-lines on the sleeve caps and bodice armscye before the sleeves have been sewn in.

Process for Fitting a Bodice

For purposes of clarity, each major step of the fitting is discussed in the directions below, followed by the different options available when fitting an existing garment or a mockup garment. The variations are placed in separate text boxes below the general directions with a boldfaced subheading. Follow the specific directions for the type of bodice you are fitting. If you are working with a rental garment, a garment that you do not want to permanently reshape, or a modern purchased garment, many adjustment suggestions will not be possible and you may need to move on to another garment option.

Be sure to fit BOTH sides of the garment equally – the best result will be an averaging of the two sides of the fit garment rather than depending on fitting one side of the garment and hoping that you have accurately kept the center line of the garment on the center line of the wearer's body.

It takes more time to fit both sides of the garment, but the result will be much more accurate.

Pin in or let out the side seams, princess seams, center seams, and/or darts or tucks to refine the fit of the bodice on the body. **The best results often are gotten by adjusting small amounts in several areas**.

Have the Actors Wear the Appropriate Accompanying Garments

This is very important. Have the actors wear the undergarments that they are slated to wear with the finished garment, including the correct type of bra or corset, body shaper, and undershirt. It is also smart to fit a bodice with a skirt shaper, petticoat, skirt, trousers, or any other garments that may impact the fit of the bodice when it is worn onstage. If the actor will wear a microphone at any point during the production, be sure to fit them in their mic belt and the battery pack, or a facsimile of the pack such as a deck of playing cards or a piece of wood or foam.

Put on the Bodice and Close It Completely

For an existing garment, fasten the closures, starting at the waistline level and working up toward the neckline. Be sure to keep the two sides level so that you don't make one side higher than the other, and to keep the closures at the center line of the body. If the bodice will not close, assess how to get the bodice completely closed. Double-check whether there is any room in the garment to let out. It may be necessary to safety-pin the garment together or even pin in a strip of additional fabric for the moment, and to move on with the rest of the bodice. If the wearer has a narrow back but a more prominent bustline than the garment will allow, I have also opened up the center front seamline of a bodice and added a decorative inset to allow it to fit. If the garment fits through the chest but cannot close at the neckline, we will adjust the neckline for comfort in the next step.

However, be realistic about whether it will be worth the time and energy to alter the garment, if you will be able to make the alteration due to time or seam allowances, or whether you need to choose a different garment for this actor.

For a mockup garment, put on the bodice. It may be easier for a beginner to fit a garment with the seams on the outside, because it is easier to see the seams and to pin them, adjust them, or unpick them as needed. In this case, and especially when fitting an asymmetrical actor, consider stitching the mockup with the seams **purposely on the outside** to make the pinned alterations easier to transfer to a finished pattern.

Begin to pin the bodice closed at the opening, starting at the waistline of the opening and working up by following the marked stitch-lines toward the neckline as high as is comfortable on the wearer's neckline. I suggest using safety pins for this, both because they are less likely to poke the wearer and also because they will not fall out during the fitting. Be sure to keep the two sides level so that you don't make one side higher than the other. You can either pin the seamlines to stick outward when the stitch-lines are lined up or fold under one seam allowance and pin the folded edge to line up with the other seam line.

Your goal is to get the center pinned closed along the marked stitch-lines, stopping at the neckline stitch-line. Assess how to get the bodice completely closed to the top if it will not close at first. You may need to pin the bodice closed further out into the seam allowances than planned in order to have enough fabric to work with. In this case, be sure **the line that you pin closed is a straight line**, especially if you intend to cut the center line on a fold. This may mean that bodice darts will need to be adjusted later in the fitting to help retain straight center lines.

Adjust the Neckline for Comfort Only

On an existing garment, if the neckline is too snug for the garment to close, you may need to remove the collar and increase the size of the neckline enough to allow the wearer to be comfortable. THIS ASSUMES THAT THE GARMENT IN QUESTION IS OWNED BY YOUR THEATRE AND THAT ANY GARMENT CUTTING WILL BE ACCEPTABLE TO THE THEATRE. As an alternative, you may be able to open the shoulder seams and/or the center front or back seams slightly where they meet the neckline, and to fold back a wider seam allowance, to make the neckline wider or deeper without clipping the garment fabric; this method works best when the too tight neckline is turned into a deeper or wider "v" shape. Or, you may decide to use the garment WITHOUT fastening it up to the neckline.

On a mockup garment, if the neckline is too snug for the garment to close, you may need to clip into the neckline seam allowances, usually starting at the center front at the base of the neck, to release the neckline and give the wearer more room. Explain what you are about to do BEFORE you place your hands on the wearer's body, get their consent, then put your hand between the tips of your shears and the wearer's neck when clipping in order to protect them. Start by cutting halfway into the seam allowance area, NOT by cutting all the way down to the marked stitch-line. Additional small clips will be about 1 ½" apart, moving outward about 4" from either side of the center front. Move slowly and assess the developing fit of the garment. If needed, continue to clip carefully toward the marked neckline stitch-line position and outward toward the shoulder line. Often, the wearer's posture will be such that the back neckline will not need to be clipped much if at all, and the finished neckline will be re-established as higher in the back and lower in the front than the original pattern. As you clip the neckline, continue to try to pin the center line until it is completely closed.

If horizontal draw-lines are radiating out of the neckline area, this may mean that the neckline is too high up on the body for the wearer's posture, that the neck is too snug for the wearer, or that the neckline/shoulder point of the wearer is higher than the slope of the garment at that point. In all cases, un-stitch the inner end of the shoulder seam to check whether revising the shoulder angle on the garment will correct the issue. If it does not, carefully begin clipping the neckline area from the center front outward on both sides to release the neckline tension.

Once the garment fits comfortably enough at the wearer's neckline to continue, proceed with the fitting. We will return to the exact shape and size of the neckline after the bodice itself is perfected.

Shoulders

Shoulders are the support points of most bodices. Usually, the shoulder seam lies in the center of the top of the wearer's shoulder area, but designs may have the seam dropped toward the front or extended at an angle toward the back armscye. Before proceeding, confirm that the shoulders are in the correct position on the actor's body according to the design drawing and the research images.

Shoulder slope: The angle of the bodice shoulders should be similar to that of the wearer's own shoulders, particularly if the garment is made of crisp fabric. If they don't match, drooping garment fabric will tell you where it is too large for the wearer. Adjusting the shoulder angles can also help if the garment neckline does not fit perfectly – see the step "Neckline and Collar" of this chapter.

If the far end of the shoulder area is hanging loose on the garment, the **bodice shoulders are too horizontal or squared** for the slope of the wearer's shoulders (Figure 8.2, left). It may be necessary to pin in the garment shoulder line near the armhole to increase the slope of the garment shoulders. This adjustment will also affect the sleeve cap for a garment with sleeves, depending on how the rest of the armscye is adjusted later in the fitting.

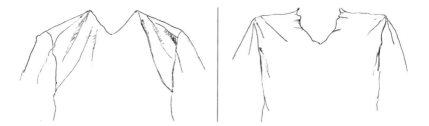

FIGURE 8.2 Shoulder angles: garment shoulders are too square (left) and too sloping (right) for the wearer's body

If the neckline end of the shoulder seam is gaping, the **bodice shoulders are too sloping** for the wearer's more squared shoulders (Figure 8.2, right). One may either pin in the angle of the seam where it gaps near the neck or open up the seam and re-pin it to let out the seam at the **outer** end of the shoulders to create a flatter angle on the garment shoulder.

On an existing garment, it may not be possible to adjust the shoulders a great deal at the outer ends except for taking them in to increase the slope. If the garment has sleeves, the adjustment will also require removing the upper part of the sleeve cap for about 6" from either side of the shoulder point on the sleeve, adjusting any fullness on the sleeve upper edges, and re-sewing the sleeves into the adjusted armscye. If the garment has a collar, it may not be possible to adjust the shoulders much at the inner ends without having to remove and replace the collar. In both cases, adding a thin shoulder pad at the outer or inner ends of the garment shoulders may be enough to adjust the shoulder angle without having to reconstruct this area.

On a mockup garment, you can un-stitch the shoulder seams and re-pin them to fit. Double-check that the angle of the shoulder seams is right for the actor, the right length from neck/shoulder to the tip of the shoulder, and is centered on the top of the wearer's shoulder bone UNLESS the design calls for a different placement.

If the garment seam lines need to be moved to a different spot, you can re-pin the intended seamlines and/or add a wedge of fabric to be incorporated into the pattern, redraw the desired seamline placement on the mockup with a different colored pencil or marker, and cross out the existing seams. When the shoulder angle of the bodice does not allow for the wearer's squared shoulders, it may be necessary to take in the shoulder seamline near the neckline AND to let out the shoulder seamline near the armhole in order to flatten the garment shoulder slope.

Remember, if the garment has sleeves, adjusting the shoulders a great deal at the outer ends will also require reshaping the upper part of the sleeve caps, and adjusting at the inner ends of the shoulder will require reshaping the neckline and collar on the garment.

Shoulder width: If the bodice's shoulder width does not match that of the wearer, it will affect where the armscye falls on the body.

If the **bodice is too narrow** for the wearer's shoulders, you will see horizontal strain lines radiating out from the armscye seam across the upper chest

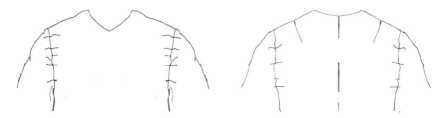

FIGURE 8.3 Bodice shoulders and armscyes too narrow for the wearer: front (left) and back (right)

(Figure 8.3), the armscye seam will fall onto the wearer's chest and the bodice may not even be able to be put onto the actor. For a trans actor, the shoulder width may be the area that determines whether or not an existing garment will be usable.

For an existing garment that is worth pursuing, the solution is to add more width to the bodice, either by letting out the armscye seam as much as possible, or by adding more room to the sleeve itself through a gusset that is added to the bodice and sleeve underarm seams to give more space for the arm muscles. If additional garment fabric is available, or a contrasting fabric is available to coordinate with the existing bodice, it is possible that the sleeves may be removed and replaced by sleeves that have more fullness at the cap. I have also added a small vertical panel of fabric to the shoulder area of the bodice to make the area broader. However, these solutions are a great deal of work and may involve re-cutting the garment; it may be more realistic to find another garment to try on.

For a mockup garment, the armscye of the bodice shoulder be redrawn further out from the bodice center lines to add the amount of extra room needed to fit the wearer. Check whether both the bodice front and back need to be adjusted. Remove the mockup sleeves, redraw the armscye stitch-lines at the correct position on the wearer's body, and re-attach the sleeves to check whether they will also need to be adjusted to fit in the new armscye.

If the bodice is **too wide** for the wearer's shoulders, the top of the armscye seam will fall onto the wearer's upper arms and you will see vertical soft folds where there is too much fabric (Figure 8.4). This extra width may be located either on the front or back armscyes, or both.

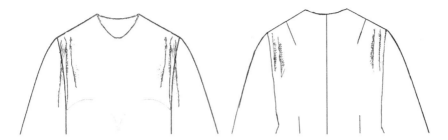

FIGURE 8.4   Bodice shoulders and armscyes too wide for the wearer: front (left) and back (right)

On an existing bodice, one may add stitching to the armscye seam to make both the bodice and sleeve seam allowance 1/8″ deeper at the shoulder tips. A quicker, reversible solution is to make decorative tucks in the shoulder seam to shorten the shoulder length. These are known as "**Opera Tucks**," sewn tucks created inside or outside the garment, which take in an area of the garment to fit a wearer. These tucks are intended to be reversible for future use and are a secret weapon to adjust borrowed costumes.

On a mockup garment, the solution is to take in the width of the bodice by re-establishing the armscye seam closer to the center of the wearer's body, following the wearer's armscye position.

Armscye

Check the position of the armscye seam as compared to the actor's chest width and arm position, as well as compared to the design drawing and research images for the garment. If the garment has sleeves, they may need to be partially or fully taken out and repositioned to adjust the armscye placement.

For a bodice whose armscyes are **too narrow across the upper chest or back**, you will see thin horizontal strain lines radiating from the armscye, which appear very much as if the bodice shoulders are too narrow (Figure 8.3). The bodice may not even be able to be tried on the actor because the armscye seam will fall onto the wearer's chest and will need to be let out as much as possible.

On an existing bodice, it may be possible to let out the armscye seam 1/8″ to gain a little more room across the chest. If the bodice has sleeves with a lot of gathering in the sleeve caps, or if the existing sleeves can be replaced by sleeves that have more fullness at the cap, this may provide enough room for the wearer's shoulders to fit within the sleeve area while the armscye seam position is falling across the chest. For a trans woman, a period bodice with full sleeves, such as the 1830s, the 1890s, or the heavily padded 1980s, may be able to accommodate the actor's shoulders within the upper sleeves.

On a mockup, remove the mockup sleeves and redraw the armscye stitch-lines at the correct position on the wearer's body. If the armscyes are too snug for the wearer because of the seam allowance depth, you may need to clip into the seam allowance in order to get the bodice to fit comfortably. Begin by clipping in at the underarms, where the fabric is folding. The area that usually needs to be clipped will be at the lowest point of the armscye, up to approximately 3″ above this point at the front and back armscye. Start slowly, because you will most likely NOT need to clip completely to the stitch-lines in all areas. Redraw the armscye stitch-line if it IS needed to clip past the stitch-line. At this point, we are trying to give the wearer enough room to move and to allow the bodice to hang properly. Allow about ½″ of extra room around the armscye to allow for the sleeve to fit smoothly.

Re-attach the sleeves to check whether they will also need to be adjusted to fit in the new armscye circumference.

For a bodice with armscyes that are **spaced too widely across the chest or back to fit the wearer**, you will see soft vertical folds in the fabric of the upper chest, similar to what you will see if the shoulders are too wide for the wearer (Figure 8.4). Correct this by reducing the chest width by small amounts by taking in the seamlines at specific places on the armscye.

For an existing garment, adjust the bodice width by increasing the seam allowance amounts on the front armscyes and upper side seams which can be done by re-stitching the armscye with the sleeve left in place if the adjustment is subtle. One may add stitching to the armscye seam to make both the bodice and sleeve seam allowance 1/8″ deeper toward the center of the body to narrow the armscye placement. A quicker, reversible solution is to make decorative vertical "opera tucks" in the shoulder seam that extend downward into the bodice, to bring the armscye closer to the bodice center line.

For a mockup, re-mark the position of the armscye to where it should fall on the wearer's armscye. This may need to be accompanied by adjusting the sleeve cap to fit the new armscye circumference with the correct added ease.

Be sure to have the actor move their arms in the bodice at this point. It is better to have a little extra bodice fabric at the armscye level to allow them to move easily.

Also remember that if the bodice is intended to have a sleeve added, you will need to leave at least ½" ease at the top of each of the side seams at the armholes in order to allow for movement, creating a total of 2" combined ease around the chest. It is tempting to over-fit a bodice without allowing for the extra room that sleeves will need. Leave at least ½–1" ease at the top of each side seam at the base of the armscyes. On a garment made of non-stretchy woven fabric, do not try to remove ALL of this fabric because approximately 1" total will be needed on each side to allow the wearer to comfortably move their arms.

For a person with rolled-forward shoulders or hunched posture (Figure 8.5), the bodice **front is often too wide** and the bodice **back is too narrow** to fit correctly. You will see the fabric on the bodice front collapse in folds between the armscyes, above the bust level, and around the front neckline. If the folds fall nearer to the wearer's front neck, the wearer may have **forward-hunched shoulders** (Figure 8.5, left) and a rounded back (Figure 8.5, upper right). On the garment back, the fabric will pull horizontally at shoulder blade level and the back neckline will stand away from the forward roll of the neckline. Angular fabric radiating around the upper bodice back is a sign of a **wearer with prominent shoulder blades** (Figure 8.5, lower right).

For an existing garment, it may not be practical to rework the shoulders to the extent discussed in the mockup directions, below. Consider adding thin padding through the shoulders, placing the pads slightly toward the front of the wearer's body on the shoulder line in order to fill in the difference between the garment and the wearer's shoulder shape. The goal is not to create a clearly padded effect but to give a slight visual lift to the area. A sleeveless, collarless garment may also have a slight horizontal tuck taken in the upper front shoulder area to shorten the excess length created by the wearer's posture.

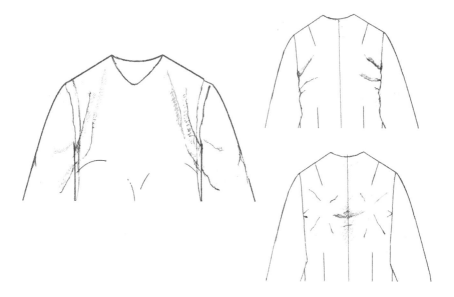

FIGURE 8.5 Bodice on a wearer with forward-rolling front shoulders (left), a rounded back (upper right), and one with prominent shoulder blades (lower right)

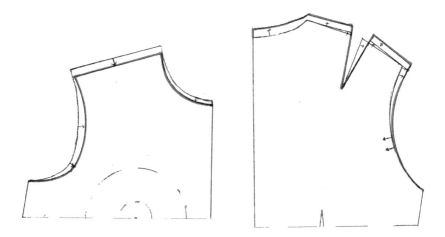

FIGURE 8.6 Patterning adjustments for Figure 8.5: forward-rolling front shoulders (left), and a rounded back or prominent shoulder blades (right). Adjusted seamline positions and dart intakes are indicated in red lines. Depending on the wearer, there may be even more taken away from and added to the armscyes to fit the body correctly than shown in this illustration

For a mockup, take IN the garment chest width across the front at the armscyes and let OUT the width at the back armscyes. On the vertical axis, the shoulder line position will need to be lowered in front (Figure 8.6), while the shoulder line will need to be raised to match the wearer's posture. Double-check whether the back neckline position is high enough to follow the wearer's neck position, as forward-rolled shoulders may require the back neckline to be raised and the front neckline to be slightly lowered to match the wearer's posture.

The shoulder seams will need to be un-stitched and adjusted to allow the garment to more accurately follow the angle of the wearer's shoulders.

Consider whether increasing (or adding) a back shoulder dart will improve the fit of a wearer with a rounded back and/or prominent shoulder blades. This will mean letting out the bodice back an additional amount across the upper back while reshaping the back shoulder line, to accommodate the larger dart intake needed to shape around prominent shoulder blades. However, do not try to **completely** fit the shoulder blades if they are so prominent that they resemble a back bustline area – take some time to get the best possible result without trying to over-fit the area, and check the adjustments from all angles before you finalize them.

Shoulder to Chest

The vertical relationship between the garment shoulders and the widest part of the chest should be accurate to the wearer's body. You may need to adjust the armscye position as well as the shoulder seam in order to get the upper chest area to fit smoothly. Double-check whether **both** the garment front and back will need to be adjusted. Many fit issues arise when wearer's posture is such that more length is needed only on either the front or back, and less is needed on the other side.

If there are rounded horizontal folds above the chest level, the garment's bust/chest level is too long for the wearer and the bustline level of the bodice is **too low** as compared to wearer's chest level (Figure 8.7, left); the horizontal folds are created because there is too much fabric length in this area. The solution is to take up the shoulders in order to reduce the length from shoulder to chest level.

On an existing garment, shorten the shoulder-to-chest length by pinching out a horizontal tuck in the upper chest below the shoulder line, or increasing the seam allowance of the shoulder seam to pull the bustline level upward, which will also affect the neckline shape and depth. However, if the bodice has a collar, a quicker, reversible solution is to take a horizontal decorative tuck out of the garment at a midpoint between the base of the neckline and the bustline level. This alteration will be less visible on a matte, small-patterned fabric. On a bodice with sleeves, this adjustment may require you to un-stitch the sleeve cap to at least 3″ above and below the tuck where it intersects the armscye, and to adjust the sleeve cap by easing it to fit the smaller, adjusted armscye.

On a mockup, the pattern may be reshaped by lowering the shoulder position on the garment, and reshaping the neckline and armscye seamline positions as needed to fit smoothly over the body. Check whether both the garment front and back will need to be adjusted. Remember to adjust the collar and sleeve to fit the adjusted bodice. You may also need to adjust the length of any darts, shaping seams, or tucks in order that they are in the correct position as compared to the fullest point on the chest/bust.

If the bodice upper chest area is vertically **too short** for the wearer (Figure 8.7, right), there will be vertical strain lines at the shoulder seam and the chest/bust level shaping such as darts or princess seams will be too high as compared to the bust points on the wearer's chest. In addition, the garment will ride up the body when the wearer moves and will not be able to fall back into place afterward.

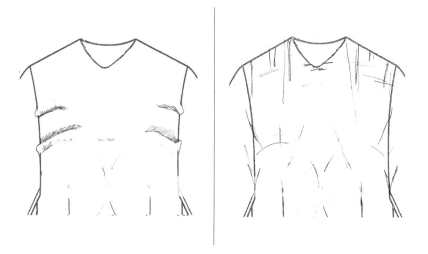

FIGURE 8.7 Upper bodice too long (left), and too short (right) for the wearer

On an existing garment, you may need to add an additional strip of fabric or a band of trim at the shoulder line or upper bodice to extend the garment length and to drop the bustline level to fit the wearer correctly. The neckline and collar will need to be reshaped, and the sleeves will need to be reshaped to fit the larger armscye, unless the bodice is also somewhat loose at the sides and can be taken in, thus raising the base of the armscye. Unless there are no other options available, try to choose a different garment.

On a mockup, gain more length from the shoulder to bustline level by un-stitching the shoulder seams. Let out enough seam allowance to allow the garment fall to the correct chest level, or add an additional strip of fabric in order to adjust this. Remember to adjust the neckline, collar, and sleeve to fit the adjusted bodice. Double-check the base of the armscye position so that it has not become too low for the design. You may also need to adjust the length of any darts, shaping seams, or tucks in order that they are in the correct position as compared to the fullest point on the chest/bust.

Fullest Chest/Bust Area

Confirm that the darts, gathers, tucks, pleats, or other dart equivalents are pointing to the fullest part of the chest. Check also the length of the darts, to see that they are pointing to the fullest part of the bust and don't go past the body curves or stop too short (Figure 8.8).

To properly fit the chest, **the dart tips should end within 1″ of the bust points, and prince(ss) seams or other dart equivalents should be close enough to the bust points to fulfill their functions.**

On an existing garment, you may have to un-stitch the darts/pleats/ tucks/seams, and reposition them to get them in the right place and to end at the right spots. Keep in mind that on a commercially sewn garment, the dart may not be able to move much because a punch hole is often put into a garment to guide the factory worker while they sew the dart. If the dart position is clearly wrong on the wearer's body, it may be better to choose a different garment to try on.

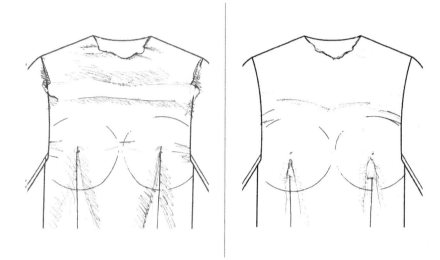

FIGURE 8.8 Dart positions too high (left), and too low (right) in relation to the wearer's bust point. A dart that ends too high on the wearer will also push some of the bodice fullness to above the bust point, creating a soft horizontal fold above the bust. However, if the bodice is long enough above the bust but the dart tip is too low, there may simply be loose fabric near the bust points

---

On a mockup, unpick the darts/pleats/tucks/seams, and re-pin them to get them in the right place and to end at the right spots. Be sure to specifically mark the position of the **bust points** on a woman's garment – ask the actor to make these marks in order to be less intrusive. You can then draw a 1″ radius circle around the bust point that indicates where the darts should end.

If there are thin horizontal draw-lines in the bodice, they will tend to point to where it is too snug. If horizontal draw-lines appear BETWEEN the bust points, ABOVE the bust AND BELOW the bust, the bodice is **too snug** for the wearer's chest (Figure 8.9, left).

For an existing garment, choose another option or purchase a replacement 1–2 sizes larger. If you have matching fabric available for a garment pulled from storage, consider adding a gusset according to the discussion below.

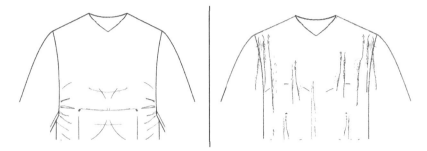

FIGURE 8.9 Bust area too snug (left) and too loose (right)

> **A mockup garment** will need to be made wider at the side seams at chest/bust level. There may be room to let out the side seams and/or you may be able to add gussets at the side seams at chest level to increase the width of the garment. Be careful when adding gussets or width to the side seams so that you do not distort the armscyes.
>
> Side seam gussets will be triangular with the widest part at the base of the armscye. If the bodice has sleeves, the gusset will need to be extended at least 1" on either side into the sleeve underarm seam to create a diamond-shaped gusset. If the bodice is snug around the body and the wearer needs to be able to raise their arms, an oval or "football" shaped gusset can be added to give more vertical room. Since this type of gusset tends to fold up into the armpit, it can be less visible than a diamond gusset. More discussion of sleeve gussets will be covered in Chapter 9, Sleeves.
>
> If the draw-lines are coming from the armscye but not the side upper seams, there may be issues with the placement of the armscye and width of the sleeve. We will look more at the armscye/sleeve relationship later in the fitting session, but one solution can be to re-mark the armscye slightly further outward in order to add a little width across both the upper chest and the upper arms to add more room in this area across both the front and the back. A more involved solution is to re-cut and sew in a new sleeve.

A bodice that is **too loose** will have **vertical, often triangular, folds** (Figure 8.9, right). The goal is to remove the extra fabric in such a way that the bodice fits closer to the shape of the wearer's body. You may need to add darts or shaping seams if they are not present in the garment, the darts or shaping seams may need to be increased on the existing garment, or the side seams may need to be taken in from chest level to taper out at the waistline level. Sometimes the best choice is to take in small amounts of fabric in SEVERAL spots.

On an existing garment, try pinching out the excess fabric from a variety of spots on the bodice to find the combination that works best in controlling the excess fabric. Consider creating a decorative vertical tuck (either on the surface or inside the garment), known as an Opera Tuck, to take out the excess fabric.

On a mockup, you may need to take in the side seams, increase dart intakes, take in the shaping seams an additional amount, or add pleats, tucks, or gathering. If folds fall from the chest level, the bodice may need darts or shaping seams added or increased on the existing garment, AND the side seams may need to be taken in from chest level to the waistline, AND/OR the angle of any darts may need to be increased if the cup size of the garment is not the same as that of the wearer. More on cup size adjustments follow later in this chapter.

Depending on the time period of the garment you are fitting, adjustments may be made by taking in princess seams an additional amount, adding pleats or gathering, or folding out a tuck of fabric that will be taken out of the pattern to reduce the excess fabric. The period style or design of the bodice can lead you to the best solution in terms of how to adjust the fabric.

Remember that it is best to let the bodice be a **little loose** at this point in order to retain wearing ease, plus to factor in the fact that the finished garment will be made of a somewhat thicker fabric than the mockup, with interfacing and internal understructure added.

If the **bodice is too rounded** for the wearer's chest, the curved areas will appear hollow and will sag. The garment will billow outward over the body and there will be triangular folds extending from the armscye with the widest ends of the triangles near the bust point on the wearer (Figure 8.10, left). On a female-identified actor, **if the cup size of the garment is too large for the wearer, the chest/bust area on the garment will be too curved**. The cup size measurement is the difference or "elevation" between the peak of the bustline and the surrounding chest walls. Many garment patterns, dress forms, and existing garments are created with a "B" cup-sized bust. If the wearer's bust is smaller than a "B," there will be excess fabric over the bust. The loose fabric creates a billowing 4-legged "starfish" effect.

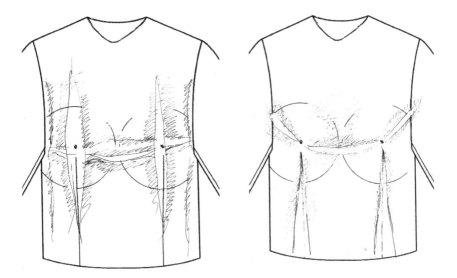

FIGURE 8.10 Bodice too rounded at the bust (left), and too flat at the bust (right)

On an existing garment, if the bustline of the garment is too rounded, taking in more fabric at the darts, princess seams, and side seams over the bust point area will help flatten it slightly. However, it is difficult to completely correct this issue on an existing garment. If the wearer is open to wearing a slightly padded bra, adding a bust pad, or a bra with more uplift, their bust may be able to be made more curved to fill in the open space. The fitting issue may be due to the bodice having a larger cup size than the wearer's bustline.

On a mockup, there will be an extra "shelf" of fabric over the bust level. Pin out the excess fabric in a horizontal fold, trying to taper it out to zero at the side seam. You may also need to pin out a vertical fold in the same manner.

On the pattern (Figure 8.11), slash through the dart intakes so that **the paper that is folded out of the bust area is equal to the position and amount of fabric pinned out of the mockup**. Redraw a new dart (center), which should have a steeper angle and less width than the original dart, due to the pattern alterations. Folding out the darts has created a large bend in bodice center front seam. Add more paper to the lower center front seam to re-establish a vertical center front line, which

> will add more width to the waistline seam. To correct the resulting seamlines after folding, the added width is taken out of the waistline dart intake (right). The resulting pattern has the same front waistline seam lengths as the original, but less volume inside the pattern.

If the bodice has one or more triangular folds extending from the armscye toward the bust point on the wearer, with the narrow points near the bust point, the garment is **too flat** for the wearer's body. On a too flat bodice chest area, the snugness over the wearer's bust creates loose wedges of fabric at the outer edges of the garment area (Figure 8.10, right; Figure 8.12, upper register).

On a female-identified actor, these "unsewn darts" may indicate that the cup size of the garment is wrong for the wearer, or that the wearer has a larger cup-sized bust than the garment will allow. Although a "C" cup or larger is more common in US women, many garment patterns, dress forms, and existing garments are created with a "B" cup-sized bust. The result is that a garment can be too flat for the curve of the wearer's chest even if the garment

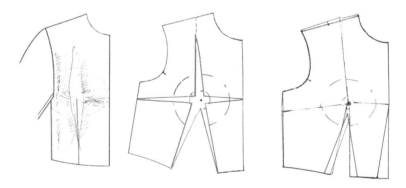

FIGURE 8.11 Pattern correction for too rounded bodice or a bodice with a too large cup size for the wearer (Figure 8.10, right): (1) image shows half of the bodice front, corresponding to the pattern front (left). (2) Red outlines indicate the areas folded out on the mockup during the fitting appointment and transferred to the paper pattern. (3) After cutting from the bust point area outward to the seamlines, the excess areas are folded to pivot them out of the pattern (blue lines, corresponding to the red lines in the center image). Because the adjustments have created a bent center front edge, the pattern must be added to at the lower center front to re-create a vertical line. The extra amount that is added at the center front is taken out by creating a wider dart intake (red lines). The resulting front waistline seam should be the exact same length as the original pattern

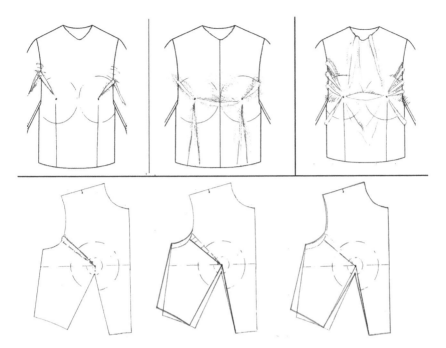

FIGURE 8.12 Pattern correction for a **too flat** bodice or a bodice with a too small cup size for the wearer (Figure 8.10, right). Upper register shows variations on a too flat bodice. Lower register shows the process for adjusting the pattern, focusing on only one of the areas needing more shaping

has been chosen or patterned to fit the bust measurement at fullest part of the wearer's chest.

On a male or non-gendered actor, a single triangular fold that extends from the armscye toward the bust point can be a sign of a wearer with developed pectoral muscles from swimming or weight-lifting.

On an existing bodice that has a small triangular fold in this area, it is better to ignore it, especially if the bodice is worn beneath a jacket, rather than attempting a tricky alteration for a small area. If the bodice has sleeves with a corresponding loose wedge of fabric, remember that some of the extra fabric will be necessary to allow the actor to move their arms. On an existing SLEEVELESS bodice, one can sew a discreet dart in the garment to take in the unsewn dart fold if desired (as shown in Figure 8.12), or one can ease the armscye around this area to pull in the excess fabric. If the bodice looks sloppy with the extra fabric, a decorative horizontal tuck that extends over the bustline area can also help mask the extra curve.

On a mockup, if the extra fabric radiating from the bust point is unacceptable, correct this by removing the sleeve from the armscye and pin out most, but not all, of the excess fabric in the bodice. The total pinned-out amounts can be added to existing darts to increase their pitch or can be used to create additional darts or shaped seams on the finished garment.

Figure 8.12, lower register, depicts this process. Red lines indicate the changes made in each step. (1) Pin out dart(s) from the excess fabric around the edge(s) of the garment along with snipping from the tip of the old dart to the bust point (Figure 8.12, lower left); (2) overlap the paper pattern by the amount of the pinned-out excess fabric, which will increase the angle of the existing dart and change the shape of the armscye and angle of the side seam area (Figure 8.12, lower center); and the final pattern after redrawing the new dart tip at the original spacing away from the bust point in the original pattern (Figure 8.12, lower right).

For the upper register images with multiple areas that are loose at the edges, you would pin out **multiple** darts of excess fabric and rotate all of that excess material to the original dart or create 1–2 additional darts to manage the excess.

If the bodice has sleeves, reduce the sleeve cap circumference by the same amount of fabric as was taken out of the bodice armscye, to retain the correct size relationship between the two pieces. For more discussion of sleeves, see Chapter 9.

If the **actor's bust is too high** and being pushed up by a bra that is too small (Figure 8.13), the first solution is to find a bra that fits better, particularly in terms of cup size. If the actor is wearing a corset, the high bustline position in Figure 8.13 is to be expected, although you should check that the corset is creating the desired effect for the period style. With a corset, high horizontal curves of upper body flesh should be planned for in the design.

For an existing bodice, if changing the bra or corset does not help, add a decorative horizontal tuck to disguise the strong horizontal body fold that is created by the upper edge of the breasts as they are pushed up toward the collarbones. One can also use a fichu, shawl, collar, or other period-specific accessories that may have been invented to cover this type of body fold.

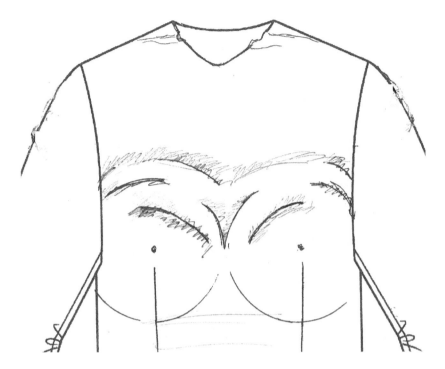

FIGURE 8.13 Bust curves pushed up too high

For a mockup, the front upper bodice needs to be shortened above the bust points. The front shoulder position can be lowered by increasing the amount of the front shoulder seam allowance to pull the bodice fabric up. This will raise the bust point level on the bodice to fit the round upper edge of the breasts as they are pushed upward toward the collar bones.

If the actor is wearing a corset, the horizontal curves of upper body flesh should be planned for in the design. Consider adding a horizontal seam, yoke, or a decorative tuck to this area.

Confirm that the darts, gathers, tucks, pleats, or other dart equivalents are pointing to the fullest part of the chest in its raised position.

You may also need to adjust the neckline position after raising the front shoulder position.

Ribcage to Waistline

Once the chest/bust area fits correctly, work from the widest chest level to the ribcage area and downward to the waistline level.

Check that the side seams are falling exactly at the sides of the body unless the intended bodice design has different seam placements. Adjusting the side

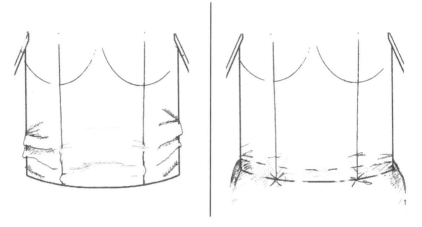

FIGURE 8.14 Ribcage-to-waistline area too long (left) and too short (right) for the wearer

seams may involve taking out the seams and repositioning them with more fabric taken out of one seam allowance and less out of the other seam allowance so that they end up in the right place on the wearer's body.

If there are horizontal folds above the waistline level on a bodice with a fitted waist, it has a ribcage area that is **too long** for the wearer (Figure 8.14, left).

For an existing garment, pinch out a horizontal tuck that can be stitched as an internal tuck and treated as a waistline yoke seam. Or remove the skirt area of the garment and re-attach it at the correct level, after taking in the vertical darts and seams to fit the wearer's waistline.

For a mockup, pinch out the excess horizontal length as a tuck. Fold out the same amount of paper in the same location to shorten the pattern.

You may also remove the skirt area of the garment and re-attach it at the correct level. Mark the correct waistline level on the garment depending on the period style or design choices of the bodice. Use a ribbon or piece of seam binding to help you preview possible waistline levels on the garment, and then clearly mark the ribbon's position on the garment. The vertical darts, shaping seams, and side seams will need to be shortened to smoothly fit the adjusted waistline position.

If there are vertical strain lines between the chest level and the waistline (Figure 8.15, right), the ribcage area is **too short** for the wearer.

For an existing garment, the waistline may be lengthened slightly by letting out the seam allowance on the lower edge of the bodice, or by adding a horizontal panel of fabric to lengthen the bodice. If the added fabric does not match or coordinate with the bodice fabric, a belt can be worn over this area.

For a mockup, let out the seam allowance at the waistline to lengthen the garment, while also letting out the darts and side seams in order to retain the correct waistline size. Another option is to cut and pin in a horizontal panel of fabric within the body of the garment. Lengthen the pattern by adding paper to the pattern that reproduces the placement and amount of added fabric on the mockup.

Mark the natural waistline on the body, and cross out any place where the marked waistline is different than where it should fall. The natural waistline is the point where the body indents when the wearer leans side-to-side and is in the vicinity of the belly button for many people. Depending on the current fashion, the natural waistline may be a distance from where the fashion waistline may lie – however, it is good to have a clear marking of this point if the bodice extends below the natural waistline.

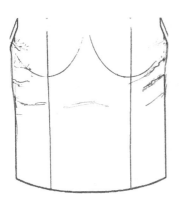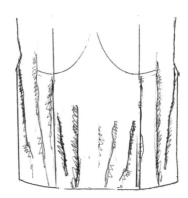

FIGURE 8.15 Bodice ribcage area too narrow (left) and too wide (right) for the wearer

If there are thin horizontal stress lines in this area (Figure 8.15, left), the garment is too snug and should be let out at the side seams and/or at any shaping darts or seams.

If there are soft vertical folds below the bustline area and above the waistline, the garment may be too large (Figure 8.15, right). This is a design decision, which should be made by the designer and their research.

Waistline

The waistline level of the bodice can be at the wearer's natural waistline, above, or below, depending on the period and design of the garment. Repositioning the skirt on a bodice will help establish a period look. For a ready-made garment, it may be possible to raise the skirt position but is often less possible to lower it on the bodice. See "Ribcage to Waistline" section for more discussion of this area.

The waistline level of a bodice made of non-stretch fabric should have at least 1″ total additional ease added BEYOND the exact size of the wearer's body at that level, WHILE they are wearing the intended undergarments, any padding, or microphone battery packs that will be worn onstage. The extra width will allow for the thickness of any skirt fabric sewn to the waistline and the understructure that will be added while constructing a fitted bodice, will prevent the garment from buckling or twisting around the body when it is worn, and will allow the wearer to breathe comfortably. If the bodice is joined to a thickly pleated skirt or is made of heavy fabric, 1 ½″ to 2″ total waistline area ease may be needed to accommodate the thick material.

If the waistline area shows horizontal draw-lines at the side seams below the bust (Figure 8.16), the area is **too snug** in one or more areas. The draw-lines that you see on the bodice fabric will point toward the area that is too snug and direct you toward which area to adjust.

On an existing garment, this may be addressed by letting out the side seams slightly and letting out the vertical darts or shaping seams if they are present. You may be able to get a total of 1″ additional room in the waistline by letting out the existing seams and darts.

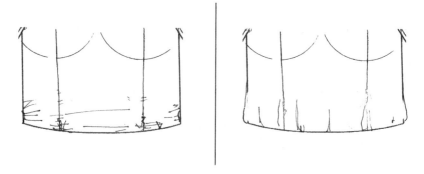

FIGURE 8.16 Waistline too snug (left) and too loose (right)

> **On a mockup**, un-stitch the waistline darts, shaping seams, and/or side seams to let them out at the areas that show the most horizontal strain lines. Unless there is a clearly rounded area on the wearer's body, you will likely need to let out a number of places on the waistline for the smoothest effect. However, unless the period style features darts that are angled, when I correct the patterns, I will redraw any pinned vertical darts so that they have center lines that are parallel to the vertical grainlines on the garment, whether or not the fabric wanted to angle during the fitting.

If the bodice has soft vertical folds below the chest level, the garment is **too loose** (Figure 8.16, right). **An existing garment or a mockup** may be taken in at the side seams and vertical darts or shaping seams if desired. For a slightly too loose garment, the waistline area may be eased slightly by soft gathers, with cross-stitched elastic to pull in the waistline, or by adding a belt.

Armscyes and Sleeves

Sleeves and armscyes must be assessed together. When fitting sleeves, it is important to consider both the shape and size of the armscye as well as the sleeve. The fit of the bodice will affect how the sleeves hang, and the sleeves will affect how the rest of the bodice fits. Chapter 9 covers sleeves in more detail. However, there are times when the sleeve itself is the issue, while the bodice fits correctly.

If the bodice has sleeves, one cause for the horizontal strain lines in the bodice may be that the sleeves are too snug across the wearer's upper arms (Figure 8.17, left).

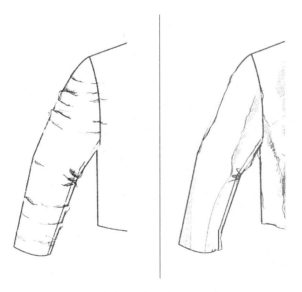

FIGURE 8.17 Sleeves too snug (left) and too loose (right)

For an existing garment, the simplest first step is to re-sew the sleeve into the armscye at a smaller seam allowance width in order to add a little width across both the upper chest and the upper arms – you may get a total of ½–¾″ more room in this area, depending on how much seam allowance width you have available. If matching fabric is available, consider adding a diamond-shaped gusset under the arm to add more overall room to the sleeve.

For a mockup, hand sew the muslin sleeves into the bodice before the fitting appointment. In addition, when conducting the FIRST FABRIC fitting, I tend to sew revised muslin sleeves into the fabric bodice so that I can confirm that the garment fits correctly BEFORE cutting the sleeves in garment fabric.

If the sleeve is too snug across the cap, it may be necessary to re-cut a new sleeve for the garment with more width across the upper arm. The sleeve cap width measurement (36), taken just above the point where the arm separates from the torso, will help in creating a sleeve wide enough to fit the shape of the wearer's arm at its widest point.

You can also create more room in the chest, which will relieve some of the binding on the sleeve cap. Widen the bodice across the upper chest area by redrawing the armscyes further apart on the pattern.

If the armscye and the sleeve are too loose (Figure 8.17, right), there will be loose vertical and triangular folds within the body of the sleeve and near the armscye on the bodice.

For an existing garment, you may take in the bodice and sleeve at the side seam and underarm seam to tighten this area. If possible, you may need to clip into the seam allowance of the altered garment at the point where the underarm of the sleeve meets the bodice side seam to reduce tension.

For a mockup, the extra fabric can be pinned out vertically in the bodice and sleeve, with the paper pattern reduced by the same amount and in the same position as the pinned-out fabric. Check that the adjusted patterns have retained the correct amount of ease on the sleeve cap to fit the corrected armscye.

Neckline and Collar

Once the bodice and any sleeves are perfected, finalize the garment neckline. Check that the neckline lies flat against the wearer's upper chest in the desired position for the design and your research.

If the design includes a collar, it depends on the bodice and neckline being perfected first. **Remove the collar in order to do any alterations and safety-pin the collar onto the neckline after the rest of the bodice has been fit.** When assessing the collar, check whether it rolls correctly around the neckline of the garment and wearer, as is intended, extends up to the right height that it is shaped correctly, that it lines up with the neckline, and that it extends to the desired point on the neckline seam. On an existing garment and a mockup, changing a collar is easier than adjusting sleeves or making many other alterations, so it is worth considering a garment that otherwise fits the wearer. More discussion of shirt collars is contained in Chapter 10.

If horizontal draw-lines are radiating out of the neckline area, this may mean that the neckline is too high up on the body for the wearer's posture, that the neck is too snug for the wearer, or that the neckline/shoulder point of the wearer is higher than the slope of the garment at that point (Figure 8.18). In all cases, adjusting the shoulders may help address this if you cannot cut into the garment to adjust the neckline itself.

For an existing garment, un-stitch the inner end of the shoulder seam. You may need to open up the shoulder seam slightly to let out the shoulder seams at the inner ends. This will raise the shoulder position near the neckline and slightly increase the size of the neckline. Or, consider whether a different style of bra will change how the breasts are pushed up in the bodice.

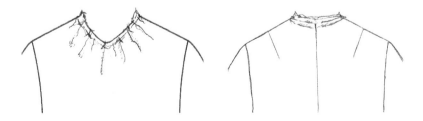

FIGURE 8.18   Neckline too high or snug, front (left) and back (right)

On a mockup, if the neckline is too small, this may be solved by clipping it carefully halfway into the seam allowances to lower and/or widen the neckline. If this does not work, or you are fitting a lowered neckline, draw the desired neckline onto the mockup according to the design and research images. I suggest sketching slightly higher and narrower outlines than the silhouette you think you want. Carefully cut to within 1", and then ½", of the drawn lines to check the fit, AND so that the remaining fabric can be folded under the drawn line. Proceed slowly on this step, as the fabric may relax more than you expect during this process when you release the tension in the seam allowances. Adjust the neckline size and shape until it is perfect front and back.

If the neckline is too loose at the shoulder/neckline points (Figure 8.19), you will see soft folds radiating from the neckline to over the upper chest, and the garment will reveal too much of the body.

For **existing garments and mockups**, the shoulders may need to be pinned snugger where the shoulder intersects the neckline area to shorten the vertical edge of the neckline and to adjust the angle of the shoulder seam. If the neckline is too large, you can also add piping to the neckline and pull up the cording to ease in the circumference of the neckline in particular spots or the entire area.

If the wearer has a posture that pushes their neck forward and rolls their back forward, the neckline of the garment will be too high in the front and gap in the back (Figure 8.20).

FIGURE 8.19 Neckline too loose and low, front (left) and back (right)

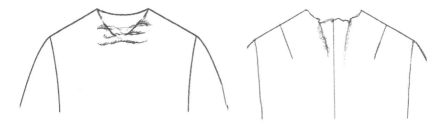

FIGURE 8.20 Forward neck (right) and bent back (left)

On an existing garment, you need to raise the back neckline and lower the front. This may involve removing the collar and re-setting it on the existing neckline, with a smaller seam allowance in the back and a deeper seam allowance in front. The altered curve on the neckline may also require re-drafting a new neckband to fit smoothly around the wearer's neck.

On a bodice without a collar, tiny darts, subtle easing, or pulled-up piping on the back neckline will help tighten up this area and keep it from gapping at the back.

For a mockup, redraw the neckline in the correct position. You may need to add fabric to the mockup at the back neckline to raise it to the right level. The back neckline curve will likely need to be higher and flatter than it was originally drawn. Make sure that the front and back neckline widths match at the shoulder seam.

Side Seams

Confirm that the side seams hang plumb at the sides of the wearer's body, starting at the lowest point of the garment armscye and continuing downward. On a mockup, you may redraw this line and adjust the pattern.

Finishing

Once you have completed the bodice fitting, be sure to look at the garment from all angles, while the actor is in motion, and while they are sitting. If the bodice allows the actor to move and it falls back into proper position when the actor is at rest, the bodice can be considered to fit correctly. Double-check all seam and dart positions, make sure that it is symmetrical (unless the design is asymmetrical), and confirm that any adjustments are clearly noted. Take photos for later reference.

If you are conducting a fitting with a designer, make sure that they approve the final result before the fitting appointment is over. Confirm your alteration plan and agree on the next steps for the garment, including whether it is worthwhile to obtain additional garments, or to construct and fit a second mockup.

9

SLEEVES

Sleeves are a secondary, albeit very important, part of a garment. The sleeves should be considered in relation to the fit of the entire garment. They hang from the armscye on a bodice, shirt, dress, or jacket. Therefore, it is most efficient to fit the torso area of a sleeved garment correctly first and then examine the shape and size of the armscye, prior to addressing the sleeves that are attached to it. However, there are times when the sleeves themselves are the issue while rest of the garment fits correctly.

This chapter is intended to be used in tandem with the bodice (Chapter 8), jackets (Chapter 11), and garments without a waistline seam (Chapter 12) chapters in the book, once those garments have been perfected. Because shirt sleeves fit differently than set-in sleeves, shirt sleeves will be part of the chapter on shirts (Chapter 10).

We will start this chapter with a summary of the parts of the sleeve, then continue to the body measurements needed to draft or check a sleeve, how to measure a sleeve to check against actor measurements before the actor tries it on, and how to conduct a fitting on existing sleeves or a muslin sleeve mockup.

Parts of the Sleeve

Figure 9.1 depicts a standard sleeve with labels in three formats: 1) sleeve pattern, 2) view of a sleeve from the front of the sleeve itself, and 3) view of a sleeve from the front of the bodice to which the sleeve is sewn.

DOI: 10.4324/9781351131353-10

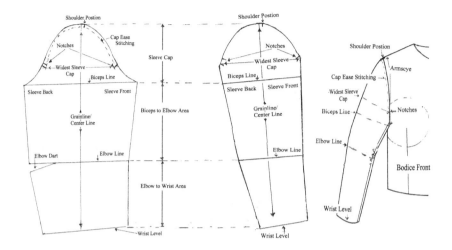

FIGURE 9.1 Sleeves with labels. Basic sleeve pattern (left), side view as seen while being worn (center), and front sleeve and bodice view (right)

Body Measurements Needed to Fit a Sleeve

The measurements below are the base measurements needed to check a ready-made sleeve. You will notice that this list is longer than the part of the list in Chapter 8 that covered sleeves, as this chapter is more specifically focused on sleeves. The numbers refer to the measurement sheet and discussion in Chapter 2.

The **wearer**'s measurements needed are the armscye (41), sleeve cap width or widest sleeve cap (36, this is a non-standard measurement), sleeve length (44), shirt sleeve length (43), sleeve cap height (42, this measurement is important in drafting a sleeve but less important in measuring an existing sleeve), biceps circumference (37), elbow circumference (38), and wrist circumference (40).

Checking an Existing Sleeved Garment before a Fitting

After taking the wearer's body measurements, a designer can use them to check a pulled or purchased garment.

1. *Armscye* around the armhole position on the garment. This is generally more comfortable for the wearer if the garment has at least ½″ more room than the person's body measurement, especially when the armscye is dropped down the upper arm for a particular design effect.
2. *Sleeve cap width* **across** the sleeve about 1″ above the point where the arm separates from the torso. On a sleeve pattern, this horizontal line is near the sleeve notches on the pattern. The sleeve will be more comfortable if there is 1″ or more ease across the upper sleeve cap. Different sleeve styles

may have much more ease in this area. This measurement is not on most standard measurement sheets, but I find it very helpful, especially when working with an actor with full upper arms.

3. *Sleeve length* from the top of the sleeve at the top of the armscye seam to the desired garment sleeve length. For a garment with an added cuff, the sleeve itself should have ½″ **or more extra length**, MINUS the depth of the cuff itself, to allow the wearer to move easily without the cuff binding on their arm; for example, for a shirt that extends 25″ from the top to the lower edge of a 2″ cuff, the sleeve above the cuff should measure 23 ½″ to allow for the extra length. For a puffed sleeve with added height in the puff, the sleeve may be need to be 1–2″ (or more) longer than a non-puffed sleeve would be.

4. *Shirt sleeve length* is an important measurement for a purchased shirt and is the length from the center back nape of the neck to the shoulder, extending around the tip of the bent elbow, to below the wrist bone on the outer edge of the arm. The garment should be the same or slightly longer than the wearer's body at this measurement.

5. *Biceps circumference* – for a sleeve that is not made of stretch fabric, there should be at least 1–2″ of room at a horizontal level, midway between the base of the armhole and the elbow level.

6. *Elbow circumference (bent)* – for a sleeve that is not made of stretch fabric, there should be at least 1–2″ of room at the elbow level when it is bent. A fitted one-piece sleeve will have an elbow dart to fit the natural bend in the arm.

7. *Wrist circumference* – for a sleeve that is not made of stretch fabric, there should be at least 1–1 ½″ of room at the wrist level. If a cuffed shirt will be worn with a wrist watch, the cuff should be at least 2″ wider from the end of the buttonhole(s) to the center of the button than the wearer's wrist measurement.

Fitting an Existing Sleeve or a Mockup

Have the wearer put on the garment. In this chapter, we are assuming that the body of the garment fits correctly, and that the focus is on the sleeve itself. On a mockup, the sleeves should be hand basted into the armscye. I also hand baste **muslin sleeves into the bodice when conducting the first fabric fitting**, to confirm that the adjusted bodice fits correctly before cutting the sleeves in garment fabric.

Check the Bodice

Begin the fitting by confirming that the shoulder seam is in the correct place, which usually follows the center of the wearer's shoulder. Next, check that the armscye seam is at the correct place on the wearer's body for the garment design. Fitting this area is discussed in detail in the chapters on bodices, shirts, and jackets. Use chalk or safety pins to mark the correct armscye location if the garment is incorrect.

> **For an existing garment**, you may decide that the garment is too far off to correct and it is more efficient to choose a different garment. If you own the garment and choose to adjust the shoulder line and armscye, remove the sleeve either partially or fully, and adjust the garment before repositioning the sleeve.

> **For a mockup**, remove the sleeve and pin or revise the shoulder position. Redraw the armscye before re-attaching the sleeve.

Hang of the Sleeve

Assess how the sleeves hang from the upper armscye by having the wearer stand up straight and let their arms fall naturally, observing whether the fabric of the sleeve falls smoothly down the wearer's arm. A correctly fitted sleeve has a centered vertical grainline that falls down the center of the wearer's arm, tilting slightly to the front at the wrist as the arm tends to hang slightly forward on many wearers. The sleeve and the arm should hang at the same angle, unless a different design decision has been made.

Figure 9.2, left, shows a standard sleeve pattern. Note that the vertical center grainline is usually placed ½″ toward the sleeve back as compared to the shoulder

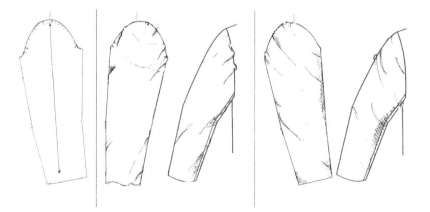

FIGURE 9.2 Twisted sleeves: sleeve pattern showing the correct position of the vertical grainline (left), two views of a sleeve that is inserted too far toward the wearer's front (center), and two views of a sleeve that is inserted too far toward the wearer's back (right)

seam position (which is indicated by a notch ½″ toward the front of the pattern's sleeve cap). This grainline position allows the sleeve to follow the typical pitch of a wearer's arm. The dotted lines indicate where ease stitching is placed on the upper sleeve cap to reduce the sleeve cap to fit the slightly smaller armscye.

The center two images on Figure 9.2 show the effects of a sleeve that is tilted too far toward the front armscye for the wearer's arm, creating soft folds on the sleeve front. The right-hand two images show a sleeve that is tilted too far toward the back armscye, creating soft folds on the sleeve back.

To correct the sleeve position, remove it from the armscye, or at least un-stitch it over the top of the sleeve cap to the position where the arm separates from the body – i.e. to the notches on the sleeve cap.

On an existing garment, you may decide that the garment is too far off to correct and it is more efficient to choose a different garment. If you own the garment, choose to rework the sleeve, and there is enough seam allowance in the garment to make this adjustment, remove it from the armscye, or at least un-stitch it over the top of the sleeve cap to the position where the arm separates from the body. Start at the top of the sleeve at the shoulder seam and remove the stitching from either side of that position until enough is released to move the sleeve cap to a better position within the armscye.

Reposition the sleeve cap as necessary to get the sleeve to hang correctly. Baste the sleeve in place, and re-check this on the wearer before sewing it in permanently.

On a mockup, unfasten and reposition the sleeve cap as necessary to get the sleeve to hang correctly. Re-pin the improved sleeve position, and have the actor move around in the bodice and move their arms to check your work. Once the position is corrected, mark the top of the sleeve where it meets the shoulder seam, and mark notches on both the sleeve and bodice approximately 3″ up from where underarm sleeve seam and the bodice side seams meet. Be sure to mark the new armhole stitch-lines if they differ from your starting position. Mark a notch at the top of the sleeve cap where it meets the correct shoulder seam position. Adjust your sleeve pattern to reflect any adjustments, and make sure that you have retained correct ease in the sleeve cap.

Fit on the Wearer's Arm

Once the sleeve is in the correct position in the armscye, you can assess the fit in the body of the sleeve itself.

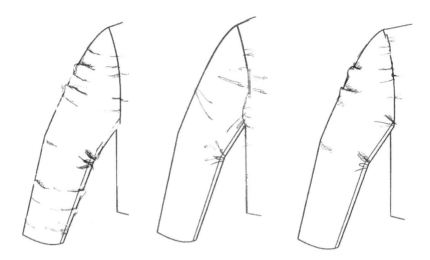

FIGURE 9.3 Sleeves too snug for wearer: too snug down entire length (left), too snug in cap, pulling the bodice out of alignment (center), and so snug through the cap that the sleeve is pulled up toward the shoulder seam

Sleeves that are too snug will have horizontal folds across the cap or forearm area and/or draw-lines originating from the seamlines (Figure 9.3, left). The horizontal folds are created because the sleeve is pulled upward to a smaller area of the arm.

If the wearer's shoulders are sloped and upper arms are very rounded, the sleeves will need their fullness distributed further around the sleeve cap to fit comfortably over the upper arms (Figure 9.3, center). For sleeves that are too snug down their entire lengths, let out the vertical underarm seam allowances or add gussets if possible. Gussets will be discussed later in this chapter.

On an existing garment, a thin shoulder pad or sleeve head can raise the sleeve cap so that a wider part of the sleeve area can be moved up to fit around the fullest part of the wearer's arm. This works only if the length from the top of the sleeve to the biceps line is long enough that the added pad does not pull the sleeve even more out of alignment.

On a mockup, un-stitch the sleeve cap from the shoulder point outward on the front and back of the sleeve, in order to allow the gathers at the top of the sleeve to reach the widest part of the arm. Distribute any fullness that is present in the sleeve cap between the armscye midpoint and the top of the sleeve rather than allowing the fullness to remain only at the top of the sleeve cap. Be sure to arrange the fullness evenly so that it lies smoothly over the arm.

If the sleeve is too small overall, add more room across by splitting the pattern vertically and adding a wedge of fabric to the entire length of the pattern piece. Or, the vertical underarm seams and upper cap curves may be expanded outward to create more room.

While the sleeve cap should fit into the garment's armscye with some ease to shape around the deltoid muscles, the relative height versus the width of the sleeve cap will affect the fit of the sleeve over the upper arm. For a person with full upper arms, the sleeve cap should be lower and wider, while for a person with thin upper arms, the sleeve cap should be higher and narrower.

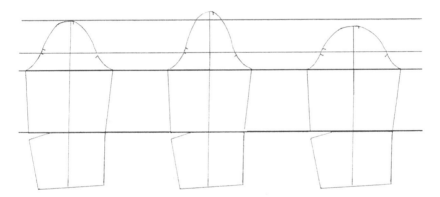

FIGURE 9.4 Sleeve cap heights and widths, all with the same overall circumference. Standard sleeve cap (left), taller sleeve cap, and wider sleeve cap

When patterning a sleeve, check the sleeve cap against the size of the armscye to ascertain whether there is the correct amount of ease. The **upper edge of the sleeve cap at the armscye** seam should have extra room, or EASE, that is **larger than the armscye seam to which it is sewn**. To fit the armscye, the sleeve is very slightly gathered into the armhole seam. The resulting billowing of the upper sleeve will allow the wearer's upper arm to fit comfortably.

A set-in sleeve made from woven non-stretch fabric should have an average of 1 ½" ease, or extra fabric, larger than the length of the armscye to which the sleeve will be sewn. For a smaller sized wearer, the sleeve should have 1–1 ¼" ease compared to the armscye, meaning that the cap of the sleeve should measure 1–1 ¼″ LONGER than the armscye seam to which it will be sewn. A medium-sized wearer should have 1 ½″ ease (ranging from 1 ¼ to 1 ¾″ depending on the garment design), and a larger-sized wearer, or one who needs more room in the upper arms, should have 1 ¾″ or more ease. For a slightly dropped armscye for a shirt sleeve, the ease is 1″. Some manufacturers skimp on the necessary ease to make the garment look tidier when it is displayed, or because easing in a sleeve can be a little more difficult than sewing it in without added ease. HOWEVER, a set-in sleeve needs ease to comfortably fit over the upper arm.

Be sure that the pattern has enough room across the lower cap at the level of the sleeve notches, to fit the wearer at the widest point of their upper arms. See Figure 9.1 for the widest sleeve cap (36) placement. This is an unusual measurement to take but it is extremely helpful to check when creating sleeve patterns. The sleeve will fit more comfortably if there is at least 1″ of ease across the widest cap area; the cap height may need to be lowered slightly to balance the width across the cap, while retaining the overall desired amount of ease in the sleeve cap, Figure 9.4 shows a standard sleeve pattern in the left-hand image, along with a tall, thin sleeve cap (center), and a low, wider sleeve cap (right). A tall, thin sleeve cap will fall smoothly from the upper armscye but may not have the room needed for a wearer with rounded upper arms. A low, wide sleeve cap will allow more comfort over the upper arms but will show some horizontal folds at the lower armscye – these folds will not be able to be completely eliminated through fitting without making the sleeve too restrictive.

The smoothest fitting sleeve will combine a sleeve cap that is ½″ taller above the pattern biceps line than the wearer's sleeve cap height meas-urement (42) with a width of the cap that is at least 1″ greater than the wearer's measurements across the upper arm at the point where the arm separates from the torso (36). At the same time, the sleeve underarm posi-tion should be placed close to the wearer's armpit to allow for the greatest range of movement.

Sleeve gussets (Figure 9.5) – gussets are an extra area of fabric that is inserted between seams to add room in a specific area. On sleeves, they are usually added to the underarm area.

If the sleeve is too snug to allow the arm to be raised comfortably, add an oval gusset between the notches and the armpit at the armpit to give more vertical room (Figure 9.5, left). If the bodice and sleeve are too snug at the side seams, add a diamond-shaped gusset in the sleeves and bodice to add 2″ or more″ total at each side seam (Figure 9.5, center). An oval gusset will tend

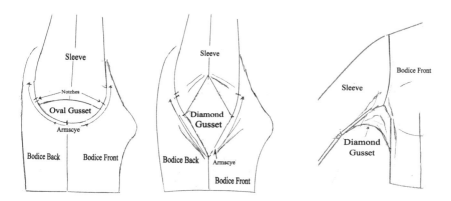

FIGURE 9.5 Gussets: an oval gusset allows more vertical lift (left); a diamond gusset allows more room across the arm and bodice (center) but is more visible (right)

to fold up into the armpit area, while a diamond gusset will be more visible to the viewer (Figure 9.5, right). Both gusset types are usually made of the same fabric as the garment. However, in productions where the actor needs to move vigorously, gussets may need to be made from Spandex-blend fabrics dyed to match the garment fabric.

> **On an existing garment**, adding a gusset is possible when you have matching fabric or can dye fabric to match the garment.

> **For a mockup**, for a garment to which you can anticipate needing to add a Spandex-blend gusset, make some dye tests to see whether the colors of the base garment and the gusset can be made to match, and whether the wearer's perspiration will change the two fabrics' color over time.

Sleeves that are too loose will have **loose, soft vertical, folds hanging from the top of the sleeve cap level and/or the elbow level** (Figure 9.6). The entire sleeve area may be too wide, creating loose folds on the lower arms (Figure 9.6, left). Or, there may be too much ease or gathering on the cap of the sleeve where it is joined to the armscye, creating a softly puffy effect (Figure 9.6, right).

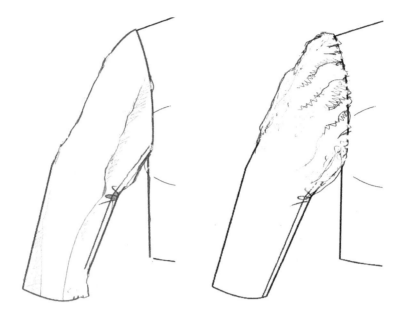

FIGURE 9.6 Sleeves too loose, throughout sleeve length (left), or at the sleep cap (right)

For an existing sleeve, take in the excess width below the biceps area by using a wider seam allowance on the vertical underarm seam. One may also adjust a period sleeve with a little too much puff in the cap by sewing five or more rows of gathering stitches horizontally across the cap area and pulling up the fabric. If you own the garment, you can un-stitch the top of the sleeve and re-stitch the sleeve into the armscye lower down on the sleeve cap, thus reducing the amount of fabric that is gathered into the armscye.

For a mockup, pin out excess fabric to create the correct silhouette. Transfer this adjustment to your pattern by folding out the pattern paper to reproduce the fabric adjustments. Redraw the cap to create a smooth curve. Double-check the sleeve cap circumference against the armhole circumference to avoid reducing the necessary sleeve cap ease with this alteration.

Sleeve Length

A full-length sleeve usually ends below the wrist bone when the wearer is bending their arm. Length adjustments can be a matter of moving a hem position, or reworking a cuff. **For a mockup** garment, the length alterations will be a simple process of either shortening or lengthening the sleeve pattern with a horizontal subtraction or addition within the body of the pattern.

Sleeves Too Long

For an existing garment, increase the hem depth to shorten the sleeves. For a close-fitting style, the elbow dart or sleeve shaping will also need to be taken out and re-sewn at the level of the wearer's elbow, so this should only be attempted if your theatre owns the garment and you can rework it.

If the sleeve has a cuff, you can take a tidy horizontal tuck out of the sleeve length along the seamline above the cuff, pressing and topstitching the edge of the tuck so that is stays folded inside the shirt. If the sleeve will be worn onstage under a jacket or onstage in a large theatre, a tidy horizontal tuck may be sewn above the elbow level to shorten the length.

For a mockup or an existing garment that may be permanently adjusted, a too long sleeve with a cuff can be altered by removing the cuff and re-sewing it slightly higher on the sleeve. If the sleeve cuff and placket will be too difficult or awkward to rework when shortening the sleeve, one may also take the sleeve out of the armscye, shorten the cap, adjust the armscye slightly by taking in the bodice side seam to retain the correct ease relationship of sleeve to armscye, and re-sew the sleeve at the new position.

Sleeves Too Short

On an existing garment, lower the hem placement if there is enough fabric in the hem allowance, or you may need to add an extra band of fabric or trim to the lower edge. If the sleeve is a close-fitting style, the elbow dart or sleeve shaping may need to be repositioned lower on the garment.

When purchasing a ready-made man's shirt, you may find that you need to purchase a shirt with a longer sleeve length than the actor's measurements would suggest in order that the sleeve is long enough to show correctly at the wrists under a jacket. As clothing has gotten more casual, the common lengths of men's shirt sleeves and hems have started to be manufactured in shorter lengths and it is increasingly difficult to find 36" or longer sleeve lengths to purchase.

For an existing garment that may be permanently adjusted, if the sleeve has a cuff, it may be necessary to cut and sew new, wider cuff to the sleeve end. If the sleeve will be worn onstage under a jacket, an additional horizontal piece of fabric may be sewn above the elbow level to lengthen the sleeve so that the correct amount of sleeve cuff shows beneath the jacket; however, the garment will not be able to be worn without a jacket after this alteration.

10

TAILORED SHIRTS AND BLOUSES

The term shirt tends to be associated with male garments with straight outlines made of cotton or cotton blend fabrics, while a blouse is associated with female garments with soft outlines made of drapier fabric. However, in the present day, the boundary of gender expression between what type of shirt or blouse one prefers to wear is not as demarcated as it once was. A tailored shirt or blouse is designed to look good on its own as well as to fit smoothly beneath a suit jacket. As jacket armholes and styles have changed over the years, so have the shirts that are intended to be worn beneath these jackets. The fashions of a period may dictate whether a particular shirt is interpreted as fitting correctly; however, the standards listed below are a baseline from which to work in evaluating these garments.

Shirts and blouses should be long enough to stay tucked in if that is the intended style. All surface patterns on the fabric should line up at the seams. Most people are flattered by darts or shaping below the bust/chest line to create a sleek body shape through the torso.

We will examine the parts of a tailored shirt and a blouse, different styles of shirts, the body measurements needed to pull or pattern a shirt or blouse, how to measure the garment to check against actor measurements before the actor tries the garment on, and the standards for how a shirt should fit on the wearer.

Parts of the Tailored Shirt

Figure 10.1 shows the parts of a standard tailored shirt, front and back.

DOI: 10.4324/9781351131353-11

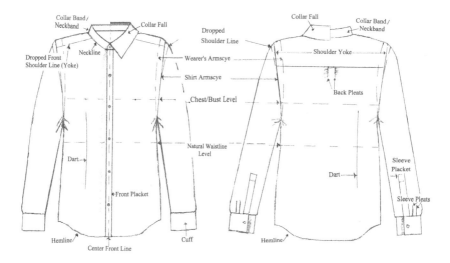

FIGURE 10.1 Shirt: front (left) and back (right)

Parts of the Blouse

Figure 10.2 shows the parts of a typical blouse, front and back. Note that the outlines of a blouse are softer and more curved than are those of a tailored shirt.

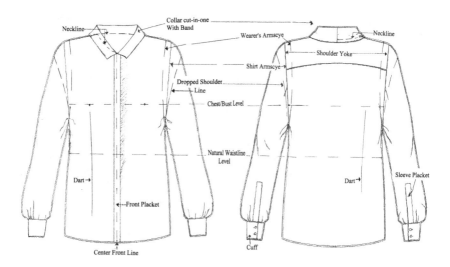

FIGURE 10.2 Blouse: front (left) and back (right)

Body Measurements Needed to Select a Shirt or Blouse

The measurements below are the essential measurements needed to check a ready-made shirt or blouse. They are listed in order of importance for these garments; the numbers refer to the measurement sheet and discussion in Chapter 2.

The body measurements needed to select a shirt are: base of the neckline circumference (1), shirt sleeve length (43), chest/bust circumference (8), back base of the neck to waist length (13b), and natural waistline circumference (11).

Checking Existing Shirts and Blouses Before a Fitting

With the wearer's body measurements, one can check a pulled or purchased shirt to assess the potential fit.

Neckline – measure horizontally across the collar band from the button position to 1/8″ from the centermost end of the buttonhole. The collar band will be most comfortable if there is 1/2″ extra ease beyond the wearer's Neck Base measurement. If the shirt neckline is 1″ or more beyond the wearer's measurements, it will be too loose to wear with a necktie knotted at the top of the shirt front (1).

Shirt sleeve length – most shirt sleeve length sizes are measured from the center back neck. Find the center back point of the shirt collar band, measure horizontally across the top of the shoulder, down the outer edge of the sleeve and to the lower edge of cuff or sleeve hem (43). Even if the shirt you are measuring has the sleeve length marked, manufacturers may err on the side of making the sleeves slightly shorter than labeled. If the shirt will be worn under a suit coat, you may need to purchase or pull a sleeve length 1″ longer than the actor's measurements to keep the cuffs from disappearing under the coat sleeve when their arm is raised.

Chest/bust circumference – the widest part of the chest at the nipple line, PLUS the appropriate amount of extra room or "ease" across the body. For a non-stretch fabric garment, there is anywhere from 3 to 4″ of ease on a standard shirt or blouse and 4–8″ or more on a loose shirt or blouse. For a garment with stretch in the fabric, the ease can be as little as 2″ at this level (8).

Back shirt length – compare to the wearer's center back length measurement from the lower seam of the collar neckband vertically down to the shirt hem. For a shirt that is being tucked in, the garment length should be at least 8″ below the body measurement from the back neck to the fashion/pant waistline level OR at least 12″ below the body measurement from the back neck to natural waistline level (13b). Modern shirts and blouses may not have the length needed to keep tucked in and may need to have extra fabric sewn to the tails.

Waistline circumference – check this width on the shirt at the lower end of the wearer's center back length measurement. Add 2–4″ to the wearer's body measurements at this level for wearing ease (11).

Fitting the Shirt or Blouse

For this chapter, I have listed the points to examine in order to assess how well the garment fits the wearer. I am assuming that the shirts and blouses being tried on can be adjusted as needed, or that other options can be purchased. Second-hand stores are good sources of shirts and blouses at reasonable prices, which can be restyled to fit. Once the shirt is tried on and the actor's widest chest/bust (or waistline) area is contained within the shirt so that it can be fastened up the center front, you can examine the shirt details.

Torso

The shirt body should fit smoothly over the torso with enough room to hide the specific contours of the wearer's figure, without having so much fabric that the sides of the shirt billow up over the waistband when tucked in, or being so snug that the fabric pulls and wrinkles horizontally away from the buttons at center front and is constricted across the tops of the sleeves. Depending on the shirt fabric, a smoothly fitting shirt will have a total of 2–4″ extra at the underarms – a shirt with stretch in the fabric can be cut closer than a non-stretchy fabric.

   The difference between chest and waistline measurements is part of the designation of the shirt "fit." A classic-fit shirt or blouse can have a 3″ difference between these two areas, a regular-fit shirt or a blouse may have a 2–4″ difference, trim fit may have 2–5″, and slim-fit may have as much as a 2–6″ difference. A classic-fit shirt will have a broader fit across shoulders, room through the body, and looser sleeves. The slim fit shirt will have closer fit in all these areas and depends on the wearer having a trimmer, more V-shaped torso.

   On any shirt or blouse, the side seams, extending into the sleeve underarm seams, can be tapered in for a smoother fit as long as the shoulder seams lie neatly on the shoulder; otherwise, the sleeves will also need to be removed and the armholes raised at the shoulder line. This is not an extremely difficult alteration, but it will result in shortening the shirt sleeve length.

Shirt Front Plackets

The front shirt placket should lie smoothly and lightly against the body, in a vertical line that does not twist or billow.

   The standard shirt front placket is an added strip of fabric, interfaced and doubled, that is used on the buttonhole side of the front opening. A mock placket may have the same effect, but is an extension of the shirt front that is turned under and machine-stitched, with a narrow vertical tuck stitched along what would otherwise be the placket seam, in order to mimic edge created by the added piece on a standard placket. A French-front placket is folded under twice to self-interface the edge. The inner edge of the fold may be machine-stitched to the front shirt to hold it in place. This is often used on the button side of a shirt, even if the buttonhole side has a standard shirt front placket.

The shirt front, no matter what type of placket that is used, must be **on-grain**. In other words, the front of the shirt should be cut with the lengthwise grainline running up the center front line of the garment. There are exceptions, such as when a separate front placket is cut on the diagonal to use a striped or plaid pattern as a decorative element. However, if the garment is inexpensive or there is not enough interfacing keeping the bias-cut placket in shape, the front edge may start to sag unevenly and the buttonholes may eventually start twisting after a few washes.

Body Fit

Since shirts tend to be cut with the body fit in proportion to the necklines and sleeve lengths, a person with long arms may end up in a shirt that is too wide through the body. For a too large body, if the neckline fits the wearer, the body may be taken in at the side seams, tapering into the underarm area of the sleeves. If you adjust the side seams, be sure to taper in at the waistlines and then flare back out to the hipline levels so that the wearer has enough room at the seat. In addition, vertical darts in the body may be slightly increased and lengthened if they already exist and can be added if there are no extant vertical darts. Look also at the width of the armscye placement of the garment in relation to the wearer's armholes. You may need to accept a somewhat too wide shirt shoulderline position in order to obtain enough sleeve length for the wearer.

Shirts should fit comfortably across the fullest part of the chest/bust. The front closures should not gape because the garment is too snug or bag because the garment is too loose. However, because a shirt usually does not fit as closely as a fitted bodice, there is some leeway in the assessing whether the chest area fits or not.

If the closures gap between the buttons, which will often happen on a woman's garment at the bustline level and can also happen at the waistline area, the garment is too snug.

On an existing garment, let out the side seams if possible, and reduce or eliminate vertical shaping darts to add more room across the body. A diamond gusset in coordinating fabric will add more room to the underarm and chest area.

If the shirt is gaping between the buttons at the bustline level, this is a sign that the cup size of the shirt is too flat, or at least that the buttons are in the wrong position for the fullest part of the bust. This is a common issue on women's shirts. Shirts button placements are measured down evenly from the neckband of the shirt but often do not fall where they are needed at the bust level of the wearer. In this case, adding a snap to the front shirt bands will allow the wearer to fasten the shirt correctly.

On a mockup, re-pin the side seams to give the wearer more room and adjust the intake on any darts. A vertical wedge of additional room may need to be added to the pattern. The underarm area of the sleeve may also be let out to help the shirt body fit better.

To avoid the shirt gaping at the bustline level for a woman's garment, mark the buttonhole placement at the bustline level, then at the desired position of the top button. Measure between these two points and break the distance into equal segments of 2 ¾–3 ½" (or inches) apart. Mark the remaining button hold centers with the equal spacing you have determined.

If the garment is baggier than you would prefer, the quickest adjustment is to reduce the width at the side seams, which may also mean reducing the width of the sleeve underarm seams. Darts may be added and increased to taper in the body.

On an existing garment, stitch the side seams inward. I usually find that this works best by continuing the side seam adjustment into the sleeve underarm seam as a continuous stitch line, tapering out to the existing sleeve seam line at the elbow level. If you would like to retain the ability to let the shirt back out for later use, don't clip at the underarm. However, if you are not concerned with future use, let out the old stitching line to release the tension at the point where the sleeve joins the shirt body at the underarm. You may find that a little clipping at this point is helpful.

On a mockup, redraw the side seams and armscye positions closer to the center of the wearer's body. It may be easier to adjust the garment by pinning out a vertical wedge of fabric and then transferring this adjustment by folding out the same amount of paper from the body of the pattern.

The body can also be refined with vertical darts. For men, back vertical diamond shaped darts are helpful in achieving a trim look. Front vertical darts are also helpful for women's garments as well as for a very tapered look for men. For a man's shirt, however, be careful that increasing the depths of front vertical darts do not create a curved bustline that appears more feminine than you intend. In that case, it is better to add a second vertical dart in the back, and/or to taper in the sides a little more.

On a woman's garment, if the wearer's cup size is greater than a "B", consider also adding a side bust dart to the pattern. This will allow much of the fullness to be controlled in a relatively efficient way and will leave the remaining vertical front dart at a moderate width. Or, consider adding creating an armhole princess seam to the garment front to achieve the same result in a tailored manner.

The torso length should allow for the shirt to stay tucked in when the arms are raised, or to hang several inches below the belt level if the shirt is worn untucked. If a shirt fits well otherwise, it is fairly simple to cut and re-hem a too long shirt length. If the shirt is too short to stay tucked in, one can sew on a lightweight fabric in a matching color to the existing tails. (As I am tall and move around a lot during a typical work day, I find that I have to sew extra fabric on all my purchased shirts and blouses to keep these garments tidily tucked in.)

A shirt that is designed to be worn untucked generally has a straight-cut hemline rather than a shaped hemline.

Collars and Bands

Correct fit on the collar unit is a marker of a good shirt. Tailored modern shirt collars are built on an interfaced band collar, functioning as the collar stand that overlaps and buttons at the center. Women's blouses or men's casual shirts may have collar that partially rolls up the back neckline without a separate stand. If the garment has a separate collar band piece it should fit smoothly around the neckline and lie at the base of the neck all the way around, neither above this point nor hanging loosely around the neck without touching it. One should be able to slip two fingers between the collar band when it is closed and the wearer's neck, which represents an extra ½″ of ease compared to the wearer's base of the neck measurement.

The lower edge of the neckband should lie in the same spot as the wearer' neck base. A neckband seam that is too snug will ride above the wearer's neckline base and will restrict the throat and/or Adam's apple (Figure 10.3, left). To correct this, the shirt will need to have a new neckband constructed and added to a slightly lowered neckline position.

A neckband that is too large for the wearer will fall below the base of the neck (Figure 8.3, right). This will cause the collar band to crumple when a necktie is worn and the shirt upper front to collapse into rounded diagonal folds. The neckband can be removed, the neckline eased to a smaller size, and a smaller collar band and collar can be sewn onto the reduced neckline area.

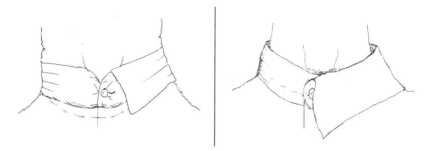

FIGURE 10.3 Collars and neckbands: too snug (left) and too loose (right)

For a quicker fix, a seam can be taken up at the center back through the neckband and collar, with the collar, band, and shirt upper back pressed very well. This alteration works best for a shirt that will be worn onstage under a jacket. If the shirt is worn open and without a necktie, the collar band or neckline can be slightly too snug or too large without it being obvious to the audience.

Collar Styles

The collar FALL, or the wide turn-over part of the collar unit, is the interfaced, shaped outer piece that extends from the band, and can have a variety of end shapes. A crisp collar will either have additional interfacing in the points, or internal or removable collar stays. The fall should end exactly at the center fronts WHERE IT IS SEWN TO THE NECKBAND, in line with the vertical buttonholes running up the center front and/or the front button positions. This allows the neckline edges of the fall to just meet at the center front when the neckband button is closed.

The shape and size of the collar ends are a matter of fashion. The spread, or the width of the gap between the collar tips on the front when the neckband collar is closed, is a matter of fashion. Different spreads will showcase different styles of necktie knots. Standard collar tips extend 1″ past the center front of the neckband and are approximately 2″ wide. For some time periods, the shape of the collar ends will differ from the standard. Sometimes replacing the collar fall with a plain crisp white collar with sturdy interfacing is enough to renew an older shirt that otherwise fits well.

Collar Styles (Figure 10.4)

1. *Standard point collar* – The standard modern man's shirt collar, with upper edges that meet at center front and outer points that frame the necktie knot. The distance between the outer tips should be evaluated in relation to the current fashion and the size of the knot on the necktie to be worn

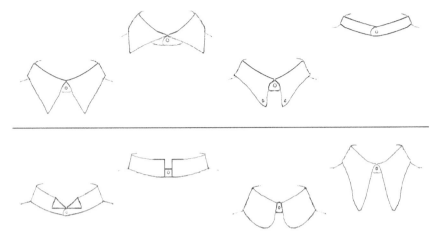

FIGURE 10.4 Collar styles: upper row, left to right: (1) standard point shirt collar, (2) spread or cutaway collar, (3) button-down collar, (4) band collar. Lower row, left to right: (5) wing collar, (6) stand collar, (7) rounded, penny, or hoover collar, (8) 1970s shirt collar

with it; a larger knot needs a wider spread. White collars and cuffs were fashionable in the 1980s, and as well as in the 1890s–1920s.

2. *Spread or cutaway collar* – The points of this collar are spread away from the center front in a wider angle than the standard collar. This collar works will with a wider necktie knot and a double-breasted suit.

3. *Button-down collar* – A point collar with buttonholes at the tips that allow the collar to be neatly buttoned in place on the shirt front.

4. *Band collar* – A collar stand without an attached collar fall. This may match or contrast with the shirt body.

5. *Wing collar* – A standing band collar that ends in pointed corners that are folded back on themselves, it is considered more formal than a shirt collar. The wing collar is often worn with a bow tie and tailcoat for current formal wear.

6. *Stand collar* – A collar band with squared ends, often with a gap between the two vertical edges.

7. *Rounded collar* – A collar fall with rounded ends, popular during the early 20th century and as a fashion option for the late 20th century. This style may be called a Penny Collar or a Hoover Collar.

8. *1970s collar* – While the back edge of the collar is similar to a regular collar fall, the front points extend longer than most styles and may have a somewhat curved shape. These collars were often worn open to showcase the wearer's chest. Generally, the collar matches the body of the shirt, but the collar underside, band, or entire collar unit may be a contrasting color or pattern.

Collar Sizes

For men's shirts that are not labeled with a specific size, the US equivalents are based on neck sizes: Small – 14–14.5; Medium – 15–15.5; Large 16–16.5; XLarge 17–17.5; XXL 18–18.5. Athletes or other people with developed necks may have a neck measurement up to 20″ or more.

Since shirts tend to be cut with the body fit in proportion to the necklines and sleeve lengths, a person with long arms may end up in a neck band that is too large. For a too large neckband, IF there is no possible shirt available with the correct neck size that also has the correct sleeve length, one can adjust the existing neckband by taking the neckband off and removing the collar fall from the band, slightly easing the remaining neckline of the shirt, and taking in the collar band at the center back in a stitched down tuck or constructing a new band in the right size.

At this point, the collar fall will be too large for the new size of the neckband, so one will need to resize the collar by either: (1) Re-cutting and stitching the ends of the collar fall to make it fit; (2) Taking in the center back of the collar fall with a tidy stitched down tuck (this works best in a larger theatre or for a shirt worn beneath a jacket); or (3) Creating a new, contrasting collar.

Shoulders and Armscyes

The horizontal shoulder seams for a classic-fit shirt can be positioned right at the upper plane of the wearer's shoulders or can be dropped toward the front by ½–1″ or more.

The armscye seams of a shirt or blouse may also vary from the anatomical armscye of the wearer (Figure 10.5). These positions are often referred to as the shoulder line positions.

The shoulder seam length on a shirt or blouse extends wider than the anatomical end of the wearer's shoulders, which is technically at the pointy shoulder bones of the wearer. This is because a shirt sleeve is traditionally cut with a

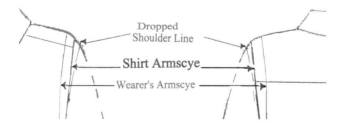

FIGURE 10.5   Shoulder line/garment armscye positions, showing parts of the shirt front (left) and back (right): Wearer's armscye, which is also the armscye position on a trim-fit shirt (blue line), standard Shirt armscye position (black line), and Dropped shoulder line/armscye (red line)

lower, wider sleeve cap and joins the sleeve top **exactly** at the point where the horizontal line of the shoulder meets the vertical line of the arm. Therefore, the shoulder length on a shirt (Figure 10.5, black line) extends at least ½–1″ past the sharp bones of the wearer's shoulder. Looser fit shirts may have a shoulder line that extends 2–3″ past the shoulder bones and drops over the top edge of the upper arm, for a "dropped shoulder" effect (Figure 10.5, red line).

A trim-fit shirt may have shoulder seams that end closer to the junction of the wearer's shoulder bones and arms (Figure 10.5, blue line). These shirts are often made of stretch fabric to allow movement despite the close fit. The closer the fit of the shirt, the narrower the extension of the shoulder line. When fitting a trim-fit shirt, be sure the wearer can move their arms comfortably.

Yokes

A yoke on a tailored shirt is a sign of quality. A yoke is a doubled piece of fabric that extends across the back shoulders and reinforces the shirt as well as slightly adding to the visual breadth of the shoulder line. A high-quality tailored shirt may have a vertical center seam to allow for better fit at the upper back, while a blouse may or may not have a yoke. The yoke is usually cut with the length-wise grainline of the fabric running perpendicular to the wearer's spine so that the yoke stands out slightly. This effect can be enhanced with a striped fabric, as the stripes will be oriented horizontally on the yoke. For fashion purposes, a yoke may also be cut with the grainline running vertically or cut on the bias in order to create diagonal chevrons at the center back. However, unless the yoke is carefully interfaced and lined with a fabric that is cut with the grain-line running horizontally or vertically, a bias-cut yoke may begin to buckle or twist after several washings.

Back Pleats

Two pleats in back at the lower edge of the yoke are common on a tradition-ally fit shirt, either a box pleat meeting at the center back or two knife pleats, each spaced close to the armscye near each end of the back yoke. The pleats each tend to take up an ½″ depth fold for a total of 1″, sewn to the yoke. A close-fitted shirt may lack a yoke, so it would also lack the added pleats. Even with a yoke, a close-fitted shirt tends NOT to have added pleats in the back. A blouse often does not have back pleats.

Sleeves

Lengths

Men's shirts are often sold by the sleeve length. The standard sleeve length is 33–35″, a shorter length is 31–32.5″, and a long length is 36–37″ or longer (which can be difficult to find in most stores). Shirts sleeves that are shorter or longer than these lengths are very challenging to locate.

Long shirt sleeves should end below the wrist bone at the top of the hands when the wearer is bending their elbow. The typical sleeve is 3/8″ longer than the straight arm in order to fit the bent arm correctly. This will result in the sleeve having a slight bagging above the top of the cuff when the wearer is holding their arms straight at their sides. A too long sleeve will billow over the top of the cuff, which is more appropriate for a period shirt or a soft blouse. A too short sleeve will inhibit movement and feel awkward.

If a shirt fits elsewhere but the sleeve length is too long, the sleeve above the cuff may be shortened. This can be done by un-stitching the sleeve from the shirt at the armhole seam, cutting down the sleeve length at the upper end, and re-attaching the sleeve to the shirt body after slightly taking in the shirt body at the underarm to fit the reduced width of the new upper edge of the shortened sleeve. If a quicker, less permanent solution is needed, one may take a small tuck at the lower end of the sleeve that is folded behind the upper edge of the cuff and topstitched in place, which will slightly reduce the length of the shirt placket. Or, one may sew a large tuck on the inside of the sleeve above the elbow length if the shirt in question is to be worn under a jacket that will hide the resulting horizontal seam.

If the sleeve length is too short, any alterations will be permanent. A sleeve may be very slightly lengthened by taking out the armhole seam and re-stitching it with a very small seam allowance, or by replacing the shirt cuff with a contrasting color cuff that is wider than the original. If the shirt is to be worn with a jacket that will hide this alteration, a piece of lightweight fabric may be added within the body of the sleeve above the elbow to add as much length as is needed.

Sleeve Cap

The traditional shirt or blouse sleeve has a cap that has been slightly shortened to work with the typical shirt armscye seam, which extends approximately 1″ past the sharp shoulder bones toward the upper arm of the wearer (Figure 10.6).

Typically, a shirt sleeve cap is shortened 1″ and the lower ends of the cap are extended to create a sleeve cap that is wider and lower than a standard sleeve. This accommodates the placement of the shirt shoulder seam, which is often extended 1″ past the placement for a fitted bodice (which has an armhole that lines up with the sharp shoulder bone at the end of the shoulder line). The lower and wider sleeve cap on a shirt sleeve will not only allow the wearer enough room to move their arm but will also create more wrinkling at the point where the sleeve seam meets the shirt underarm than might be found in a high-and-slim fitted bodice sleeve. Because a shirt's armscye base is placed

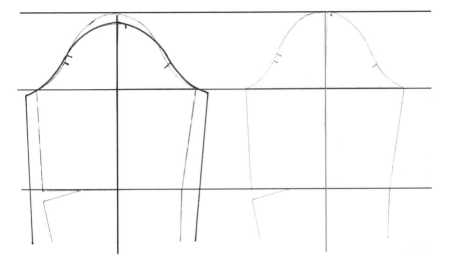

FIGURE 10.6 Shirt sleeve (left) compared to a standard bodice sleeve (right, and half-tone outlines superimposed on the shirt sleeve)

lower than that of a standard bodice, it can affect the fit of a jacket worn over it. Therefore, if a shirt is intended to be worn with a jacket on stage, the shirt fitting appointment should include trying on the jacket to check the fit of the garments together.

Sleeve Width

A tailored shirt sleeve should have approximately 2–4″ extra room around the arm so that the fabric hangs smoothly without pulling across the upper arm or elbow, or billowing around the arm at the lower end above the cuff. Sleeve ends are usually larger than the cuff circumference, so the extra sleeve fabric will be taken up with one to two shallow pleats at the outer edge of the wrist or with soft gathers on a blouse sleeve. Period shirt or blouse sleeves may have even more fullness at the cuff seam, so be sure to fit the shirt with a jacket if that is how the garment will be worn.

Cuffs

Traditionally, men's tailored shirts worn with a jacket should show ½″ below the lower edge of the jacket sleeve. For theatre, I tend to ignore this rule and work with ¼″ of the cuff showing when the wearer's arms are hanging straight. When the wearer has their arms bent, the jacket sleeve ends will pull up enough to show ½–5/8″ of cuff. If the jacket is already ½″ shorter than the shirt cuff, when the actor moves around there is a danger than the jacket sleeves will pull up and get caught on the top of the shirt cuff, creating a very awkward effect. This is especially common on a shirt with French cuffs. Be sure that the jacket sleeve end is WIDE enough to accommodate the width of the shirt cuffs **plus** at least 1″ extra for room.

A standard shirt cuff is the most common option on modern shirts. The cuff is 2 1/2′–2 7/8″ wide cuff, overlaps approximately ¾″, and fastens with one to two buttons, often with two horizontal button positions in order to allow a cuff to be fastened tighter or looser (Figure 10.7, left). Tailored sleeve cuffs should be 1 1/2–2″ larger than the wrist bones when they are worn, so that there is space between the cuff and the wrist. In addition, the cuff should be an **additional 1″** longer for the button and buttonhole. When worn, the closed cuffs should be able to slide over the hand if tugged on but should not slip off easily or constrict the wrist. If the wearer is wearing a wrist watch, the cuffs should allow for the watch to fit without pulling, which means that the cuff may need to be even longer than if there is no watch worn.

For a tall blouse cuff that extends up the forearm, the cuff will need to be tapered to fit comfortably both at the top and at the wrist level of the cuff when worn, with at least 1″ ease plus another 1″ to allow for the closure overlap (Figure 10.7, second from right). In this case, the upper and lower edges of the cuff will curve.

A French cuff is twice as deep as a regular modern cuff so that it can fold back on itself, roughly 6″ wide (Figure 10.6, far right). It has two sets of two buttonholes so that the cuff can be fastened with cufflinks. French cuffs also have a 2″ rather than the standard 1″ overlap to allow for the cufflinks. This is the standard cuff choice for men's modern formalwear and is the period-correct choice for wealthy men's shirts from the 19th century onward.

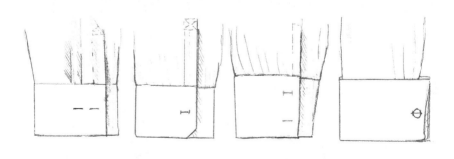

FIGURE 10.7 Styles of shirt and blouse cuffs. From left: (1) standard cuff with two buttoning positions, (2) cuff with diagonally cut corners, (3) tall cuff with two vertical button positions and a tapered fit which is often used for blouses, and (4) French cuff

11

SUIT JACKETS, SPORTS COATS, BLAZERS, AND PERIOD INDOOR COATS

Suit jackets, sports coats, blazers, and other period-specific indoor coats are important garments for creating an established and elegant appearance, onstage or in real life. They are labor- and time-intensive to create and can be expensive to purchase. They are an important resource in a theatre's costume stock because many plays include characters who need to be dressed in a tailored jacket of some sort. By understanding how a jacket should fit, a designer can make the best choices when pulling, purchasing, and trying jackets on an actor.

While this chapter most directly covers modern jackets, most of the information in the chapter can be used when measuring and fitting a period coat or jacket, such as a frock coat, cutaway, justaucorps, tuxedo, tailcoat, or other types of indoor coat. The differences tend to be in where the shoulder line falls on the wearer's body, the armscye placement and upper sleeve fullness, whether shoulder pads will be added, the shape of the collar, the hem lengths and shapes, whether there is a lapel or revers or not, whether there is a waistline seam or not, and how high the coat fastens. Be sure to have accurate research images in the room when you are fitting a period coat.

Suit jackets, sports coats, blazers, and period coats are garments that are designed to be worn over other garments, such as tailored shirts, blouses, thin sweaters, knit shirts, and/or waistcoats, depending on the time period. They are often the outermost upper body layer worn inside a building, and may also be a lightweight outer garment worn out of doors, with or without an additional overcoat added on top. Because these garments are layered over other garments, jackets should be tried on while the wearer is dressed in their other layers in order to get an accurate sense of how the jacket will lie when

DOI: 10.4324/9781351131353-12

worn as intended. While this book does not discuss overcoats or outerwear in detail, an overcoat will have similar elements as an indoor jacket, but **the amount of wearing ease on an overcoat is generally double that of the indoor jacket**.

We will start by defining different types of jackets, then move on to the standards of fit for various jackets categories, the body measurements needed to pull or pattern a jacket, how to measure existing jackets to check against actor measurements before a fitting appointment, jacket structure, and how to conduct a fitting for an existing jacket or a mockup garment.

Parts of the Jacket

Figure 11.1 shows the standard parts of a jacket.

Types of Jackets

A **Sack** or drape coat is the most common modern jacket worn by men, having started as a jacket style in the mid-19th century. It is characterized by NOT having a waistline seam but is softly fitted through the body because of the use of vertical darts and/or shaped seams.

A **Suit Jacket** is a type of sack coat. It is a tailored garment that is intended to be worn with matching trousers or skirts and may also have a matching vest, creating a "suite," or suit. The suit jacket is usually made of a tightly

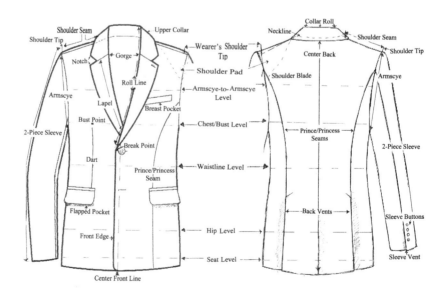

FIGURE 11.1 Parts of a jacket with labels: front (left) and back (right)

woven fabric such as a worsted wool, gabardine, linen, or cotton twill. Suit jackets fasten with buttons with holes and tend to be made in neutral colors, so that the choice of shirt, necktie, top, or blouse will make the primary color statement in the ensemble.

A **Sports Coat** is a jacket that does not match the trousers or skirt being worn and is often created of slightly heavier fabric than is used for a tailored suit, such as tweed, woolen, herringbone, corduroy, velveteen, velvet, suede, or leather. A sports coat tends to be in a wider range of colors than is available in a suit and has a slightly looser fit in order to allow layers such as medium-to-heavy sweaters to be worn underneath. It is more likely to have patch pockets than a suit jacket, may have a contrasting upper collar, pick stitching or topstitching on the upper collar and lapels, and may have elbow patches. Sports coats tend to have shanked buttons of leather or metal, or horn buttons with holes.

A **Blazer** is a specific type of sports coat that is traditionally made of navy or striped wool or of solid- or wide-striped linen, often with metal buttons for the closure and on the sleeves. A blazer has a dressier appearance than a sports coat but is not as formal as a suit jacket.

A **Tuxedo** coat is a formal sack coat, made in black or dark navy, with a shawl, notch, or peak collar lapel that is often made of contrast fabric. It is usually paired with matching trousers with a decorative side seam stripe.

A **Tailcoat** has a short front that ends near the wearer's waistline and longer back pieces known as "tails." In the 20th and 21st centuries, tailcoats are worn as the most formal dress available to men. In their modern iteration, tailcoats are black, made of wool, and the front buttons are not functional because the edges do not meet. In the 19th century, tailcoats could be made of a variety of different colors of wool or other fabric and could be single- or double-breasted and have extended shoulder lines, puffed sleeve tops, and deep upper collars. Tailcoats usually have a separate upper collar and lapels which may or may not be made of contrasting fabric.

A **Frock Coat** is THE formal day coat of the 19th century and is a precursor of the modern suit jacket. A frock is distinguished by a waistline seam which allows it to be tailored to fit the wearer's waist. The frock is generally closed in the front and usually has an upper collar and lapels. It extends to roughly knee-length, although the length and width of the skirts will vary by decade. The skirt backs tend to have pleats and a center back vent.

A **Cutaway** coat is similar to a frock coat but the front skirts are "cut away" to create an open lower front that rounds away from the jacket torso. A familiar version of a cutaway is the "Morning Coat" that is still used for some formal occasions.

A **Justaucorps** coat is a fitted coat of the late 17th and 18th centuries, which has a close fit through the upper body and long skirts. Depending on the decade of the coat, the shapes and lengths of the lower skirts may be wide, narrow, or swept back while the upper fronts may or may not meet. Period suits of the 18th century with justaucorps coats may be made of silk or brocade.

Categories of Modern Men's Jackets by Fit

When fitting a jacket, the time period of the production and the character wearing the jacket may affect some of your choices. It is helpful to understand the differences between the various styles of modern jackets from which you might choose.

A **Classic-fit jacket** has room under the arms because of slightly lowered armholes, a sloping shoulder line that may be slightly extended past the wearer's shoulder tips, can be slightly tapered inward for subtle shaping at the waistline, and has a medium-width notched lapel and a center back vent that covers the wearer's seat.

An **American-fit Sack jacket** is cut without front darts in the body and hangs loosely from the shoulders. It often has a single back vent and covers the seat completely in the back.

Modern-fit or **British-fit jackets** fit higher under the arm and have a softer shoulder line with a slightly higher squared padding and a bit less extension of the shoulder line than the classic jacket. This means that the shoulder is a bit higher and narrower than the classic-fit jacket. The chest has interfacing with slight padding in the upper area and the waistline is a bit more tapered. All of this creates the look of a broad chest and a V-silhouette. The back of the jacket ends slightly higher up the wearer's seat, generally with two vents, and the lapels are a bit narrower than the classic style.

French tailoring and **Northern Italian tailoring** from Milan and Florence are cut similarly to the British style, with a slightly extended padded shoulder.

A **Southern Italian or Neapolitan-fit** jacket may have three buttons with the lapels gently shaped to roll so that the top button and hole lie in the fold line of the lapel. The top button is not intended to be fastened in this style, also known as a **three-roll-two** button style. A soft shoulder or natural shoulder without any padding is also most typically seen in Neapolitan tailoring, resulting in a relaxed look. The gorge or notch placement is slightly higher than a classic jacket style. These jackets generally have two back vents, although some have no back vents in order to have a sleek back view.

Contemporary or **Trendy jackets** may have a combination of narrower lapels, slightly shinier fabric that may have some stretch, a higher and narrower shoulder line, and more fit through the waistline. The back of the jacket ends slightly higher up the wearer's seat, generally with two vents, while a less expensive version of this type of jacket tends to have no back vents. The narrower contemporary jacket styling tends to flatter a younger wearer, and the trendy look is continued by being worn layered with casual shirts, T-shirts, sweaters, or hoodies.

A **Shrunken-fit jacket** is the most extreme form of the contemporary style, with a tight fit that shows off the wearer's body and a short length that shows half of the wearer's seat. This style needs to be made in a fabric with some stretch in order to allow the wearer to move. This style was popular in the 2010s and early 2020s.

An **Athletic-fit jacket** will have broad shoulders and looser upper sleeves to fit a wearer with developed chest and arm muscles. The waist is usually tapered inward, and the flare of the jacket skirt is a little wider to accommodate more developed thigh muscles.

An **Executive-fit jacket** will have a medium-width shoulder line, with a looser chest and waistline area than the classic jacket. It often has two back vents. The presumed wearer tends to be a little older with a less pronounced V-shape in the torso area, so they need the extra room through the jacket torso.

A **Paddock jacket** is cut for horseback riding, with a flared jacket skirt area to accommodate the wearer's hips when sitting on a horse. This jacket has two buttons that are placed higher up the body front in order to be comfortable while riding. The buttons are usually both buttoned because the lower button is at the natural waistline level rather than below the waistline as on other jacket styles. The lower pockets on a paddock jacket are flapped and are sewn with the outer ends lower than the inner ends, so that the pockets will be parallel to the ground while the wearer is riding a horse. Because this style is designed to fit over body curves, **Women's jackets** may be cut similarly to paddock jackets.

Body Measurements Needed to Fit a Jacket Body

The measurements below are the base measurements needed to check an existing suit jacket, sports coat, blazer, or period coat. They are listed in order of importance; the numbers refer to the measurement sheet and discussion as represented in Chapter 2.

The wearer's measurements needed are as follows: chest/bust circumference (8), shoulder tip to shoulder tip (4f and 4b), around top of arms (5f and 5b), armscye to armscye (6f and 6b), base of the neck to natural waist level (13b), fullest seat depth (25), shirt sleeve length (43), and sleeve length (44).

Checking an Existing Jacket Prior to a Fitting

After taking the wearer's body measurements, one can check an existing jacket to assess the potential fit on a specific wearer.

1. *Chest*: Fasten the front buttons. Measure across the chest level line, which is approximately **1″** below the base of the armholes. Double this measurement to get the full chest circumference. Jacket styles will have different

amounts of wearing ease; 3–5″ extra room in the chest is standard in order to allow for movement and comfort. The chest circumference of the jacket should be at least **2″** wider than the wearer's measurements for a very fitted style, which is often made of fabric with some stretch. For a baggy jacket, there may be up **to 6″** of extra room.

2. *Shoulder tip to tip*: Measure horizontally across the jacket from tip to tip, across the outer ends of the shoulder pads of the garment to where the shoulder line intersects with the armscye seam. This measurement should be at least 1″ (shrunken fit) and is usually closer to **2–3″, wider than the wearer's body measurement from shoulder tip to shoulder tip** – note the different points on the illustration in Figure 11.1 for the location of the jacket shoulder tip and the wearer's shoulder tip. Be sure to measure both the front and back of the garment, as the roll of the wearer's back may be such that a garment that seems to fit in the front will be too narrow across the back.

   Unless the jacket is intended to fit snugly through the shoulders, I also like to check the jacket against the wearer's around upper arm measurements (5f and 5b). A jacket should be **at least 1″ wider than the wearer's around upper arm measurement** to account for shoulder pads in the jacket.

3. *Armscye to armscye*: Measure horizontally across the jacket midway between the shoulder tips and the chest level, which should be at the furthest indent of the armhole curve on the garment. The garment should be **½–1″ wider** than the wearer's body measurements. Be sure to measure both the front and back of the garment when comparing it to the wearer's measurements.

4. *Base of the neck to waist level*: Measure the back vertically from the lower seam of the jacket collar where it is sewn to the neckline, to the indent on the back seam just before it starts to flare back out over the seat. If there is a back vent, the top of the vent is approximately 3″ below the waistline level. The back waistline of the jacket will often line up with the wearer's natural waist, rather than the fashion/pant waist.

5. *Garment body length*: Measure the vertical center back seam, from the lower seam of the jacket collar to the lower edge of the jacket hem. This measurement should be the same as the wearer's fullest seat depth measurement plus an **additional 2–4″ of length** to cover the seat fully. For a period-style coat or a specially designed jacket, the additional length may be more or less than a modern jacket style.

   A conventional man's jacket length will cover his seat and will end at the side seams **at the point where his fingers lie when bent inward at a 90-degree angle**. A shrunken-fit jacket or a young man's jacket may show off part of the wearer's lower seat; however, this is a specialized fit that may not work for all characters or be accurate to most time periods.

A woman's jacket length will vary with the prevailing fashion, from the mid-thigh or longer jacket lengths of the 1990s to the high pelvic bone-level lengths of the early 2010s.

6. *Waistline circumference*: With the front buttons closed, measure across the waist level, which is where the jacket is most tapered inward at the sides. Double this measurement. The total waist measurement of the jacket should be at least **2″ larger than the wearer's measurement at the natural waist** (rather than at the fashion/pant waist) of the wearer.

7. *Jacket sleeve*: From the center back of the jacket collar at the neckline seam, over the outer tip of the shoulder pad, and down to the lower edge of the sleeve hem at the button vent. Jackets should be approximately **1–1½″ longer** than the wearer's shirt sleeve measurement to accommodate the jacket's shoulder pads. If ordering a jacket, you may also need the jacket sleeve measurement, which is taken from the armscye seam at the top of the sleeve to the lower edge of the sleeve.

8. *Hip circumference*: If the wearer has a full, rounded seat or hip area and the jacket needs to fit over that, it makes sense to check this measurement. At a point that is the same level as the wearer's fullest hip measurement, or approximately 10″ below the natural waistline level, measure the jacket circumference while it is buttoned closed. Jackets should be approximately **4″ (range of 2–6″ depending on fit) larger than the wearer's measurements**.

Jacket Structure

This book is not intended as a guide to tailoring, but it is helpful to keep the structure of the jacket in mind as you choose jackets to try on an actor, or if you are planning to fit a muslin jacket that will be formally tailored when it is constructed.

Interfacing – Interfacing is a support fabric that helps reinforce and add structure to the jacket body. The best jacket interfacing is called a **canvas**, which is a layered construction made of wool and horsehair (a linen fabric with horizontal nylon threads for stiffness) that sits between the suit fabric and the lining. The purpose of the canvas is to help a jacket hang correctly and maintain its shape over a lifetime of many wearings. The canvas is hand-stitched to the inside of the front body of the jacket so that it supports the fabric from the full shoulder, chest, and lapel area down to a narrower strip at the front openings and extends to the hem area. Additional interfacing is added to the upper shoulder area in the back, and at the hemlines of the sleeves and jacket hems. Inserting a canvas correctly is time-intensive, so less expensive jackets may be half canvassed (covering only the chest and lapels) or have a fused iron-on interfacing. A fused interfacing will tend to bubble over time due to its glue coming unsecured.

Shoulder pads – On a 19th- to 21st-century jacket, the extra width of the jacket shoulders in relation to the wearer's shoulders will be supported by a moderate shoulder pad and/or a sleeve-head pad. The padding will help fill in the curve at the top of the arm and create a clean angle where the shoulder and sleeve meet. The shoulder pad is part of the armature of the jacket and should create a crisp strong line from which the rest of the garment will fall.

Almost all tailored jackets of the 19th–21st centuries will have shoulder pads, even for most women's jackets. A pad will also create a smooth line at the shoulder by filling in the natural dip in the middle of the wearer's shoulder and will prevent the garment from sagging above the chest level. The very large set-in shoulder pads of the 1980s and the very large raglan shoulder pads of the 1990s have spooked some designers into eliminating pads altogether in order to avoid an oversized effect. However, classic tailoring depends on a thin-to-moderate pad in the jacket shoulder to fill out the natural dip in most wearer's shoulder lines, and/or a small line of padding in the upper area of the armscye seam to fill out the upper edge of the sleeve.

Lining – Lining adds structure to a suit jacket, helping it hang well on the body by placing a thin layer between the suit fabric and other garments to keep the jacket from catching on the other garments. Lining also covers the understructure of the jacket and keeps the insides looking tidy. It should be made from rayon such as Bemberg or Cupro rayon which is breathable, allowing the wearer's body heat to dissipate while they are moving around. Polyester or nylon lining is very uncomfortable to wear and should be avoided if possible or replaced with rayon if the jacket is otherwise worth the labor involved. Summer or more casual jackets are sometimes half-lined or unlined but should have their exposed seams finished with rayon or silk seam binding. However, the jacket sleeves should ALWAYS be lined in order to allow the sleeves to fall smoothly while wearing. Traditionally, jacket body lining fabric is the same color as the jacket body fabric, with a white, striped lining in the sleeves. Modern jackets may have colorful and/or printed linings.

Fitting a Jacket

Be sure that the wearer has on all the underlayers such as the shirt, blouse, or waistcoat that are intended to be worn with the jacket as well as the sweater, trousers, skirt, skirt shaper, correct type of bra or corset, shoes, or any other garments that are intended to be worn with the finished jacket. A jacket that appears correct on its own may look odd with the rest of the ensemble if the garments have not been fit as a group, because the proportions and lengths of each garment will impact all the others. For a mockup fitting, it is important to have the other garments worn with the jacket available in order to avoid any issues later.

For a mockup, remember that the finished jacket will be built over the understructure discussed above. Therefore, be sure not to over-fit the muslin mockup so closely to the wearer's body that it will be too snug once it is built in the correct fabric and with all the layers. If possible, I like to fit a jacket mockup sewn out of cotton twill, canvas, corduroy, or other fabric that is heavier than the muslin that is often used for mockup garments. I have also used inexpensive felt for a mockup jacket that was intended to be built of leather or tweed and to fit loosely. Use a light-colored, non-patterned fabric so that you can see your fitting marks when it is time to revise the pattern. The seam allowances should be at least 1" wide so that the garment may be readily adjusted. Use the longest machine stitch or a hand-running stitch to construct the garment, and backstitch the ends or tie a knot so that the seams do not come apart during the fitting session.

Before putting on the jacket, be sure that the seams and darts are sewn accurately. Mark all the stitch-lines for future references. Mark the center back of the jacket if it has been cut on the fold. Make the hemlines, neckline stitch-line, and the vertical center front line, as these makings will help you during the fitting. Also be sure you have marked the stitch-lines on the sleeve cap and the armhole stitch-lines before the sleeve has been sewn in. With all the marking to be done, use different colors for stitch-lines versus center lines versus darts to avoid later confusion and choose yet another color for the marking pencil or pen to be used during the fitting.

Insert any shoulder pads that you plan to use in the finished jacket. You can slide them into the jacket and safety pin them from the outside.

Fasten the Jacket Closures

Even if a jacket is intended to be worn open, a modern jacket should appear as if it could be closed smoothly. The garment should appear balanced, with the shoulder seam lying along the center of the wearer's shoulders. The jacket should drape evenly down the front of the chest and over the back without pulling to the front or back of the body, and without riding up or sagging down at any point. Fasten the jacket to start the fitting session.

For an existing garment, if the garment does not fasten, determine whether moving the button placement ¼–3/8" further out toward the front edge will create enough space to allow the garment to close smoothly. If not, choose another jacket.

For a mockup, it may be easier to fit the jacket with the seams on the outside and with the shoulder pads between the mockup and the wearer's body.

A 19th- to 21st-century jacket should be patterned with an approximately 1″ extension past center front line on both sides to accommodate the buttons and horizontal buttonholes. For a double-breasted jacket, there may be a 5″ extension.

Pin the jacket closed on the marked center front stitch-line, starting at the waistline of the opening and working up toward the chest level to the top of the intended buttons. Be sure to keep the two sides level so that you don't make one side higher than the other. If you cannot get the jacket closed completely, you may have to adjust or clip the side seams to get it to lie properly on the body. With the center front lines perfectly lined up, on a man's jacket, the wearer's left side overlaps the right side, while on a woman's jacket, the wearer's right side overlaps the left side. Be sure to fit both sides of the garment equally – the best result will be an averaging of the two sides of the fit garment, rather than depending on fitting one side of the garment and hoping that you have accurately kept the center line of the garment on the center line of the wearer's body.

Chest Area

The jacket chest should fit smoothly with approximately **4″ of ease**. This means that at the chest level of the jacket near the base of the armholes, the jacket should be 4″ larger than the body measurements at the widest point of the chest. The amount of fabric in the chest area, also known as the **drape**, will affect the fit. A suit jacket with a lot of drape has a fuller cut and more room in the chest. Jackets with noticeable drape are seen as more laid-back but are not as trim as a closer fitting jacket style. A period coat may have less drape; a late 18th-century justaucorps will not be able to meet at the upper fronts and the garment back will be snug as well.

Shaping methods: Modern jacket fronts may be shaped with darts, which usually end at or somewhat below the outer ends of the lower front pockets. The darts should point to the fullest part of the wearer's chest or bust and add some contouring to the shape of the jacket. A man's tailored jacket often combines a front vertical dart with shaped back **prince seams**, with or without shaped side panel seams. Panels with subtly shaped seams will also contour the jacket to follow the body. However, men's classic fit, sack jackets, and some period coats may not have front vertical darts.

A woman's tailored jacket may contain darts, shaped panels, princess seams, waistline seams, and/or easing to contour the jacket torso to follow the line of the wearer's body. A non-binary tailored jacket can be fit within the middle of the ranges of measurements and options contained in this chapter; I recommend using a front vertical dart, back prince(ss) seams, and a shaped side panel for fitting the torso. Consider starting with a modern-fit man's jacket or a paddock jacket, depending on the relative proportions of the wearer's measurements.

> **For a mockup,** consult your research images for the correct types of shaping seams or darts for the type of jacket that you are fitting. Check that the darts or the fullness of the shaping seams are in the right place for the wearer's chest and waistline, and that they take up the right amount of fabric. You may have to unpick and re-pin them to get them in the right place. Check also the length of the darts, to see that they are pointing to the fullest part of the chest/bust, pelvic bones, and hips, and don't go past the body curves or stop too short. Redraw and re-pin the darts, and mark clearly.

The jacket should fall easily over the chest and down toward the waistline. When buttoned, the jacket should fall back into place after the wearer raises and lowers their arms. A too snug jacket will create an "X" shape when the fastenings are closed (Figure 11.2). The buttons should not gap at center front when fastened. If there are horizontal wrinkles or bowed-out lines when the jacket is buttoned, the jacket is too snug.

There should be enough room in the chest to allow the jacket lapels to lay flat. If the lapels bend outward and create a space between the jacket and the

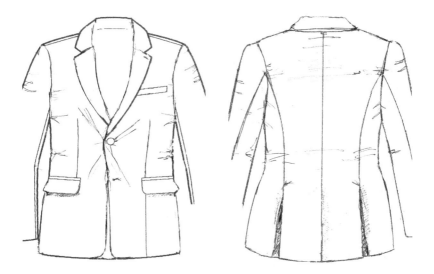

FIGURE 11.2 Jacket too snug over the chest, waistline, and seat, front (left) and back (right)

shirt, the chest width is too tight (Figure 11.2, left). Tension in the upper back and underarms can also result from a too snug chest.

Also check whether the jacket itself is the correct length for the wearer from shoulder to the closures. If the garment waistline is too long or short for the wearer, the garment closures may be at the wrong position on the wearer's body.

For an existing garment, if any of these issues occur, choose a larger sized jacket or a looser cut style. Also consider whether choosing a longer or shorter version of the same jacket would solve the issue. If the issue is slight, consider whether moving the front buttons toward the jacket front edge ¼" or so will resolve the issue without upsetting the balance of the garment fronts.

For a mockup, if the waistline area is too snug, let out the side seams and any waistline shaping in the jacket front. It is often best to let out small amounts in several areas for the smoothest result, unless there is one obvious area that is causing the problem. Consider also if raising or lowering the shoulder position will help move the closures to the correct position for the wearer's body. If the jacket fits reasonably well in the chest area at this point, go on to the shoulders and then re-evaluate chest and lapels.

If there are vertical folds or sagging lines when the jacket is buttoned, the jacket is too loose (Figure 11.3). A too loose jacket will collapse and create soft vertical folds. The shoulders may also extend past the wearer's shoulders and sag downward if the shoulder position is too wide for the wearer.

For an existing garment, if the jacket is slightly loose at the lower chest or waistline, the front buttons can be moved about ¼" horizontally away from the front edges, the waistline areas of the side or side back seams may be slightly tapered in, and/or the inner edge of the back vents can be hand-stitched closed to keep them from flapping. If the jacket is only SLIGHTLY loose in one or two spots, consider leaving the extra room intact to accommodate actor movement and comfort.

However, if the jacket visibly sags, it may be taken in very carefully at the back prince(ss) seams or side seams. This alteration should only be attempted if the jacket is made of natural materials, a heavy steam iron is available, and you have the time and skill to complete the task. If the upper back needs to be altered, you may also need to remove the upper back sleeve seam and rework the entire area. In many cases, it will make more sense to choose another jacket.

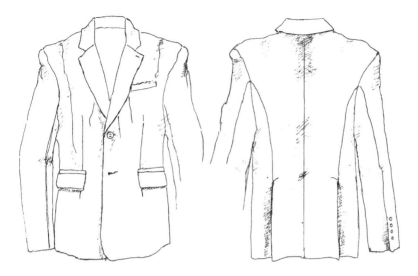

FIGURE 11.3 Jacket too loose in front (left) and back (right)

On a mockup, if the fit of the garment is baggy, you can take more fabric in at the darts or shaping seams, either front or back of the body or both. However, it is best to let the jacket be a little loose at this point in order to retain the necessary wearing ease, plus to factor in the thicker fabric, interfacing, and internal understructure that will be used on the finished garment.

Start first with the darts and/or prince(ss) seams in the front, and then in the back. Pin in the vertical darts and/or shaping seams to adjust the fit. If there are no front darts, the back prince(ss) seams are a good place from which to adjust the jacket; however, make sure the wearer can move their arms smoothly once the sleeves have been pinned back in place. It is better to have a slightly looser fit in the upper back to allow for actor movement.

You can continue fitting the chest by slightly adjusting the placement of the armhole area, although be sure to leave approximately ¾–1″ of looseness in the jacket body at the chest/bust level of the armscyes in order to have sufficient room for the sleeves in the completed garment.

If the over-all fit on the mockup is too loose, you may also pin out vertical amounts of fabric from the body of the jacket. As long as the pinned-out areas reach from one seamline to another, or from shoulder seam to the hemline, the amount of fabric pinned out in the mockup can be folded out of the pattern to transfer the alteration.

In certain situations, it can be helpful to add thin-profile padding in the upper back shoulders of the jacket to fill out that area where if the wearer has pulled-back shoulder blades.

FIGURE 11.4 Fit issues with women's jackets: from left: (1) shoulder-to-waistline level of the jacket is too long for the wearer, (2) button placement is too low for the wearer's bustline, and (3) jacket is too snug at the center front. The right-hand image (4) shows a jacket that fits correctly with the top button at the correct height for the wearer

For a woman's jacket (Figure 11.4), the upper torso area may gap when the buttons are fastened, particularly when the wearer is seated. There are several causes for this, which have their own solutions as long as the gaping is slight – if the gaping is pronounced, it is better to look for a different jacket.

If the shoulder-to-waistline area of the garment is too long for the wearer (Figure 11.4(1)), this may be corrected by adding a shoulder pad to raise the shoulder position of the jacket and remove the slack from the jacket front.

If the jacket button stance is too low (Figure 11.4(2)) for the wearer's figure, the jacket will gape open around the wearer's bust. This may be addressed by wearing the jacket open only, or by selecting a different jacket with a higher button stance. Trying to add another button to a jacket front is almost never successful because the button position is built into the essential shape of the jacket during patterning.

If the jacket is too snug to fit smoothly over the waistline and bust area (Figure 11.4(3)), it will create an "X" effect when wrinkles radiate out from the buttons. In this case, one can slightly move the button positions closer to the vertical front edges of the garment to create more room at the center front, or only wear the jacket open.

A jacket that buttons at or near the bust point level of the wearer's body (Figure 11.4(4)) will stay in place over the bust and create a tidy effect.

Shoulders

The shoulders are the support point of the entire garment, and once the chest area is determined to be the right size, the shoulders will determine how the jacket hangs. **Poorly fitting shoulders are a clear marker of a jacket that does not fit.** If the shoulders do not fit on the jacket, the jacket will look shabby.

A jacket's shoulder width should be carefully assessed in relation to the wearer's own shoulders and to the desired style of the jacket. Jacket shoulders should fit smoothly along the top of the wearer's shoulder line. The length of the jacket shoulder seam, where it meets the armscye seam of the jacket, should **extend past the end of sharp shoulder bones on the wearer's shoulder tip and stop just before the arm drops vertically** (Figure 11.5, upper register). Note the difference in this illustration between the blue lines of the wearer's shoulders/armscyes and the black lines of the jacket's shoulders/armscyes. **Shoulder pads** (crosshatched in Figure 11.5) are necessary to support the space between the jacket and the wearer's body. The difference between the wearer's armscye and the armscye on a jacket is filled out with a shoulder pad, which extends very slightly past the jacket armscye and into the upper sleeve to help support it.

The exact position for the end of the jacket shoulder seam will vary with the time period of the jacket. Despite the changes of fashion or period style, the usual goal is that the sleeve will hang vertically and will neither reveal a bulge at the upper arm nor collapse inward at the upper arm (Figure 11.5, lower register). In the later 20th century, one rule of thumb was for top of the

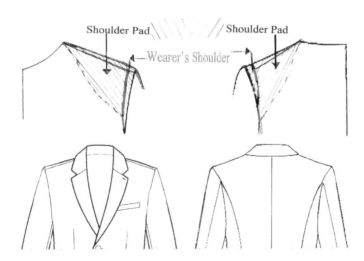

FIGURE 11.5 Jacket shoulder and armscye positions: upper register: jacket shoulders and armscyes (black lines) as compared to the wearer's shoulders and armscyes (blue lines). Shoulder pads (cross-hatching) support the space between the jacket and the wearer's body. Lower register: jacket with correct shoulder position, front and back

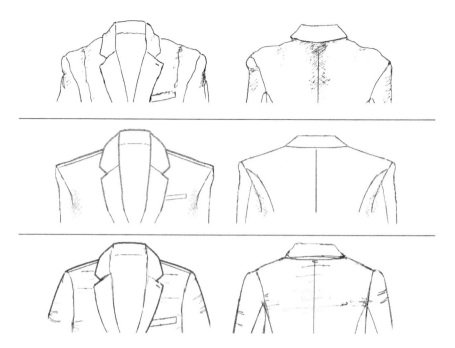

FIGURE 11.6 Jacket shoulder line positions: shoulders too wide for the wearer and sagging (upper register); shoulders with too large pads but not enough room in the upper sleeves (center register); and shoulders too narrow for the wearer (lower register)

armscye seam to fall on an implied vertical line from the furthest out curve of the wearer's upper arm.

If the jacket shoulders, or the shoulder pads in the jacket, are too wide for wearer, the upper sleeves will collapse in at the upper arm (Figure 11.6, upper register).

For an oversized jacket with heavy shoulder pads, the extra width of the shoulders extends ½–1″ or more past the standard bodice armscye position into the upper arm area. In this case, the upper sleeve will fall straighter because **the extended shoulder is doing part of the work of the upper sleeve**. Because of this, the upper sleeve of a jacket with extended shoulders will have less ease relative to the armhole than a jacket with a narrow shoulder, because the extended shoulder is taking up part of the area normally reserved for the upper sleeve. However, when the wearer is moving their arms, a jacket with extended shoulders can restrict the movement of the upper arms and may look awkward because the upper sleeve will collapse below the extended shelf of extra padding (Figure 11.6, center register).

For a slim-fitted jacket, the shoulder line may be set slightly narrower than usual, with the armscye seam ¼–½″ closer to the center front than for a conventional modern jacket. In this case, the upper sleeves will slightly round outward from the armscye seam in order to accommodate the upper arms (Figure 11.6, lower register). In fitting a slim–fit jacket, be sure to ask the wearer to move their arms around in order to ascertain whether they have enough room to move.

On an existing garment, if the jacket shoulders are obviously incorrect when the jacket is put onto the wearer, look for another jacket option. Shoulders are difficult to alter and will require taking out the sleeves at least partially to make the alteration.

If the jacket shoulders are slightly too wide, you may replace the existing shoulder pad with one that extends further into the upper sleeve in order to support the extra fabric. If the shoulders are too narrow, the jacket will never fit correctly and should not be used.

On a mockup, if the neckline end of the shoulder seam is bowing or sagging, the garment shoulder angle is too angled as compared to that of the wearer. You may either replace the existing shoulder pad with a thinner pad to change the seam angle at the outer end, open up the seam at the outer end and re-pin it to let out the seam and create a flatter angle, or re-pin the inner/neckline end of the seam to match the angle of wearer's shoulders. However, if you need to adjust the inner end of the shoulder seam, it will likely also require removing the jacket collar in that area, which can be re-evaluated later in the fitting session.

If the sleeve end of the shoulder seam is collapsing, there is too much height on the shoulder angle at the outer end. You may add a larger shoulder pad and/or a sleeve head (a small crescent-shaped pad that supports the upper half of the armscye seam). If these solutions do not work, remove the sleeve for approximately 4" each on the front and back of the armhole seam in order to pin in the excess of the shoulder seam and create a more sloped seam. In either case, if you open up the sleeve and adjust the shoulder seam, you will need to adjust the sleeve cap by an equal amount in the pattern. However, if the wearer's shoulders are sloped and the upper arms are very rounded or developed, it may be that more fullness in the sleeve cap is necessary to fit comfortably over the upper arms and the extra sleeve fullness generated by taking in the shoulder angle can be redistributed within the sleeve cap to fit the wearer's arms.

The shoulder seam should fall correctly in the center of the top of the wearer's shoulder line unless the jacket is designed differently. For a jacket since the 18th and 19th centuries, the shoulder seam may extend from the front and fall at an angle on the garment back, with the lower edges of the angle touching the armscye seams.

On a mockup jacket, you may need to redraw the shoulder seam placement if it is incorrect. Be sure to cross out the old seam position in order to avoid confusion later, when correcting the pattern.

Finally, shoulder pads are useful for correcting small fitting issues. If the jacket shoulders are of the correct width but the upper chest area collapses, this may be remedied by adding a thin shoulder pad to raise the angle of the shoulder line – the pad helps create a smooth line at the shoulder and prevents sagging of the garment above the chest, the upper arms, and the back shoulder blades. If the wearer has one shoulder that is higher than the other, adding a thin pad on the low side can equalize the shoulders. Have some tailoring shoulder pads as well as thin shoulder pads available when fitting a jacket in order to check whether the addition of a pad will enhance the fit of the jacket.

Torso

Once the shoulders are of the right widths and at the right positions, proceed down the garment. We have already determined that the jacket has the correct amount of room in the chest area itself; if not, try another jacket or check your alteration notes on the mockup. **Many of the fit issues that you may encounter will mirror those of bodices, as discussed in Chapter 8.** For existing jackets, if there are noticeable issues with length and width in this area, the jacket will not be fixable and an alternate jacket should be found. For mockups, you will be moving seamline positions in or out to correct the problems.

If the jacket shows rounded horizontal folds between the shoulder and bust/chest area, the upper chest is too long.

On an existing garment, consider whether adding a thin shoulder pad will raise this area so that it does not collapse on the wearer.

On a mockup, this may be addressed by pinning up the excess length at the shoulder seamline, or by pinning out a fold of fabric that is left pinned and later folded out of the pattern. The collar and neckline area will also need to be reshaped.

If the mockup shows thin vertical strain-lines, the area between the shoulder and bust/chest is too short.

On an existing garment, the jacket will not be able to fit correctly on the wearer. Try a different jacket.

On a mockup, the shoulders seams need to be let out to extend the body length. Open up the shoulder seamline to add more length, or note how much extra length to add in the pattern between the shoulders and the chest. Again, the collar and neckline area will also need to be reshaped.

If horizontal strain-lines point across the chest toward the arms, the armscye might be positioned too narrowly to fit on the wearer. The lapels will also bow outward from the chest surface.

On a mockup, begin by clipping into the seam allowances at the base of the armholes, working outward up from the underarm seam to release some of the tension. If the strain-lines persist across the upper chest, this will require un-stitching the armscye seams at the locations where the strain-lines originate and repositioning the sleeves themselves slightly further away from the body center lines to increase the room across the chest. We will continue working with the sleeves themselves later in the fitting process.

Look at the jacket back at the upper chest. If the jacket seems to bow outward at the shoulder blade level, the wearer's shoulder blades are protruding and the jacket needs a back shoulder dart or to have the fabric eased into the back shoulder seam at the same time that more fabric is added to the pattern in the upper back area at the armscye. The effect will be similar to Figure 8.10 in the chapter on bodices. See the patterning diagrams in Figure 8.11. Pin in the side seams or center back seams to refine the fit of the jacket on the body. A fine tailored jacket, especially for a man, tends to have a shaped center back seam, so even if the mockup was cut on a center back fold, you may find it to your advantage to convert the center back to a seam.

If the fabric collapses at the shoulder blade, the shoulder blade is flat. The effect will be similar to Figure 8.12. If there is a back shoulder dart in the jacket pattern, it can be reduced or removed and converted into ease at the back seam, with the excess fabric taken out of the pattern in the upper back area at the armscye. See the patterning diagrams in Figure 8.13.

In both cases, adding a back prince(ss) line seam to the design may be an excellent solution because it puts a shaping seam in the shoulder area. The upper back of the center back jacket seam may also need to be reshaped slightly to help with fitting the shoulder blade area.

Check that any side seams are falling exactly at the sides of the body. Redraw the seams and cross out any seams that are in the wrong place.

Collar

A well-fitted collar is another key attribute of a well-fitted jacket. The jacket's upper collar should fit smoothly around a shirt or blouse collar, without gaping or straining. If the jacket has an upper collar that is designed to fold over, the outer edge of the jacket's upper collar should hide the jacket neckline seam from the center back to the shoulder seams.

Check that the neckline fits smoothly around the shirt collar that is intended to be worn with the jacket. This means the jacket neckline is **1/4″–3/8″ lower** than the shirt collar neckline. The jacket neckline should follow the base of the wearer's neckline from center back to the shoulders, but will begin to fold away from the wearer's neckline in the front, where it turns back with the lapels. We will discuss the lapels later in this chapter.

The collar neckline seam in back should fall smoothly across the top of the wearer's spine, neither pulling in so tightly to create a ripple across the upper back of the jacket, nor gaping loosely compared to the curve of the wearer's neck.

If the collar neckline seam sits lower than the top of the wearer's spine, the collar will gape at its upper edge and the back neckline will seem awkwardly low (Figure 11.7, upper and lower left). If the back neckline is too low due

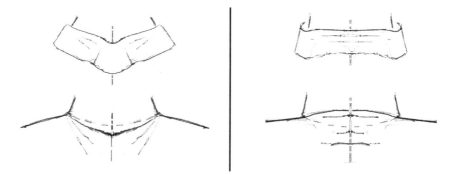

FIGURE 11.7 Back necklines and collars: neckline too low at center back so that the collar bows downward (upper and lower, left), and neckline too high and flat and center back so that the collar rides up the neckline (upper and lower, right). Dashed outlines on the images indicate the wearer's back neckline position

to the wearer rolling their neck forward or rolling their shoulders, the upper edge of the back collar may point away from the wearer's neck. A wearer with rolled-forward neck or shoulder posture can present a challenge when fitting this area of the jacket because they will need the jacket center back raised to accommodate their posture.

For an existing garment, the collar seam position needs to be raised slightly at the center back but the extra fabric needed at this point may not be available. (It is possible to slightly lower the back collar position on an existing jacket but it is very difficult to raise it.) Check whether adding thin shoulder pads raises the shoulders enough to bring the neckline up to the correct spot.

For a mockup, the collar may have been taken off to allow for earlier shoulder adjustments. If so, pin it back onto the neckline. Start with the neckline fitting and continue on to the collar.

A too low back neckline will need to be repositioned higher in the back than the original pattern, into the back seam allowance area. The neckline may also need to be lowered slightly in the center front, depending on the wearer's posture. The collar itself will need to be shortened at each end to fit the adjusted neckline and may also need to be reshaped.

If the collar neckline seam sits higher than the top of the wearer's spine, the extra length on the center back of the jacket body will collapse and create a soft horizontal fold below the collar seam where the upper jacket is being pushed downward by the collar (Figure 11.7, upper and lower right).

For an existing jacket, a too high back collar may be able to be carefully removed at the center back, steamed to slightly stretch the collar width, and the collar repositioned slightly lower down the body while tucking the jacket a tiny bit into the collar area, before hand-stitching this area back together.

For a mockup, a too high back neckline will need to be lowered at the back and the neckline, often by clipping into the seam allowance from center back outward toward the shoulders in order to release the jacket neckline and allow it to sit correctly on the wearer. The clips will be about

> 1 ½" apart but may not reach the marked stitch-line. The collar itself will need to be lengthened at both ends in order to fit the adjusted neckline and will also need to be reshaped.

Once the neckline shape and position are correct, consider the collar itself. It should roll up the wearer's back neck area for 1–1 ¼". The folded-over outer edge should cover the back neckline seam by at least ¼". It should not buckle across the shoulders, which indicates that the shape of the collar is too narrow to fit the shoulder angle. Confirm that the shape and width of the collar front ends match the garment design and research.

Gorge Seam

Once the collar shape is correct, check that the collar lies smoothly in the front upper chest area where it is joined to the lapel at the **gorge seam, which connects the upper collar to the upper end of the lapels**. This assumes that the jacket has a lapel, which was not common until the end of the 18th century. If the collar bows outward at this point, the shoulders and the collar seam do not fit the shape of the wearer's chest and/or shoulders. On an existing jacket, this is a sure sign that you need to look for another option.

> **On a mockup,** the collar shape and placement at the gorge seam can be remedied by detaching the collar from the neckline from the shoulders to the center front, and adjusting the angle of where the collar and neckline are joined, before re-pinning the collar to the jacket.

If the notched lapels on a 20th- or 21st-century jacket were to be folded over one another to cover the chest, the gorge seam connecting the upper collar to the lapel would roughly follow the base of the wearer's neck (Figure 11.9, center). Folding the lapel back into place, the gorge should rest on the collarbone area. However, **the exact placement of this seam can vary**.

Different modern jacket styles will place the gorge in slightly different positions for different effects (Figure 11.8). Suits from the early- to mid-20th century tend to have a lower gorge and a very low gorge was fashionable in the 1980s (Figure 11.8, center). A slightly higher gorge can make a jacket look sleeker, and in the late 2010s, the gorge upper edge was closer to the top of the shoulder. For most 19th-century coats, the gorge placement will be affected by the number of front buttons and the shape of the upper collar and lapels (Figure 11.12).

The gorge seam placement should be seen in relation to the jacket's button stance and the wearer's proportions. A higher gorge is typically balanced with

FIGURE 11.8 Jacket gorge seam positions: (1) standard late 20ᵗʰ- and early 21ˢᵗ-century gorge position on a two-button jacket (far left), (2) high gorge seam position on a high-buttoning jacket (second from left), (3) low gorge seam position on a low-buttoning jacket (center), (4) low gorge seam position on a high-buttoning jacket (second from right), and (5) high gorge seam position on a low buttoning jacket (far right)

a higher buttoning stance (Figure 11.8, second from left), but a slight adjustment of the gorge in relation to the stance can be made to flatter the wearer. A lower gorge and slightly higher buttoning point will make the lapels look short which, with the resulting longer closed fronts, will add visual weight to a tall, thin wearer (Figure 11.8, second from right). A slightly higher gorge and a lower buttoning point can be flattering to a shorter person by elongating the vertical line of the lapels (Figure 11.8, far right). In both cases, be sure that there is enough material below the buttoning point to balance the overall effect so that the jacket skirts don't look oddly short.

> **On an existing jacket**, double-check that the gorge position and angle are consistent with the time period you are costuming, and that all the jackets in the production have similar gorges.

> **On a mockup**, double-check the jacket design and especially the research images when you are evaluating the gorge position and angle. The gorge can be adjusted to the jacket's button stance and the wearer's proportions, as a slight adjustment of the gorge in relation to the stance can be made to flatter the wearer, according to the discussion above.

Lapels

Lapels are also known as **Revers**, as they are the REVERSE side of the jacket fronts, folded back to reveal the facing on the inner fronts (Figure 11.9). On a

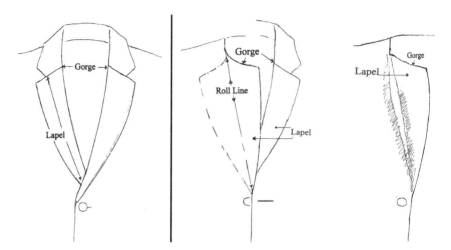

FIGURE 11.9 Parts of the lapel and roll line (left); underside of the lapel (center); extra fabric along the roll line (right), which usually needs to be taken out in a dart

late 18th-century coat, the revers folded completely back from the coat center front, were not intended to meet at the center front, and could be faced in a different color than the coat, most notably in the white revers on British military coats. On other types of 18th-century coats, there may be no revers/lapels at all.

The fold line that extends from the upper collar to just above the highest center front button is called the **Roll Line** or Lapel Roll (Figure 11.9, center). A strong lapel roll raises the lapel slightly away from the chest, creating a **hollow** under it. The lapel roll is seen as a sign of high-quality tailoring; a smoothly rounded roll is a sign of good tailoring, whereas a flat thin fold in this area is a sign of a cheaper, mass-produced suit.

The Roll Line position, height, and shape are created in the patterning and construction of the jacket, so the mockup fitting is the time to perfect them by **adjusting the angle of the seam where the upper collar meets the lapel.** The angle of the roll line is also tied to the number of buttons on a jacket front, because the higher the roll line, the more buttons will be needed on the front. Since a jacket's lapel ends at the point where you button it, a single-breasted jacket with three buttons will have a shorter lapel and a higher top button than a single-breasted jacket with two buttons.

The Roll Line position is created in the patterning and construction of the jacket and cannot be changed easily. I have repeatedly tried to alter this over the years when I wanted to have one additional or one fewer button on the jacket front for a particular time period, and the result has **never** been entirely successful. The exact angles of the upper collar and the Roll Line are built into the jacket and force the Roll Line into a particular height and shape that is not changeable, much as we may try to change it.

On a mockup (or a jacket during construction), make sure that the roll line position ends exactly where the research images and design drawings indicate. Remember to look both at the point at the base of the area opened up between the lapels and at the width of the lower edges of the lapels themselves when the jacket is fastened. Check how visible the top button will be when the lower edge of the lapels cross and the jacket front is fastened.

When the lapels roll back on themselves, there is often a bubble of fabric that develops on the jacket chest under the lapel. This is because the fabric at the inner surface of the roll needs to be slightly reduced to fit an area that is smaller than that of the outer surface of the lapel roll (Figure 11.9, right). This excess can be taken out with a long dart, either diamond-shaped or with the wider area at the shoulder end, beneath the lapel area. If you examine an existing jacket, you will often see a dart in this position at the Roll Line.

If the lapels wrinkle and pull outward from the jacket center line, this indicates that the wearer has too rounded a chest for this style or size of jacket (Figure 11.10, left). It may also be a sign that the top button on the jacket is in the wrong position for the wearer.

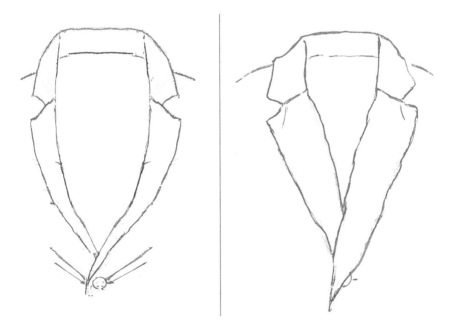

FIGURE 11.10   Lapels rolling outward (left) and collapsing inward (right)

On an existing garment, a larger jacket size may be needed. A different bra style that slightly flattens the bustline may help on a woman's jacket.

Try unfastening the top button to see if the lapels hang better, which may indicate that the top button is in the wrong position. If you intend the top button to be closed, choose another jacket.

On a mockup, check the amount that has been pinned out for the under-Roll Line dart. The angles of the collar and lapel where they meet at the gorge seam may also need to be adjusted, which usually means lengthening the edge of the upper collar where it meets the lapel.

More fabric may need to be added to the upper chest, either by moving the armscye position further outward, raising the shoulder seam position to lengthen the area, or adding a vertical wedge of fabric to the chest area. As long as the added amount begins and ends at seamlines, this adjustment should work.

Be sure that you are conducting the fitting with the shoulder pads inserted into the garment to get an accurate idea of the eventual shape of this area.

If the lapels collapse inward along the roll line, the chest of the garment is too loose or the Roll Line is too slack (Figure 11.10, right).

On an existing garment, a different jacket size may be needed, or a shoulder pad can be used to fill raise and smooth out a too large area by pulling slightly higher on the wearer. A bra style that lifts and rounds the bustline may help by increasing the size of the chest.

On a mockup, check the amount that has been pinned out for the under-Roll Line dart. The angles of the collar and lapel where they meet at the gorge seam may also need to be adjusted, which usually means reducing the amount of fabric at the edge of the upper collar where it meets the lapel to tighten up the roll line. Or, some of the excess chest fabric may need to be pinned out, usually at the armscye and shoulder area of the garment.

Be sure that you are conducting the fitting with the shoulder pads inserted into the garment to get an accurate idea of the eventual shape of this area. Otherwise, it is easy to over-fit the upper chest and lapel area.

Lapel styles (Figure 11.11) – The standard lapel shapes from the late 19th through the early 21st century are the Notch or Peak, with the Shawl collar as an additional option for formal-wear tuxedo jackets, men's period coats, or women's jackets. M-lapels are characteristic of men's period coats from the early 19th century.

A **Notch,** or **Stepped** lapel (Figure 11.11, far left) has an approximately 90-degree angle between the outer end of the upper collar and the start of the lapel. This is the standard traditional choice for most suits, dating back to the mid-1800s and is the most economical choice when purchasing jackets for stock as this style is versatile for many time periods. Lapels and/or upper collars may be of contrasting fabric or leather in sports coats.

A **Peak** or **Pointed** lapel (Figure 11.11, second from left) has a higher, pointed upper end of the lapel and is derived from formal wear such as tail-coats. Peak lapels are common for coats from the early 1800s to the 1820s. This is the less traditional choice for 20th- and 21st-century daywear, although it may be seen in suits from the 1940s (where the peak of the lapel extends closer to the armscye, the upper edge of the peak area creates a close-to-horizontal line, and the lapel has a broad curve) and the 1980s (where the peaks point a bit more toward the ends of the shoulders) to the 1990s (where the peak is slightly narrower than the 1980s). The peak is used more often for double-breasted suits.

The **Shawl** lapel (Figure 11.11, second from right) has a curved edge that originates at the center back of the neckline and blends to the roll line and vertical edge of the coat front. There is no seam between an upper collar and lapel

FIGURE 11.11 Lapel styles, from left to right: notch, peak, shawl, and M styles. Note that the shawl lapel has no gorge seam, as it has no upper collar

as the collar is a continuous area cut-in-one with the coat front. This lapel is most commonly seen in men's tuxedos, dinner, or smoking jackets in the 20th and 21st centuries and for women's jackets, although it was also common in the 1840s and 1850s, especially for men's waistcoats.

An **M-shaped** lapel (Figure 11.11, far right) has a shaped intersection between the lapel and upper collar with an added small point in between these two areas, creating a sideways M shape. This subgroup of notched lapels is very specific to the early decades of the 19th century.

Lapel widths – Lapel width can be quite period-specific, so check any design drawing and research images very carefully. The lapels often extend halfway across the chest from where they are folded back at the roll line to the point of the notch or peak lapel.

The lapel width on the jacket, as with the gorge placement, should be considered in relation to the chest width, shoulder width, and the height of the wearer in addition to the period research.

Lapel width on a modern jacket can vary from skinny (as narrow as 2″) to quite wide (4 ½″). Very thin or very wide lapels can be quite period-specific and make a jacket less useful for future use in a theatre costume stock. Visually, the **standard jacket lapel should extend roughly halfway across the chest** (the area from the roll line to the armscye seam) **from where it is folded back at the roll line to the point of the notch or peak lapel.**

The lapel width is measured at a 90-degree angle from the roll line of the jacket, in a straight line across the upper edge of the lapel to the tip of the lapel. **As many of the following numbers have been taken from men's tailoring, the measurements should be adjusted as needed for the wearer and the coat design, particularly for women's jackets**. However, this size range is useful as a starting point:

- A **Narrow** lapel ranges from 2 to 2 ¾″ wide.
- A **Standard** lapel ranges from 3 to 3 ½″ with the average width being 3 ¼″.
- A **Wide** lapel is 3 5/8–4″ up to 4 ½″.
- A **Peak** lapel tends to be wider, usually in the 4″ range at the widest point.

The chest width and height of the wearer will have an impact on which lapel width looks best within each range of sizes. Narrower lapels create the impression of wider shoulders by leaving visual space between the lapel and the sleeve seam. Wide lapels make the chest look wider as compared to the shoulders – if the lapel fills that space, the shoulders may appear narrower. Thin wearers will look more proportional with narrower lapels, while wider lapels can appear to be oversized on them. Tall or broad wearers will look better with wider lapels while narrow lapels may appear as if the jacket itself is too small for the wearer.

Lapel width should also be considered in relation to the width of the shirt collar and neckwear, usually matching the relative widths of all three items. As it is easier to adapt the shirt and tie than the jacket lapel width, choose a narrow shirt collar and a skinny necktie to go with a narrow lapel, and a taller collar and a wider necktie to go with a wide lapel. As a rule, notch lapels in the range of 3 ¼–3 ½″ look good on many men, as they balance with the average necktie width of 3–3 ½″.

Interfacing – Check that the interfacing (underlayer of support fabric inside the lapels and the front of the chest) does not cause ridges in the roll of the lapel or puckers in the chest. This can be the sign of poorly applied fusible interfacing and can be made worse if one steams a jacket with fusible interfacing in this area. In this case, use a press cloth between the jacket and a heavy iron, and carefully press the jacket fronts and lapels **without** steam to ease out the puckers. This only works on a very good jacket that has mistakenly been steamed, but it is not worth trying on a jacket that has come to you with puckered interfacing. The best jackets have interfacing that is all, or mostly, hand pad-stitched into the jacket fronts and collar, with little or no fused interfacing.

Buttons

When fastened, a jacket should fall back into place after raising and lowering the arms. It should not function as a corset by being too snug. There should be 3–4″ or more ease at the chest level to the waistline area. Be sure any functional buttons do not gap at center front when fastened, and check that the back vents lie closed. If the jacket fits otherwise, the front buttons can be moved about ¼″ more toward the front edges and the inner edge of the back vents can be hand-stitched closed. However, keep a sharp eye out for additional issues that may crop up and render the jacket too much work to be worth the alteration time.

The **Break point** is the spot where the jacket's curved lapels blend into the vertical front edge (see Figure 11.1, left), while the buttoning point or **Button Stance** is the height of the top front button. These two points are positioned very close to one another. A jacket's lapel ends at the point where you button it, so a single-breasted jacket with three buttons will have a shorter lapel and a higher buttoning stance than a single-breasted jacket with two buttons. Figure 11.12 shows a range of buttoning styles and the effect on the break point position.

FIGURE 11.12 Button stances: one-, two-, three-, and four-button jackets. The more buttons, the higher the buttoning stance and the less that the garments worn beneath the jacket will be visible

The more buttons, the higher the button stance and the less visible the garments worn beneath the jacket will be. A lower button stance elongates the lapels and creates a longer triangle of exposed shirt, which makes the wearer appear taller and thinner. Therefore, a heavier male wearer may be flattered by a lower button stance because the longer exposed shirt triangle has an elongating effect, **as long as the buttons close neatly and the lapels lie smoothly on the body**. However, a female wearer with a rounded bustline will be more flattered by a higher button stance because buttons placed at or near the bust point level will keep the front jacket edges in place, rather than allowing them to spread open and frame the bustline.

A very tall, lean wearer may be flattered by a higher button stance to shorten the triangle of exposed chest. A higher button stance will make the lapels look wider in contrast to the shorter exposed triangle of chest. Higher button stances visually broaden the chest if the wearer is lean because of the horizontal effect of the lapel edges in contrast to the vertical coat edges. At the same time, a higher buttoning line can be flattering for many wearers by covering the midsection and creating a vertical button line, **as long as the buttons fit well over the body**.

Check your research images when looking at the buttoning area of the jacket you are fitting.

One-button jackets (Figure 11.12, far left) appear more casual and work well for a casual 1950s' and 1960s' style.

Two buttons are the most common and classic on 20th- and 21st-century jackets (Figure 11.12, second from left) and are a traditional late 20th- and early 21st-century man's business style.

Three buttons are traditional, work well for most of the first half of the 20th century, and are a fashionable choice for the first decade of the 21st century (Figure 11.12, second from right).

Four buttons are common for the end of the 19th and early 20th centuries (Figure 11.12, far right), and have come back into fashion in the middle of the 20th and the early 21st centuries for zoot suits or other styles. The four buttons are placed closer together than a three-button jacket, and the lower buttons are not intended to be closed.

Double-breasted jackets have a greater variety of button possibilities, such as 6 × 2, 6 × 3, 6 × 1, or 4 × 2 jackets (the first number represents the total number of buttons on the front, with the second number representing how many of those can be fastened.). The 6 × 2 is most common in modern jackets, followed by the 4 × 2. The more buttons, the more formal the effect. The placement of the buttons can create two vertical rows or two rows that flare out as they travel up the body.

On a mockup, check the design and research images carefully when determining the placement and spacing of the front buttons. Draw the button placement on the mockup garment after the jacket body has been completely fit. The top front button and hole are placed where the lapel ends at center front.

Buttoning the Jacket – This information is less about fitting, and more about period style onstage. However, a costume fitting appointment is an excellent time to teach an actor how to wear the costume in character.

Traditionally, a man **buttons his jacket when he stands and unbuttons it when he sits**. However, the time period of the jacket and the number of buttons on the jacket will dictate how the jacket is fastened. For women, jacket-wearing traditions are not as codified so there is more leeway in how and when they fasten their jackets.

A **one-button jacket** is buttoned when standing; the exception to this is IF the man is wearing a matching vest with the single-button jacket, he may leave the jacket button open at all times.

A **two-button jacket** is fastened at the top button and the lower button is left unbuttoned, except in the 1920s when both buttons were closed.

A **three-button jacket** in the early 21st century is usually fastened at the middle button AND often at the top button, while in the early 20th century, it was fastened at the top button, and in the 1920s and 1930s, it might be fastened at all three buttons.

A **four-button jacket**, stylish in the late 19th century, was buttoned at the top three buttons if the jacket skirt had closed quarters as with a frock coat, or at the top button only if the jacket skirt had open quarters as with a cutaway.

On a **double-breasted jacket**, the wearer **always fastens the appropriate buttons when standing**. Two-button double-breasted jackets were popular for suit jackets in the 1980s; a tuxedo is the most common two-button double-breasted jacket in the 21st century. **The number of buttons on the**

double-breasted jacket and the time period of the coat will deter-mine the finer points of buttoning etiquette. See below.

On a 4 × 2 jacket, depending on how high or low on the body the buttons are placed, the wearer may fasten the top OR lower one or two buttons, whichever looks better. For a more casual appearance in the early 21ˢᵗ century, a double-breasted jacket is only buttoned on the top one or on both. Because double-breasted jackets are often fastened with inside buttons on the right-hand row of vertical buttons, a 4 × 2 button jacket is often kept buttoned while sitting as well as standing because of the awkwardness of re-fastening the inner buttons.

Traditionally, a double-breasted 6 × 4 jacket with peak lapels is a more formal style and all four active buttons are closed at all times. A double-breasted 6 × 2 notch lapel jacket is often fastened at the two buttons in the middle row. The bottom one is only undone when sitting in order that the jacket hangs smoothly on the sitting body.

Onstage, blocking may involve the actor getting up and sitting repeatedly within the space of a few minutes. In that case, reason may dictate that the actor keeps their jacket either closed or open for most of the play, depending on what looks better on the wearer, in order to avoid spending their entire scene dealing with jacket closures.

Jacket Lower Torso

Waist suppression refers to how much the waist area of the jacket is tapered in, creating the impression of wider shoulders through visual contrast. Usually, at least a slight suppression at the waistline is flattering to the wearer's figure, although that depends on the wearer's particular shape. Waist suppression on a modern man's suit is related to **suit drop**, which is the number indicating the difference between the size of the jacket, based on the chest size, and the waist size of the suit pants. For a size 42 jacket, a 36″ waist size pant would be a "drop 6" suit, which is a standard chest-to-waist proportion offered in a man's suit. A slimmer cut suit may be a "drop 7" or even "drop 8." A drop 7 or drop 8 suit will be slimmer than a drop 6 suit because, given the same chest size, the drop 8 suit will have a slimmer fit through the waistline of the jacket and a smaller waistline on the suit pants. The suit pants in a slimmer suit are also more likely to be cut WITHOUT waistline pleats.

Jacket skirt – The jacket **Skirt** is its lower half below the waistline level. On tailcoats, cutaways, or frock coats, the skirt is joined to the chest area of the garment with a waistline seam. At the front, the two flaps of the jacket skirt that meet at the waist button are known as the front **Quarters**. The flaps can lie nearly straight down below the waistline (closed quarters, used for frock coats) or spread apart below the waistline (open quarters, used for cutaways, and tail coats). In theory, closed quarters maintain emphasis on the shoulders because the hip area appears narrow since it is covered. However, this is only the case if the jacket skirt fits with enough room over the wearer's hips and thighs to hang smoothly and vertically.

Jackets with open quarters, such as cutaway or tailed styles, may be used to balance out very broad shoulders. Open quarters can make the lower body look wider because the trousers or skirt are revealed. For a wearer with narrow shoulders and/or a rounded tummy or thighs, open Quarters may frame and emphasize a rounded lower body. When fitting a jacket with open Quarters at the front edges, be sure that the edges do not twist. This area should be well interfaced and the edges should be taped with tailor's tape during construction to keep their shape.

Vents: On the back of the jacket skirt, there are usually one or more vertical vents (Figure 11.13). Jackets should fit smoothly without binding over the seat or flapping loose in back. Check the placement of any back vents, and whether they hang closed when the wearer stands while allowing enough room when they sit. Vents should only open up slightly to allow the jacket to fall smoothly when the wearer sits or puts their hands in their pockets; the jacket's back vents are not spread so far open that the garments below the vent can be seen. However, a wearer with a rounded seat may need the vents to be hand-stitched into place, and/or to wear a jacket that is slightly looser fitting through the hip area to allow for the vents to hang correctly.

Classic or American-fit jackets, frock, cutaway, and tailcoats have a single center back vent. Overall, 17th- and 18th-century coats may have two vents at the side seams and many modern jackets have two vents below the back prince(ss) seams. Fashionable modern jackets may not have any back vents because the vents add to the cost of construction, and dinner jackets and tuxedo jackets are usually ventless to create a streamlined effect.

Women's jackets do not necessarily have a back vent if the jacket length is worn to the hip level or shorter. Because vents open up on a wearer with curved hips or seat, vents are sometimes sewn closed to keep the jacket looking tidy in the back.

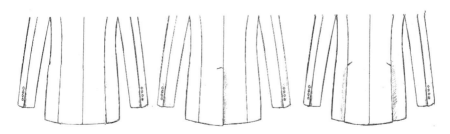

FIGURE 11.13 Jacket back vents: ventless (left), single vent (center), and double vent (right)

Body length: The jacket length should be checked against any research images or information. When wearing a classic-fit modern jacket, the tip of the wearer's relaxed thumb, or the point where the finger tips touch the thighs when the fingers are folded inward at a 90-degree angle, should be on a level with the jacket's lower edge. This generally means that a modern jacket skirt will cover most or all of the wearer's seat. However, the length of a man's jacket will differ based on the time period.

For an early 21st-century shrunken jacket style, the jacket length will be shorter. Jackets from the early 1960s were slightly shorter in order to create a longer leg proportion and taller impression as compared to 1950s' styles, while 1940s' jackets were slightly longer to create a heavier, more substantial effect. For 19th-century and earlier coats and jackets, lengths will vary. Overall, 17th- and 18th-century coats were nearly knee length, while 19th-century coats varied from above the knee to mid-thigh length depending on the decade.

The jacket hemline should be level front to back or very slightly longer in the front for a man's garment, unless the garment is designed to sweep back. Assess the length of a jacket after the wearer has relaxed their posture, as a person who slumps may need the back hem adjusted a bit to maintain the illusion of a level jacket hem when they are standing naturally.

Sleeves

Sleeves are discussed in more detail in Chapter 9. However, jacket sleeves present specific fit issues. Once you are sure the jacket fits correctly through the shoulders, move on to considering the jacket sleeves.

A good-quality jacket will have two-piece sleeves, with shaped outer/upper and inner/lower vertical panels. The two-sleeve panels allow the sleeve to curve slightly in order to shape around the elbow and to fit smoothly around the natural bend of the wearer's arm. The upper end of the sleeve unit will have a slight amount of easing to allow for the width of the deltoid muscles, but the ease should not be visible unless the time period of the jacket requires a gathered sleeve cap, such as for the 1830s–1840s for men and the 1830s and 1890s for women. Because jacket tailoring was historically developed with wool as the main material, it assumes that fabric can be slightly shrunk in with a hot iron at certain points to conform to body curves without the easing being visible.

Sleeve pitch (Figure 11.14) – Jacket sleeves should follow the line of the wearer's arm, with the fabric's lengthwise grain dropping from the top of the sleeves at the shoulder seams to the front center of the wearer's wrists (Figure 11.14, left). Check the hang of the sleeves by having the wearer stand up straight and let their arms fall naturally. The fabric of the sleeve should fall smoothly down their arm. If the jacket sleeve twists on the wearer, check whether the sleeve itself is large enough for the wearer's arm, shirt, and cuffs, OR whether the sleeve lining has been sewn incorrectly to the sleeve hemline.

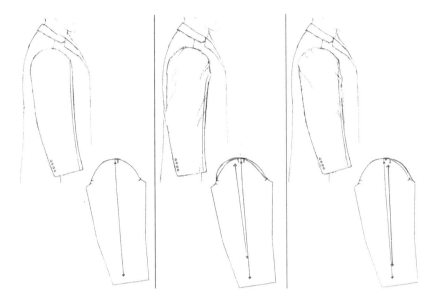

FIGURE 11.14   Sleeve pitch: sleeve pattern with the grainline drawn, in the correct position (left). Sleeve inserted with the grainline tilted too much toward the garment front, with possible pattern adjustments in red (center). Sleeve inserted with the grainline tilted too much toward the garment back, with possible pattern adjustments in red (right)

If the jacket sleeve is large enough and the lining is sewn correctly, the twists will either be a result of (1) the sleeve is sewn into the armscye at an angle that doesn't follow the angle of the wearer's arms, and/or (2) the sleeve cap does not have the correct curve to fit the shape of the wearer's upper arm. If the sleeve is hanging incorrectly, it can be un-stitched and slightly rotated before being re-inserted. However, this is a difficult alteration and should only be attempted by a skilled stitcher, with enough time to complete the job without rushing. An existing jacket with twisting sleeves should be eliminated from consideration if there are any other options available.

On a mockup, reposition the sleeve cap within the armscye to get the sleeve to hang correctly. Figure 11.14 shows twists on sleeves which are sewn incorrectly into their armscyes. Possible adjustments to the grainline position, shoulder seam position in relation to the jacket, and reshaping the sleeve cap are shown in red on the adjacent upper sleeve patterns. Not all of these adjustments may be necessary to solve the issue, but all may be tried during the fitting appointment.

Figure 11.14, center panel, shows a sleeve that is angled too much toward the jacket front. If the sleeve fabric is pulling toward the front of the armscye, the wearer may round their shoulders which will mean needing more fabric across the cap back and reshaping the cap front.

Figure 11.14, right panel, shows a sleeve that is angled too much toward the jacket back. This is usually not a matter of the wearer's posture. The sleeve may be sewn incorrectly or the cap shape may not fit the curve of the wearer's upper arm.

Mark the top of the sleeve where it meets the corrected shoulder seam position. Be sure you mark the new armhole stitch-lines if they differ from your starting positions.

If the wearer has naturally full upper arms, the sleeve may have horizontal draw-lines across the cap area (Figure 11.15, left). Redistribute the cap ease stitching to move more of the fullness across the widest part of the arm rather than at the top of the sleeve cap (a jacket sleeve is often cut with the fullness eased in at the top of the sleeve pattern). Distribute any fullness in the sleeve cap between the outer ends of the upper sleeve cap and the top of the sleeve. Refer to the widest

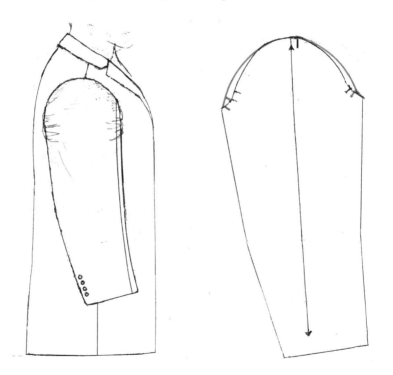

FIGURE 11.15 Jacket sleeves too snug across the upper arm, with possible pattern adjustments in red (right)

cap arm measurement for the wearer. You may also need to simply add more width across this area (Figure 11.15, left). Be sure to arrange the fullness evenly so that it lies smoothly over the arm, remembering that a shoulder pad and sleeve head will help support the fabric, add structure, and fill out what may seem like too much sleeve fullness when you are looking at the muslin garment.

Sleeve length – Sleeve length should extend to the indent below the wrist bones at the top of the hand. For a stage jacket, double-check this length when the arms are raised to chest level and bent – since actors are in motion almost constantly, sleeves are more often seen with the arms bent than hanging at the sides. Some style guides recommend that ½″ of shirt sleeve extend below the lower edge of the jacket sleeve, while other guides recommend ¼″. I suggest using the ¼″ shirt sleeve length, as the jacket sleeves will move up while the actor moves their arms. For reference, the jacket sleeve ends should hit ½″ above the lower edge of the wrist bone, or at the widest point of the wrist bone, when the arms are bent.

Sleeve width – Jacket sleeves should follow the line of the wearer's arm when they are standing with the arms hanging vertically, neither binding nor sagging loosely. There should be enough room for shirt sleeves to hang smoothly under the jacket sleeve, which means that a jacket should be tried on while wearing the shirt that is intended to be worn beneath the jacket onstage. A jacket sleeve **will** slightly inhibit the movement of the wearer's arms but should not bind across the arms. The sleeve width at the wrists should be large enough to accommodate the width of the cuffs, plus a wrist watch or bracelet if they are to be worn with the jacket. If the wearer will be wearing French cuffs, be sure to fit the jacket over these cuffs, as these extended cuffs and their cufflinks will need enough room to avoid the jacket sleeves hitching up and resting on top of the French cuff once the arms are in motion.

The lowest position of the jacket sleeve armhole should be approximately 2″ below the armpit and allow the shirt sleeve to fit comfortably beneath the jacket. An armhole that is too high can be restrictive but an armhole that is too low also restricts arm movement, dates the jacket as being from the 1980s or 1990s, and can make the jacket body hang oddly when the arms are in motion, especially while the jacket is buttoned. If the jacket armholes are comfortable for the wearer and look good but are too high for the shirt sleeve worn beneath it, alter the shirt sleeve to fit the jacket.

On a mockup, the goal is to give the wearer enough room to move and to allow the body of the jacket to hang properly, while getting the sleeves to fit as discussed in this section.

A jacket mockup may be easier to fit while being worn inside out, or with the sleeves purposely sewn with the armscye seam allowances on the outside, for easier adjustment.

> Because a mockup often has a large seam allowance in the armscye, you may need to clip the armholes into the seam allowance in order to get the jacket to fit comfortably across the chest. Begin by clipping in at the underarms. The area that usually needs to be clipped will be at the lowest point of the armhole, up to approximately 3" above this point at the front and back armhole. Start slowly, and realize that you will most likely NOT need to clip completely to the stitch-lines in all areas. If you work slowly, you will most likely be able to clip the seam allowances of the armhole and the sleeve without having to reposition the sleeve itself. Redraw the arm-hole stitch-line if it is necessary to clip past the stitch-line. Remember that you can add a small sleeve head (a 1 to 1 1/2" wide folded piece of tailoring fleece or of cotton flannel that is approximately 12" long and is sewn just past the stitch-line in the seam allowance of the sleeve cap) to support the width of the sleeve and create a crisper outline.

Sleeve vents and buttons – A well-made jacket sleeve, from the 19th century to the present day, should have a placket at the outer wrist edge. There are usually three to four buttons sewn vertically at this position. Vent buttons on the sleeves originally were paired with working buttonholes, although this is not necessarily true for modern jackets. If the buttonholes are functional and allow the jacket sleeves to be rolled up when the buttons are un-fastened, they are known as **Surgeon's sleeves**, after the 19th-century doctors who would perform surgery while dressed in a tailored jacket. An eccentric styling trick is to unbutton the lowest button on the sleeve placket to show off that the jacket has a working placket and is presumably custom-made.

The number and spacing of modern jacket sleeve placket buttons will vary. The center of the lowest button on the jacket sleeve is often 1 5/8" above the lower edge of the hem but can range from 1 ¼ to 2 ½", especially on a wom-an's jacket. For a casual jacket, two-sleeve buttons are common. For a regular jacket or blazer, three buttons are common. Four buttons are the most formal and are a sign of elegance. In terms of spacing, jacket sleeve buttons should be placed close together. Four-hole buttons will either touch ("kissing" buttons, common on British tailoring), or have less than 1/16" spacing (non-kissing buttons, the classic style), and may even overlap ¼ of the way over the next button up ("stacked kissing" or "waterfall" buttons, more common on Italian tailoring). Other jackets may have open space between the sleeve buttons.

Pockets

Jacket pockets come in a variety of shapes and placements. Lower front pockets on a late 19th- to 21st-century jacket tend to be lined up with the pelvic bone level on the wearer's body. Earlier coats, such as 17th- and early 18th-century justaucorps coats, have lower pockets placed at the top of the thigh in a coat with wide skirts.

For a mockup, check the placement of pockets on the garment against your research images, as well as where the actor will need them onstage. If the actor needs to carry any props in their pockets, be sure to try them during the fitting appointment.

Pocket styles (Figure 11.16) – **Flapless**, also known as **Besom** or **Jetted pockets**, have a sleek look because the thin double welts edging the pocket opening are not hidden by a flap. They create a simple line that does not add bulk to the figure. The welts can be made of the jacket body fabric or a contrasting fabric and are mostly seen on suit or tuxedo jackets, since they are considered to look best on jackets worn with matching trousers. Jacket pocket welts tend to be created in a set of two welts, which average ¼" wide each and 5–5 1/2" total length. Jetted jacket pockets are commonly located at the same level as the bottom button of a jacket that has more than one front button.

Flap pockets have a narrow, doubled, and interfaced piece of fabric added beneath the upper welt of jetted pockets. Flap pockets are considered less formal than jetted pockets but are more practical because the flaps keep the pockets' contents from falling out. They add slight bulk to the wearer's figure where the flaps are sewn but can also make the waistline look smaller in contrast. To create the effect of a jetted pocket, the flaps can be neatly tucked inside the welts when worn.

The flaps may be rectangles or shaped like parallelograms, flaring away from center front at the lower edges. The lower ends may be sharp corners or slightly rounded. Flap depth may change with fashions, following lapel width. Hip pocket flap depth is approximately two-thirds the width of the lapels. Flap pockets are typically positioned so that either the top of the pocket is aligned

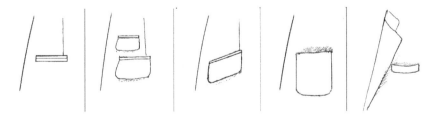

FIGURE 11.16 Pocket styles: from left to right: flapless besom/jetted (far left), flapped (second from left), ticket pocket (above second from left), hacking/slanted (center), patch (second from right), and Barchetta breast welt (far right, shown with the lapel)

with the bottom button or so that middle of the pocket flap is aligned with the bottom button.

An additional smaller flap pocket placed above the wearer's right side flap pocket near the natural waistline level is called a **Ticket pocket** and is the mark of an early 20th-century suit (used for train tickets) or a more expensive contemporary jacket. The ticket pocket is slightly narrower than the pocket below it. It can be straight or slanted to match the angles of the other pockets. This pocket is best used on a taller wearer, since jacket fronts with two stacked pockets can look crowded on a shorter person.

When flapped pockets, with or without a ticket pocket, are tilted downward at the outer edges, they are called **Hacking pockets** or **Slanted pockets** (developed for horse riding because the angled pockets will sit level when one is riding a horse). Slanted pockets can help shorter or broader wearers appear taller and leaner due to the angle, which draws the viewer's eye upward and inward. However, straight pockets, level to the floor, are the classic choice for most jackets.

Patch pockets are made from separate pieces of the jacket fabric and are sewn onto the exterior of the jacket body rather than existing between the outer shell and the jacket lining. They may be topstitched onto the jacket or partially hand- and machine-stitched from the inside of the pocket itself for a more elegant effect. This pocket is a mark of a relaxed jacket such as a sport coat, blazer, or an informal suit such as a linen summer suit.

Patch pockets may have a **vertical center pleat** for a more informal coat such as a **Norfolk jacket**, **hunting**, or **safari** jacket. The pleat reinforces the pocket and adds more volume to the pocket interior. Patch pockets may also have a flap on the top. These flaps are often shaped, with a point at the center of the lower edge, and have a buttonhole to secure them when closed.

Breast pockets are located on the wearer's left side of the jacket's chest. The standard breast pocket style is a single-welt pocket that has a wide piece of fabric sewn to hide the pocket opening. The breast pocket welt usually has a straight upper edge and is placed at a slightly slant downward toward the center front line of the jacket, but with the vertical edges plumb to the floor. Breast pockets tend to match the shape of the lower pockets. Jackets with patch pockets commonly have a matching breast pocket; open patch hip pockets often have an open patch breast pocket.

The **Barchetta** breast pocket is a subtly curved welt pocket commonly found on southern Italian suit jackets. The upper and lower edges of these pockets slightly dip lower at their horizontal centers.

A **Flapped breast pocket** is less common on a jacket but may be found on a sports jacket, or on both sides of the front on a Norfolk jacket, to accompany similarly shaped lower pockets.

One other detail that can add to a jacket's appearance is **picque stitching**. This is a small hand-stitched outline near the edge of the upper collar, lapels, jacket fronts, pocket flaps, and/or the breast pocket. **Machine topstitching**, which is usually placed ¼″ from the garment edges, is a less exclusive version of this detail, and can sometimes be used to control the edges of a jacket that has not been trimmed or pressed correctly during construction. On an elegant jacket, it is much preferable to press the jacket edges with a press cloth and pound with a maple block to get them to roll under slightly toward the wearer's body than to use topstitching to force the edges into place.

12

FITTED GARMENTS WITHOUT A WAISTLINE SEAM

A close-fitting tunic, dress, or jumpsuit that is made of a woven fabric **without** a waistline seam poses specific fitting challenges. The natural waistline area on a person is a convergence of a number of curved areas that meet from different angles. Therefore, to fit smoothly, a garment that extends from the upper torso to past the waistline area into the hip area often **depends on a waistline seam to create a close fit**. This seam helps join two different garment areas together into a curved line at the waistline (Figure 12.1).

In general, a garment without a waistline seam may be approached during a fitting much as you would a bodice and skirt or trousers, with or without sleeves. In order to avoid repeating material that is presented elsewhere in the book, please refer to the appropriate sections on body measurements and fitting existing garments or mockups in the chapters for bodices (Chapter 8), skirts (Chapter 13), and/or trousers (Chapter 14).

In this chapter, we will focus on what the lack of a waistline seam means for how to conduct a fitting.

A waistline seam allows a bodice front (which covers a curved body area that requires a relatively large amount of dart intake to shape over the bust/chest area) to join a skirt or trouser front (which requires small, if any, darts to shape over the front abdomen). In the garment back, a waistline seam allows the relatively flat bodice back to join a skirt or trouser back that requires more dart intake to shape over the buttocks and hips. In other words, the front bodice needs more shaping with darts than does the front skirt, and the back skirt needs more shaping than the back bodice. **The waistline seam allows two pieces with different volumes of darts at the pattern edges to be sewn into a smooth line, as long as the edges that are sewn together are the same lengths after any darts are sewn closed**. Without a waistline

DOI: 10.4324/9781351131353-13

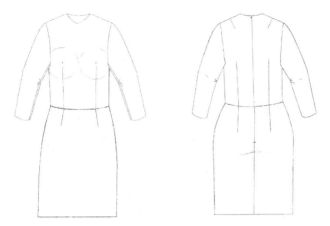

FIGURE 12.1 Dress with a waistline seam, front and back

seam, the upper and lower segments of a garment that extends from the chest to below the hips will not be able to fit together both closely and smoothly.

When looking at a bodice and skirt or trouser patterns (Figure 12.2), one will notice that the waistline often curves downward in the centers, depending on where the wearer carries their waistline weight and on their posture.

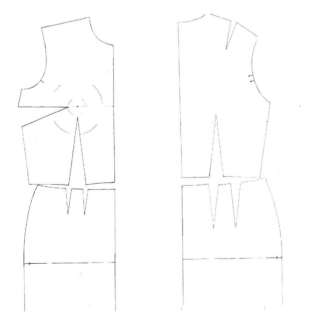

FIGURE 12.2 Bodice and skirt patterns joined, with extra space at the waistline due to the shape of the garment pattern pieces. The extra space is commonly controlled by the shaped seam at the waistline

Depending on the curves on the bodice waistline versus the curves on the skirt or trouser waistline, there may be a gap between the two pieces that would otherwise be resolved by joining them with a waistline seam when lining up the two pattern pieces on a vertical center line.

The waistline seams act like a **horizontal ring of darts around the wearer's body** when the lower bodice edge is joined to the upper skirt or trouser edge. Without the waistline seam, the bodice section blends into the lower body portion of the garment, **including the unsewn area that would have been taken out with the seam**. Therefore, a garment without a waistline seam is slightly LONGER in some sections than it would be with a waistline seam and puffs up a little at the waistline.

The dart adjustments that would be needed to blend the bodice and skirt pieces together without a waistline seam are shown in blue outlines (Figure 12.3). The front vertical bust dart intake is much larger than the intakes

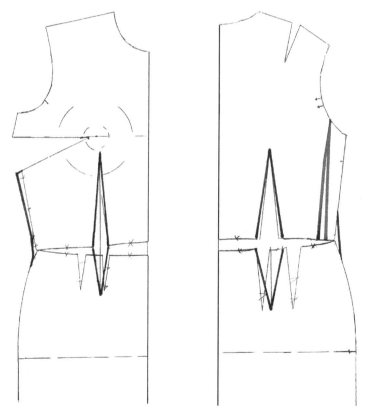

FIGURE 12.3 Bodice and skirt pattern adjustments to blend the bodice and skirts: front (left) and back (right). Dart adjustments are shown in blue ink and side back alteration in red ink

on the front skirt or trouser darts because of the greater curve in the bust/chest area of the bodice than over the abdomen area of the skirt. Therefore, it is necessary to DECREASE the bodice vertical dart intake by converting some of the front waistline dart into an additional side bust dart. This is achieved by rotating part of the original waistline dart into a side bust dart. The resulting vertical bust dart now takes up the same amount of dart intake as the combination of the two front skirt darts, and the vertical darts on the bodice and skirt fronts can be combined into one long, double-ended dart that extends through the two pieces.

On the garment back, the two back skirt darts are combined into one dart. In order to fit the garment over the wearer's hips, the back skirt dart intake is larger than the back bodice dart intake. Therefore, the bodice back vertical dart intake needs to be INCREASED to take up the same amount as the combined back skirt dart. This means that the bodice side back needs to be rotated outward enough to retain the original amount of un-darted fabric, so that the back bodice and skirt waistlines will continue to be the same length and fit one another. The wedge drawn in red at the side back bodice represents the added fabric.

The final garment (Figure 12.4) has soft horizontal folds that rest in parts of the waistline area of the wearer's body where the garment is too long because of the adjustments needed to line up darts, but where it doesn't have the width to fall lower down the body.

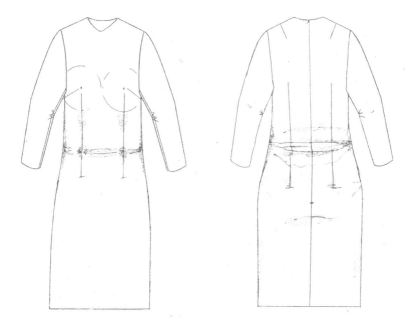

FIGURE 12.4 Dress with waistline folds

Of course, there are times where a waistline seam may not be necessary. For an actor who does not have a noticeable indentation at the waist, or who has a waistline that is larger than their chest/bust area, a waistline seam may not be necessary to create a flattering effect.

If you are faced with horizontal folds at the waistline area of a garment with no seamline, the temptation may be to increase the intake of the vertical darts. However, this often results in reducing the depth of the horizontal folds only partially while also increasing the number of horizontal strain-lines between the darts and side seams. **Therefore, if you are intent on avoiding a waistline seam on a close-fitting torso-length garment**, it may be necessary to REDUCE the vertical waistline darts so that **the garment is looser through the waistline**. The garment will then be able to fall softly over the waist area, transitioning from the width of the chest/bust and then back outward to the width of the hip/seat area.

Depending on the actor's figure, I have sometimes created a horizontal dart or waistline seam ONLY at the back waistline of a dress or jacket, which helps reduce the "shelf" of excess fabric that sits at the back waist of a person with rounded buttocks, high rounded hips, or who stands with their tummy forward and buttocks tipped upward in the back. However, for a jumpsuit that combines a bodice with trousers, I find it best to leave the extra fabric in place so that the wearer has enough vertical room to sit down without the garment pulling up into the seat and creating a "wedgie" effect. In fact, it is often necessary to INCREASE the length of the lower bodice, particularly in the garment back, for the wearer's comfort when the bodice is joined to trousers in a jumpsuit. A final styling solution to the extra room at the waistline area is to add a belt to the garment. The result will be soft folds above and below the belt.

Because of the extra waistline folds on a garment without a waistline seam, it is more flattering to the wearer to construct the garment out of fabric that falls softly over the body. For example, rayon or silk charmeuse will drape languidly if it is not too snug. If the garment is cut on the bias, it is possible to eliminate many of the vertical darts and to get a soft drape over the body. Stretchy woven fabric can be fit closer to the body with fewer folds and strain lines than a non-stretch woven fabric that is cut on the vertical grainline. Knit fabric (particularly knits with a higher Spandex content) can be pulled even closer to the body than can woven fabric, although a knit garment on a curvy wearer will still show some folds and strain lines at the side seams, around the bustline, and may tend to "puddle" in horizontal folds at the back waistline area.

Due to the challenges created by a garment with no waistline seam, **I tend to include a waistline seam in most of the garments I design if I want the garment to follow the wearer's body closely**. The extra step of joining a bodice to a skirt or to trousers is worth the time because it gives a smoother result. However, if the design is such that it is important to avoid the waistline seam, be thoughtful about how the garment is manipulated on the wearer during a fitting appointment, and consider striving for a silhouette that softly **skims** the figure rather than hugging it closely.

13

SKIRTS

Skirts have been a traditional garment for female-identified people in many parts of the world for much of history, and for male-identified people in many times and places as well. Fitting a skirt is much simpler than fitting trousers, with most of the difficulty arising in controlling the amount of fabric that is contained in the body of the skirt. While some skirts may take more fabric to build than trousers (thus being more expensive to construct) and rely on specific undergarments, if you are a young and inexperienced designer or technician, it makes sense to choose skirts rather than trousers when you can in order to simplify some areas of your task. As you get more experience fitting skirts, you will find that much of the skirt fitting processes will transfer to fitting trousers.

Parts of a Skirt

Figure 13.1 shows the parts of a skirt without added width at the side seams.

Body Measurements Needed to Fit a Skirt

The measurements below are the essential measurements needed to check an existing skirt. They are listed in order of importance with some added notes specific to skirts; the numbers refer to the measurement sheet and discussion in Chapter 2.

The body measurements needed are as follows: widest hip circumference – if in doubt, take the measurement **twice** to confirm that the measurement is accurate. Do not be tempted, or pressured, to flatter the wearer by recording an inaccurate measurement for this point of the body (23); fullest seat

DOI: 10.4324/9781351131353-14

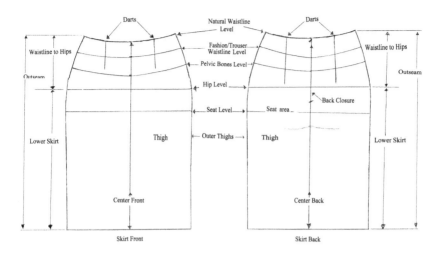

FIGURE 13.1 Parts of the skirt: front (left) and back (right)

circumference – compare to the widest hip and use the larger of the two measurements when measuring existing garments (24); hip level from the desired
waistline level (21); waistline circumference at the desired level (20 or 21); and
outseam from the desired waistline level down to the desired length of the
skirt (32 or 33). While it would seem most important to check the skirt length
first, if the garment does not fit over the fullest hip and seam measurements, it
will not be able to be tried on.

Checking an Existing Skirt Prior to a Fitting

After taking the wearer's body measurements, a designer can check a pulled or
purchased skirt to assess the potential fit on a specific wearer. Check the fiber
content of the garment to judge how much ease to allow when comparing the
body measurements to the garment. Also, be sure to check the seam allowances available at the side seams and center seams and in any dart intakes in
order to allow for alterations.

1. *Hip circumference at the widest point of the skirt hips:* With the closures fastened, measure horizontally at the widest part of the skirt, which aver-
   ages about 8″ below the waist. Double this measurement. The garment
   should be at least 1″ wider than the body measurements, and often 2″
   larger will be optimal to allow for stage movement. If the skirt is made of
   non-stretch fabric, the measurement of the garment should be 1–2″ wider
   than the wearer's body measurements for a close fit, or 2–4″ for a looser
   fit. HOWEVER, if there is Spandex/Lycra in the fabric, be sure to stretch
   the garment gently at the hipline when measuring; if the skirt is made of

stretch fabric with 5% Spandex, the hip circumference of the garment can be the same as the wearer's body measurements or ½″–1″ wider than the wearer's body measurements. If the skirt is made of performance knit fabric or with 10% or more Spandex, the hip circumference of the garment can be up to 2″ smaller than the wearer's body measurements. Look carefully at the skirt during the fitting; it should not creep up the body as the wearer moves around, sits, and bends.

2. *Waistline circumference:* **Determine the waistline level of the skirt in relation to where it will fall on the wearer's body**. Measure around the top of the skirt or the center of the waistband from the button, pant bar, or snap to the far end of the buttonhole, pant hook end, or snap. I recommend having 1″ extra width compared to the body measurements. If the skirt is intended to have a shirt tucked into the waistline, or if the skirt is made of heavy fabric, you may need 2″ of total ease. However, if the skirt style is intended to compress the waistline and fit closely, as with a very low-cut skirt, or a garment with 5% or more Spandex in the fabric, the waistline of the skirt may be the same size as or slightly smaller than the body measurements at the same level of the wearer's body. If the skirt fits otherwise but is too small in the waistline, check whether there is sufficient fabric in the seam allowances at the seams or darts to be let out prior to the fitting. This alteration will also require letting out the waistband if possible, or removing the waistband and adding more fabric to the end to fit the expanded skirt. I recommend basting on the extended waistband for the fitting, as the skirt will fit slightly differently with a waistband than without one, and it is best to see the actual fit during the fitting.

3. *Outseam:* Measure the side seam of the skirt vertically from the top of the waistband to the lower edge of the hemline. Also, check the depth of the available hem if the garment will need to be lengthened. Keep in mind that a lowered hem may not be able to have the original fold line pressed out or that there may be a visible line where the fold line is slightly faded. It may be necessary to add a band of trim to cover the old fold line.

Fitting a Skirt

Have the wearer wear the garments that they are slated to wear with the finished garment, including the correct type of body shaper or shaping hosiery, shirt/blouse, sweater, undershirt, or any other garments that may create fitting issues in the future. Assess the fit with all the elements as a whole. Skirts should be fit in the same shoes that will be worn with the garment on stage, or a pair with the same heel height.

Because a skirt and trousers share some fitting issues, check the chapter on trousers if some of your questions are not answered in this chapter.

Try on the Skirt and Fasten the Closures

For an existing garment, check the garment prior to the fitting appointment. Be sure to let out the seams and re-stitch with a basting stitch at the point where the garment needs to be adjusted to fit the wearer. If possible, avoid moving the position of a zipper closure by adjusting any other darts or seamlines first.

Closures should lie flat and add as little bulk as possible, so pay attention to them when they are closed. The waistband should fit smoothly, without binding or gaping when the closures are fastened. If the skirt closures do not fasten, assess whether there is sufficient extra fabric in the other seam allowances to out.

For a mockup, be sure that the seams and darts are sewn correctly, using a long stitch so that the seams can be easily changed or removed if needed. Mark all the stitch-lines for future references. Mark the center front and the center back of the skirt if either of these seams have been cut on the fold. Mark the horizontal hip level line on a mockup for a slim-fitting skirt so that it is clear whether it is staying in the right spot on the wearer during the fitting. Mark the waistline stitch-line. The waistband may be hand basted onto the skirt upper edge so that it can be easily adjusted as needed.

Be sure to fit BOTH sides of the garment equally – the best result will be an averaging of the two sides of the mockup.

It may be easier for a beginner to fit the skirt with the seams on the outside; label "right" and "left" sides to avoid confusion. Otherwise, put the skirt on right-side out.

Pin the skirt closed at the seam opening, starting at the base of the opening and working up toward the top of the garment as high as comfortable for the wearer. You can either pin these seamlines to stick outward or fold under one seam allowance and pin the folded edge to line up with the other seamline. In any case, be very careful that the two sides of the skirt are lined up accurately and meet at the intended stitch-lines.

Check the Fit at the Hips

With a slim skirt, fit the widest part of the body first, which will be the hips and the seat. The fabric should fit smoothly over the widest part of the hips, stomach, and seat. Look at the back view of the skirt to be sure that the garment does not bind over the body, as it is better to have the garment slightly loose than too tight. Be sure to have the wearer sit down to check that the garment is not too snug for them to move comfortably. After the wearer stands up, the garment fabric should fall smoothly down the body without staying hitched up on the body, which would indicate that the garment is too snug through the hips and seat.

Look at the side and back views of the skirt to assess fit, making sure the fabric does not bunch, bind, or stretch over the body. Check the hang of the garment to be sure the horizontal balance line is sitting level on the wearer at the widest part of the hips and is parallel to the floor.

The use of stretch fabrics for garments has altered the calculus of whether a garment is too tight when it is first put on. If the fabric has 2–5% Lycra/Spandex, allow the wearer to move and sit for a few minutes before determining whether the skirt will actually be too snug to use onstage. In this situation, look carefully at your research materials to evaluate the correct fit for the era and character that you are designing.

A full skirt should be evaluated by consulting the research images and design sketches. A full skirt is usually balanced from front to back or has more fullness in the back. Check that the fullness falls smoothly over any skirt shapers or petticoats. Also, look at the proportion of the skirt with the other garments that will be worn together. In this chapter, all of the fitting images will be of a straight, fitted skirt, as this type of skirt requires the most attention to detail. On a full skirt, the main areas to fit will be the waistline, amount of fullness, and length.

If the garment is **too snug**, the skirt will show thin horizontal "draw-line" folds that radiate out from the area that is too small for the wearer (Figure 13.2). The draw-lines may also be accompanied by softer horizontal folds if the skirt is being pushed upward so that the too tight area can rest on a spot where it fits the wearer.

On an existing garment, let the side seams out at the tight areas and taper the adjustment back into the original seamline where the skirt fits well. If there are center seams or princess seams, these can also be adjusted to help with the fit. Moving a zipper placement is the last resort. Better to un-stitch the vertical seams and re-pin as needed until the strain-lines disappear.

If there is not enough seam allowance available to let out the skirt to fit, consider whether removing the waistband and re-establishing the waistline at a lower level is possible. This will raise a wider area of the skirt up to the hip level of the wearer. If your theatre owns the garment and you are willing to make the alteration, you will either need to add fabric to the waistband to fit what will be a wider waistline circumference or you may add a yoke or waistline facing to the new upper edge of the skirt. This alteration will shorten the skirt length.

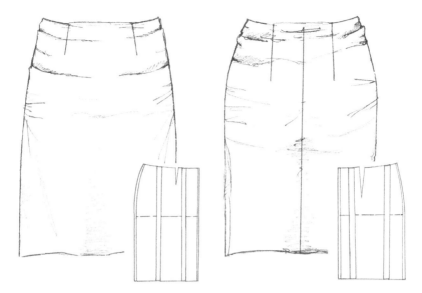

FIGURE 13.2 Skirt too snug: front (left) and back (right), with pattern adjustments in red indicating **areas to be added to the patterns** to add more fabric

On a mockup, let out the seams so that more skirt fabric is available over the hips. This will allow the garment to fall smoothly and vertically. There should not be discernable pulling on the fabric across the thighs; curvy outer thighs or rounded hips will need the side seams to be let out at the hip level, tapering the seam smoothly back into the existing seams above and below the hips.

The pattern adjustment may be made by adding more width at the seamlines to reflect how the mockup is re-pined. Additional adjustments should be made by slashing and adding more width in the center of each panel of the pattern pieces if a straight slice or wedge of added room will solve the fitting issue. The small pattern pieces in Figure 13.2 show adjustments made by adding to the center front and side seams of the pattern, as well as the addition of vertical, red-outlined areas added within the body of the pattern piece to increase the size of the pattern.

If the garment is **too loose**, fabric will fall in loose, soft vertical, folds hanging from the waistline and/or hip/seat level (Figure 13.3). If that is NOT the desired look for the garment and/or the design does not include loose fullness, the skirt is too loose. Before determining whether the skirt needs to be taken in, be sure to have the wearer walk around, sit, and climb stairs to see if the extra fabric is necessary for movement and comfort.

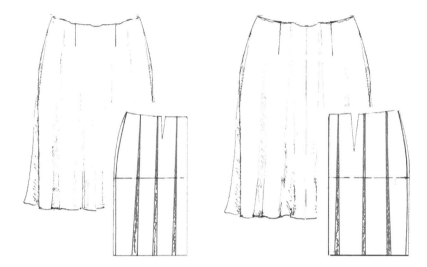

FIGURE 13.3 Skirt too loose: front (left) and back (right) with pattern adjustments in red, indicating areas to be taken out of the patterns to reduce excess fabric

An existing garment can be taken in at the side seams, and/or the center seams, which may involve adding a center seam where one had not existed, or creating decorative vertical tucks in the garment, or even removing a panel of fabric. Pin in the vertical seams to narrow in the area that is too loose, tapering out to the original side seam at the upper and lower ends of this alteration. As a last resort, one may rework the seam containing the garment closure.

For a mockup, the excess can be addressed by pinning out the excess fabric at the seamlines, or by pinning out tucks of excess fabric as long as the tuck has straight edges and originates and ends at the outer edges of the garment.

For the garment pattern, the adjustments may be made by reducing the pattern at the seamlines, or a vertical tuck can be folded out of the skirt pattern **as long as the tuck has straight edges and originates and ends at the outer edges of the pattern piece**. Other adjustments with darts or seam-shaping may need to be added. The small pattern pieces in Figure 13.3 show areas in red where the excess fabric from the center of the garment piece may be folded out from the pattern, which reduces the overall size while retaining the essential shape of the piece.

Check the Seat

The shape of the wearer's buttocks and their posture will affect how the skirt fits their body in the back. A too tight seat may crawl up the body and settle in folds above the buttocks when walking or sitting. It will also tend to bag at the seat once it has been worn a few times.

The amount of fabric at the hipline level, the height and shape of the waistline curve, and the amount of the dart intakes will be the three factors to be adjusted when fitting the seat area.

A wearer who has rounded buttocks and tilts their abdomen forward (Figure 13.4) will need a skirt with more room across the seat, and the back waist darts will need to be increased to accommodate their body curves. In this image, the seat area of the skirt is no longer level to the floor, the distance from the seat to the waistline is affected, and side seams may no longer be perpendicular to the floor.

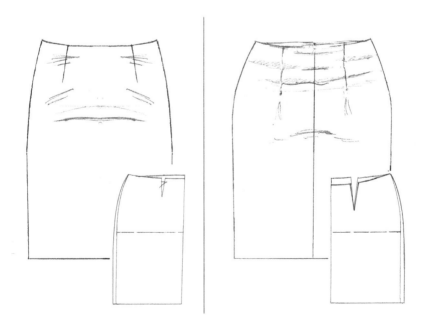

FIGURE 13.4 Skirt with tilted posture, forward abdomen and rounded buttocks: front (right), back (left) and pattern adjustments

For an existing skirt, it may be necessary to pick a skirt one size larger in order to have enough fabric available across the seat. The waistline in this case may be too large, so the waistband can be taken in with small darts sewn through all layers to taper in at the back.

The back waistline level may need to be shortened to raise the widest part of the skirt back to accommodate the seat and to sit smoothly at the back waistline without pulling up in the back and pulling across the stomach (Figure 13.4, right). If the garment is worth the alteration, one may un-stitch the back of the waistband from center back to the side seams, slide the skirt up into the waistline area while easing the upper edge slightly to fit or increasing the width of the darts, and topstitch the waistband back into place at a slightly lowered position at the center back.

For a mockup, the shape of the wearer's buttocks and their position will affect how the skirt fits their seat. Look at the marked horizontal hip-level line on the mockup to confirm that the skirt is level and that the hipline is parallel to the floor.

Begin by letting out the side seams to fit smoothly across the seat. The goal is for the upper back skirt to sit smoothly at the back waistline without creating horizontal folds at the back above the seat or pulling across the stomach. Front darts may need to be let out and the back darts may need to be taken in more to create a more pronounced curve from waistline to seat. Remove the waistband and adjust the waistline placement until the skirt falls smoothly over the body. In Figure 13.4, the skirt front needs to have the waistline position raised and the front darts should be eliminated to accommodate the stomach curve, while the back waistline needs to be dropped slightly, the dart intake needs to be increased, and the side seams need to be let out slightly to fit the curved seat.

Double-check that the alterations have not pulled the side seams out of their correct position perpendicular to the floor and in the center of the sides (Figure 13.8). If this has occurred, cross out the side seams on the mockup and redraw the correct position. Transfer these alterations to your pattern.

Check the Waistline

Once the hips and seat fit, move up to the support point of the waistline. If the garment is worn at the natural waistline, the fabric should fit smoothly around the waistline without pulling across the stomach or the upper buttocks. If the garment is worn at a lower waistline level, it may be worn slightly snug at the upper edge so that it does not slip down the body. The waistband should fit closely to the waist so that a shirt will stay tucked in, but not so tightly that the fabric strains across the top of the garment. There is generally a total of 1″ space between a fitted waistband and the wearer's body.

If the skirt is **too snug** at the waistline (Figure 13.5, three images on left), the solution is to expand the area of the waist.

For an existing garment, remove the waistband or waistline facing. You can reduce the amount of the dart intakes, eliminate the darts, or let out the vertical seams a small amount and press well. Avoid adjusting the seamline that contains the zipper.

If it is possible to move the waistline level while the skirt remains the right length for the wearer, remove the waistband and reposition the waistline position lower on the body of the skirt. This will place the waist at a wider circumference. Un-stitch the side and center seamlines down to the new waistline position. Again, avoid adjusting the seamline containing the zipper.

After adjusting the waistline, lengthen the waistband to fit the expanded waistline by adding more fabric to the underlap of the waistband, and/or covering any added fabric with a belt. You may also decide to use a waistline facing instead of a waistband, to avoid trying to match the original garment fabric.

FIGURE 13.5 Skirt waistlines: too snug (three images on the left side), and front pattern with red lines for pattern adjustments (right). The back pattern would be altered in the same manner

For a mockup, the vertical center, side, and any princess seams can be let out at the waistline and blended back into the existing seamlines, approximately 4" below the lower edge of the waistband. If there are darts in the skirt, adjust their intakes or eliminate some or all of them (Figure 13.8, right. The image shows the pattern front, the back would be adjusted in the same manner).

You may also re-establish the waistline at a lower position on the skirt, which will result in a wider circumference. Starting at the center front, clip the waistline seam allowances of the mockup skirt into the seam allowance, not quite cutting down to the original marked stitch-line. Your clips will be about 1 ½" apart. Continue to clip carefully toward the marked stitch-line. The wearer's posture may be such that the back waistline will not need to be clipped much if at all, and the finished waistline may be higher in the back and lower in the front than the original draft/draping. Or, the wearer may have a slight sway back, so that the back waistline is lowered in the back and not adjusted in the front. In this case, the back waistline will need to be clipped past the drawn waistline in order to lift the skirt up to the wearer's waist (Figure 13.4, right). Redraw the waistline in the new position, which will be at the base of the clips you have just made.

Skirt darts and side seams may need to be adjusted to fit the wearer's waistline at the new skirt waistline position. Double-check that the hipline curve is at the right level on the wearer, adjusting if necessary. Adjust the waistband to fit the new waistline circumference.

If the skirt is **too loose** at the waistline, the waistline can be taken in slightly at each dart, or darts can be added. The quickest adjustment is to take a tuck through the waistband on the side seam, extending slightly into the upper end of the side seam. This is a good way to adjust a rental costume. One may also adjust the placement of the button or hook closure at the waistband, or take small darts in the waistband at the back.

If the skirt fits at the waistline level but the waistband gaps in the back (Figure 13.6), the waistband needs to be cut on a curve to fit the differences in the wearer's circumference at the upper and lower edges of the waistband.

On an existing garment, a quick alteration is to take in tiny darts or tucks in 2–4 spots THROUGH the back waistband while it is attached to the garment, with up to ½" total intake each. This works well on a rental garment that must be returned to its original size. The same alteration can be used for a wearer with a small waist and fuller hips, to make the back waistline fit better without changing the fit through the seat. This results in a more curved shape to the back waistband.

For a less-temporary adjustment, the waistband can be removed from the skirt and the waistband opened up with the facing removed. Take in the side seams on the waistband and create small darts in the back waistband; repeat the alterations in the waistband facing and re-attach the facing to the waistband. The waistband can then be re-stitched to the upper edge of the skirt.

On a mockup, remove the waistband and take in the skirt darts a little more. If more adjustment is needed, the vertical center, princess, and side seams can be taken in at the waist and blended back into the existing seams approximately 4″ below the lower edge of the waistband. Shorten the waistband to fit the adjusted waistline.

If the waistband fits the waistline but there is a gap between the top of the waistband and the wearer's back, pin in small darts to reshape it. Transfer these small folds to the waistband pattern to create a curved pattern piece (Figure 13.6, three right images).

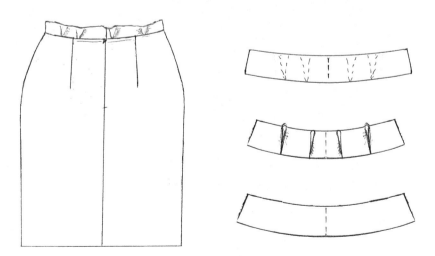

FIGURE 13.6 Waistline gaping: garment gaping in back (left) and garment/pattern adjustments (right three images)

Side Seams

After correcting the garment at the waistline, look at the fit overall. Any diagonal or horizontal folds tend to point toward the area of the skirt that does not fit over the body. Also, re-examine the garment placement and fit over the hips and seat to check whether any waistline adjustments have affected these areas.

There should be no discernable pulling on the fabric at the side seams at the pelvic bones, hips, or across the thighs. Figure 13.7 shows a skirt with that is too narrow for the outer thighs. To accommodate the body curves, it may mean choosing a larger sized garment to fit the widest part of the body, and taking in the waistline to fit closer in those areas.

For both an existing garment or a mockup, if there is enough seam allowance in the existing garment or mockup, let out the side seams where the fabric pulls across the body. Taper the altered seam smoothly back into the existing seams above and below the altered area.

The side seams should hang plumb from the waistline and perpendicular to the floor, falling vertically on the wearer's body UNLESS a tilted side seam is part of the design or your research. Look at the garment from the sides to check this. The side seam will angle toward the skirt panel that is **too narrow**. Figure 13.8, left, shows a skirt where the side seam is pulled away from the vertical side position on the wearer, drawn in red, and toward the wearer's

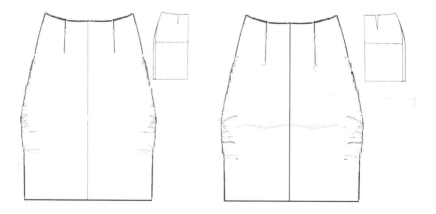

FIGURE 13.7 Curved hips at side seams: front (left), back (center), and patterns with red lines for pattern adjustments to increase the amount of fabric in the side seams (left)

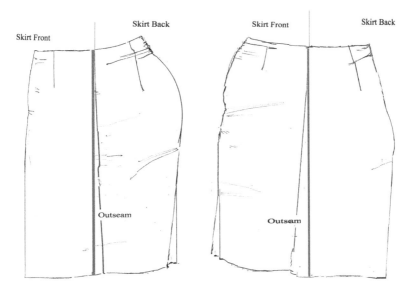

FIGURE 13.8 Side seams tilted: pulling toward the back (left) and toward the front (right), with plumb side positions indicated in red

back where the skirt is too snug. Figure 13.8, right, shows a skirt where the side seam is pulled toward the wearer's front.

On an existing garment, the easiest solution is to choose a different garment. If possible, choose a larger sized version of the garment in order to fit the widest area of the wearer's figure, and taper in the seams elsewhere to fit. You may need to adjust the waistline placement and the darts to help keep the skirt level and the side seam plumb. This amount of alteration should be used on a garment that the theatre owns, not on a rental costume.

A wearer with clearly tilted posture may be more flattered with a softly flared skirt so that the side seam can fall to the floor with gravity.

On a mockup, start by **adjusting the side seams to fit the wearer's figure** smoothly with the right amount of ease for them to move and sit comfortably.

The darts may be adjusted in and out to help raise the garment waistline on its low side and lower it on the high side so that the side seams hang vertically. It may be necessary to add more height on the waistline where it is too low and lower the waistline in areas where it is too high on the body. The goal is for the waistline to lie level around the body.

If this does not correct the hang of the skirt side seams, one of the seam allowances should let out more than the other to create a vertical side seam. If there is not enough existing seam allowance, draw the correct side seam position and transfer the information to the patterns. For Figure 13.8, left, the extra fabric would be added on the back panel; for Figure 13.8, right, the extra fabric would be added on the front panel. On a skirt that has previously been adjusted to fit smoothly on the body, you would adjust one panel by reducing it by the same amount that the other panel has been increased.

Pockets and Details

Look at any pockets to make sure that they fit flat against the body when the wearer is standing, sitting, and moving. If vertical or side seam pockets stick out slightly from the body, this may be corrected by hand stitching or machine topstitching ¼″ of the upper and/or lower ends through all layers to keep the pocket in place. Or, this may mean that the skirt is a little snug across the body at pocket level and needs to be let out at the side seams if there is enough fabric available.

Pocket linings may be cut out and sewn closed if they are too bulky, or a thick lining may be replaced with a thinner fabric. The pockets should have enough room inside to carry intended items, and to allow the wearer to put at least part of their hands into the pockets. If the actor needs to carry items in their pockets, have similar items on hand to try with the garment during the fitting. If the pockets are too shallow, extra lining can be added. If the pockets are not needed, they may be stitched closed if that creates a more flattering effect (or helps prevent an actor from using the pockets when they need to keep their hands OUT of the pockets).

If the skirt is designed with yokes or decorative seams, check that they fall correctly on the wearer's body and that they neither pull too snugly or fall too loosely.

Skirt Shape and Width

These aspects will be determined by the garment design, period style, wearer flattery, and the fabric the garment is made of. Be sure to check with the design reference or the research materials when fitting. Step back and look at the totality of the actor's body shape and proportions when evaluating skirt shapes and widths.

Be sure to consider all of the garments that will be worn with the skirt to check the overall proportions of the ensemble as a whole. If the skirt is to be worn with skirt shapers underneath, those items need to be worn during the fitting.

Full skirts may not need to be carefully fit other than at the waistline and length; in this case, check that the garment fabric falls evenly in the folds or pleats and is balanced front-to-back or has more fullness toward the back. Double-check that the skirt is correct according to the research and design images.

Have the actor walk around and sit in the garment during the fitting to check whether the skirt allows for movement. Also, check whether the actor can climb stairs. A skirt that is long and narrow at the foot can inhibit how well the wearer can climb stairs; while there may not be stairs onstage, the actor may need to deal with stairs backstage or during their walk from the dressing room to the stage.

Length

Skirt hem levels tend to be a matter of the design of the costume and the fashion standards of a time period as well as what appears to flatter the wearer's body. Hems can be adjusted up and down as long as there is enough fabric available. In order to get enough length to fit a tall actor in a purchased skirt, it is often necessary to choose a larger sized garment and to take it in.

Try the skirt on with the intended footwear. Allow the wearer to relax into their natural posture. I also recommend looking at the skirt from the position that it will be seen by most of the audience. For example, if designing for a stage that is higher than the audience's eye level, I tend to lie on the fitting room floor to check the hem level in addition to viewing it from chair. A skirt that is seen from below will appear shorter than one that is seen straight on and should be checked to see if there are undergarments or body areas under the skirt that will be visible to the audience from their perspective. Conversely, in a theatre where the stage is below the audience's eye level, a skirt will appear longer than one that is seen straight on. If you are designing for a theatre in which the audience is seated at multiple levels in relation to the stage floor, be sure to check the skirt length from a variety of angles before you finalize the hem position.

Mark the hemline. Instruct the wearer not to look down as you work, as this will alter the way the skirt hangs and will throw off the balance of the hem level. However, if the actor's posture will be hunched or tilted onstage when wearing the garment, either because the wearer naturally has this posture or because the posture is a character choice, you will save time if you have the actor adopt this posture while you mark the hem.

The hem should be level or may angle toward the back when seen in profile. It is usually best to mark the hem by measuring up from the floor (while the wearer is dressed in the correct shoes and undergarments and with the other garments in the costume) or in relation to marks that are made where the skirt hits the floor, rather than measuring down from the waistline.

If the measuring device is too short to reach the intended hem level above the floor, mark an even length on the skirt with the understanding that this level line is a set amount ABOVE OR BELOW the desired hem level.

For an existing skirt which is very full as well as **too long**, a decorative horizontal tuck can be added to the skirt above the upper edge of the hem. Use several narrow tucks of up to 1″ depth (taking up 2″ total in each tuck) if you need to shorten the skirt a considerable amount. The tuck(s) can be sewn to be visible or can be sewn so that the tuck is on the inside of the garment. This is especially helpful if the skirt is hanging unevenly on the wearer and needs to be taken up in different amounts in different spots. This works well for quick adjustments on a rented garment.

For a skirt that is **too short**, you may be able to add a matching or coordinating panel or ruffle to the lower edge of the garment.

On a mockup, a skirt that is too long can be shortened at the lower edge of the garment or a band of horizontal length can be pinned out. A skirt that is too short can be lengthened at the lower edge of the pattern or a band of horizontal length can be added within the pattern. These adjustments can be transferred to the pattern by subtracting or adding paper to the lower edge or within the body of the pattern.

Consider whether your adjustments on the skirt length will inadvertently change the shape of the skirt. Also, be sure to check that the seamlines on all adjacent pieces are of the same lengths after the pattern alterations are made. Where practical, a skirt that will be added to costume stock and is expected to be reused for future productions should have at least 3″ or more fabric left in the hem.

Finally, have the actor move around in the garment to check their ability to perform their stage movement, walk comfortably, and sit without the skirt crawling up their body. Once the garment has been approved, record all of your notes and take photos for future reference.

14

TROUSERS AND JEANS

Trousers, also known as slacks or pants in various parts of the world, are an important modern garment. Since different localities use **Trousers, Slacks, and Pants** as the name for a variety of garments, this book will use the term **Trousers** for a bifurcated garment that covers the legs.

This chapter covers both Trousers (Figure 14.1) and Jeans (Figure 14.2), to avoid repeating the many fitting aspects that are common between them. Where the two types of garments differ, I will note the differences in the text. For sake of brevity, I will use the term Trousers in general and Jeans when I am specifically addressing jeans.

Depending on style, the differences between trousers and jeans can include:

1. The fabrication – Jeans are traditionally made of indigo-dyed cotton or cotton blend fabric with a twill weave, known as denim, but not all jeans are made of denim or are dyed indigo. Many modern jeans include stretchy Spandex fibers in their fabrication for a close fit.
2. The pockets – Jeans are traditionally cut with high curved front pockets, often with an additional small watch pocket included in the wearer's right front pocket area, and with patch pockets on the back. However, jeans may also be cut as "denim trousers" with front slant side pockets and flapped or welt pockets in the back.
3. The construction – Due to their origin as heavy-duty work trousers for miners and sailors, jeans traditionally include flat-felled seams on the curved crotch seam, inseams and/or outseams; a narrow turn-and-turn hemline; and bar-tacking and copper welts to reinforce seams that are likely to be stressed during wear. Due to the time period in

DOI: 10.4324/9781351131353-15

which jeans were developed, they may also use a 19th century button fly closure rather than a modern zipper. However, jeans may be designed with only some of these elements, and to feature details such as embroidery, decorative topstitching, sequins, and brand-specific embellishments that make them into fashion statements rather than utility garments.

In decades of fitting actors and clients, I have frequently heard a variation on the phrase "I am hard to fit in trousers/jeans, my body is weird" from almost every woman and many of the men with whom I have worked. We can't ALL have weird bodies, so the problem is likely with the trousers and not the wearers. **The trousers work for the wearer, the wearer does not work for the trousers.** Any fit issues have to do with the trousers, not the wearer's body.

Different companies use different fit models when developing their garment patterns. Therefore, **a company that uses a fit model that is close to a particular wearer's proportions will tend to fit that wearer better.** I will often ask an actor which brands of trousers or jeans they feel fit them best, as a starting point when I am shopping for their costumes. Fitting jeans is one case where it makes sense to ask the wearer the brands and styles that work best for them in daily life, because jeans have such a close fit that it is helpful to get this sort of head start. When working on a contemporary show, the actor may actually have a better sense of the intricacies of current fashion than the designer. The show budget may not accommodate the purchase of expensive

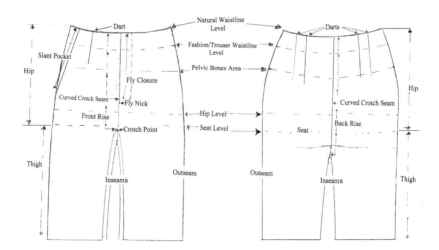

FIGURE 14.1 Parts of trousers: front (left) and back (right)

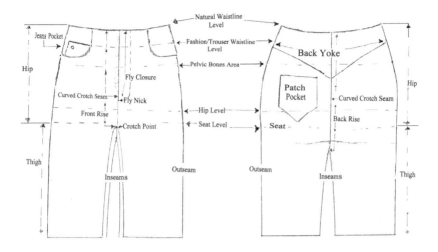

FIGURE 14.2 Parts of jeans: front (left) and back (right)

jeans, but there may be some elements of the actor's preferred brands that can be found in lower priced options.

Trousers and jeans can be difficult to fit because they cover a part of the body that has a variety of angles and curves coming together at particular places, while the garment itself needs to allow for comfortable movement. This chapter is intended to help you fit trousers and jeans correctly. We will cover the body measurements needed to pull or pattern the garments, how to measure existing garments to check against actor measurements before the actor tries them on, and how to conduct a fitting on existing garments and a muslin mockup. You will notice that there is some similarity in these directions to the directions for skirts in Chapter 13, but with the added complexity of crotch curve seams and inseams on trousers. Refer to Chapter 13 if the discussion in this chapter does not cover some issues that you see during the fitting appointment. This chapter contains more examples of pattern adjustments than other chapters, due to the complexity of fitting trousers.

The time period of the trousers or jeans to be fit will contribute to fitting considerations. Late 18th and early 19th century trousers were intended to fit quite snugly, without the addition of stretch fibers in the fabric – this requires careful attention to the proportions and cut of the trousers. Mid-to-late 19th and early 20th century trousers tend to fit with more ease than early 19th and late 20th century trousers. Since the 1960s, and especially with the inclusion of Spandex fibers in fabrics, trousers and jeans have tended to be worn close to the body in at least some areas. Be clear about the correct trouser proportions for the time period for which you are fitting so that you can accurately reproduce them.

Body Measurements Needed to Fit Existing Trousers and Jeans

The measurements below are the essential measurements needed to check an existing garment. They are listed in order of importance with some added notes specific to jeans; the numbers refer to the measurement sheet and discussion in Chapter 2.

The body measurements needed are: hip and/or seat circumference (compare the two measurements and use whichever is **larger** [23 and 24]); hip and/or seat level (from the desired waistline level to the **widest** point of the hips or seat [21 or 25]); waistline (at the desired level of the trouser waistline [11, 12, or 22]); half girth (26); front rise (27); back rise (28); deepest crotch depth (29, this is a non-standard measurement); crotch level depth (30, this book suggests a different method for taking this measurement); inseam (34); outseam (32); and leg circumferences (depending on the style of the trousers, it may be necessary to take the upper thigh, around the bent knee, under knee, calf, and/or ankle [31]).

Checking an Existing Garment Prior to a Fitting

After taking the wearer's body measurements, check pulled or purchased trousers to assess the potential fit on a specific wearer. **Also, be sure to check the seam allowances available at the center back seam, waistline, crotch curve, inseams and hem in order to allow for alterations.**

Check the fiber content of the garment to judge how much ease to allow when comparing the horizontal body measurements to the garment. If you are purchasing trousers, consider purchasing them one size larger in order to give yourself more room to make adjustments during the fitting appointment, because purchased trousers often have very small seam allowances at the inseams, outseams, and other adjustment points. However, men's trousers will sometimes have an additional 1 ½" of seam allowance on available on each side of the center back seam for potential waistline adjustments.

Hip Circumference at the Widest Point of the Trouser Hips

With the closures fastened, measure horizontally at the widest part of the trousers, which is usually somewhere between the base of the fly to the point where the legs separate from the trunk. Double this measurement. **The garment circumference should be at least 1" wider than the body measurements, and 2" larger will be optimal to allow for stage movement.** If the trousers are made of non-stretch fabric, the measurement of the garment should be 1–2" wider than the wearer's body measurements for a close fit, or 2–4" for a loose fit. For jeans, there may not be much ease at the hip level line, as denim fabric tends to stretch to fit around the body during wearing.

HOWEVER, if there is Spandex/Lycra in the fabric, be sure to stretch the garment firmly at the hipline when measuring. For fabric containing 5% Spandex, the hip circumference of the garment can be the same as the wearer's body measurements or ½–1″ wider than the wearer's body measurements. If the garment is made of performance knit fabric or with 10% or more Spandex, measure this hip circumference while the fabric is being stretched, as the hip circumference of the garment can be somewhat **smaller** than the wearer's body measurements. However, if the garment is made of fabric with polyester fibers and contains no Spandex, there will be NO stretch in the fabric and you will need the standard 2–4″ ease in the garment.

Trunk Measurements (Figure 2.2)

With the fastenings closed, lay the trousers front side up and flat. **Determine the waistline level of the trousers in relation to where it will fall on the wearer's body**, as this will affect the following lengths:

a. *Front rise* – measure from the desired waistline level at center front, along the curved crotch seam, down to where the inseams meet the curved crotch seam (the crotch point). For snug-fitting trousers or jeans, this measurement should be ¼–½″ longer than the body measurements. For men's standard trousers, this measurement should be ¾–1″ or more than the body measurements.

b. *Back rise* – measure from the desired waistline level at center back, along the curved crotch seam, down to where the inseams meet at the crotch point. For snug-fitting trousers or jeans, this measurement should be ¼–½″ longer than the body measurements. For standard men's trousers, this measurement should be ¾–1″ or more than the body measurements.

c. *Deepest crotch depth* – measure from the top of the center back waistband along the crotch curve seam to the **lowest point of the crotch curve**, which is where the trousers will begin to curve back upward toward the front waistline level. This measurement should be the same as or up to 1″ longer than the wearer's body measurement, depending on how closely the garment should fit to the wearer's body.

d. *Crotch level depth* – having located the deepest crotch depth point, measure from that level along the side seam upward to the top of the waistline at the side seam. This measurement on the garment should be the same as or up to 1″ longer than the body measurement, depending on how closely the garment should fit to the wearer's body. If the other rise and crotch depth measurements are close to the body, the crotch level depth should be similarly close to the body.

Waistline Circumference

Determine the waistline level of the trousers in relation to where it will fall on the wearer's body. Measure around the top of the trousers or the center of the waistband from the trouser closure to the far end of the buttonhole or other trouser closure. The garment measurement should be 1″ larger than the wearer's body measurement for trousers made of non-stretch woven fabric. Be sure to compare the front rise measurement of the wearer to the trousers to assess whether the garment waistline will fit **at the level at which it will sit on the wearer.** If the trousers will be worn with a shirt or sweater tucked into the waistline, they may need an additional 1″ or more of extra room to fit the shirt. If the trousers fit otherwise but are too small in the waistline, check whether there is sufficient fabric in the seam allowances at the center back to be let out prior to the fitting. Well-made men's trousers tend to have up to 3″ of extra fabric in this area to allow for alterations.

Jeans may be 1–2″ SMALLER than the body measurements at the waistline level of the wearer's body, especially if they are intended to compress the waistline and fit closely, are very low-cut, or contain 5% or more Spandex in the fabric. This is an important distinction to make when you are checking existing garments – an actor may give you their jeans size and be surprised when trousers are too snug, because the two types of garments should fit differently.

Outseam

Measure the side seam of the trousers vertically from the top of the waistband to the lower edge of the hemline. If the outseam measurement was taken to the floor on the wearer while they were wearing shoes, subtract 2″ or more from the body measurements to be accurate to where the garment should end.

Inseam

Measure vertically from the crotch point down the inseam to the lower edge of the hemline. Since the crotch level of trousers varies with style of pants and wearer preference, this measurement may not be consistent in all cases. I tend to use the outseam measurement more often than the inseam measurement when measuring existing garments.

Leg Circumferences

Depending on the style of the trousers, especially for skinny jeans or leggings, measure the thigh circumference at the top of the thigh, knee circumference, calf circumference, and ankle circumference of the garment against the thigh, bent knee, calf, and ankle circumference measurements of the wearer. For medium fit trousers, or for trousers made of non-stretch woven fabrics, the garment should be at least 2″ larger than the body measurements at those points. For close-fit jeans, the garment should be roughly 1″ larger. If the trousers are made of stretch fabric with up to 5% Spandex, the thigh circumference of the garment can be the same as the wearer's body measurements or ½–1″ wider than the wearer's body measurements. If the trousers are made of performance knit fabric or with 10% or more Spandex, the garment may be 1–2″ SMALLER than the wearer.

Fitting Trousers and Jeans

Fitting trousers and jeans can be an art. Current fashionable notions of how trousers should fit will have to be balanced with the standards of the **production** time period and the specifics of character, along with the actor's input.

Trouser fitting and patterning have been transformed in the past several decades due to the use of fabrics with stretch fibers in trouser construction. Whereas trousers once needed to fit precisely around the hips with some added ease, stretch fabric has allowed trousers, and especially jeans, to function as girdles to compress the body over the stomach and hips. Consider the style and time period of the trousers that you are trying on, as well as the fabric they are created from, when assessing the fit.

Trousers should be tried on in the same shoes and/or foundation or undergarments that the trousers are intended to be worn with. Assess the fit with ALL the elements as a whole, including the shirt or top that will be worn with the garment. Take photos from all angles of each pair of trousers you try on, so that you can calmly evaluate your choices after the fitting session.

For existing garments, have a range of options on hand during the fitting. A garment that seems promising might not look good on the actor once it is tried on, and it is important to have back-up garments.

The use of stretch fabrics for trousers has also altered the calculus of whether a garment is actually too tight or not when it is first put on. If the fabric contains 2–5% Lycra/Spandex, allow the wearer to move and sit for a few minutes before determining whether the trousers are really too snug to use onstage. In this situation, look carefully at your research materials to determine the correct fit standards for the era and character that you are designing.

For a mockup, the garment should be constructed with at least 1″ wide seam allowances to allow leeway for adjustments during the fitting appointment. I also like to keep extra muslin available to pin onto the mockup if extra room is needed beyond the seam allowance amounts.

Before putting on the trousers, check that the seams and darts are sewn correctly, using a long stitch so that the seams can be easily changed or removed if needed. Mark all the stitch-lines for future reference. Mark the waistline stitch-line. For a first trouser muslin fitting, the waistband may be hand basted onto the trouser upper edge so that it can be easily adjusted during the fitting.

Put on the Trousers and Fasten the Closures

Modern trousers use either a zipper or button fly closure. Button closures were used on men's trousers from the 18th to the 20th century, while zip flies became most common on men's trousers after the mid-20th century. However, if the trousers fit smoothly, the exact type of closure may not be visible to the audience.

The waistband should fit smoothly, without binding or gaping when the closures are fastened. If the actor is wearing a body mic during the show, they should also wear it during the fitting.

For an existing garment, check the garment measurements prior to the fitting appointment, let out the center back seam if needed, and re-stitch the seam with a basting stitch so that the garment will be the right circumference for the wearer (including the added ease needed). For a new pair of men's dress trousers, part of the back crotch curve may have been left unsewn in order to facilitate fitting.

Fasten the closures. Closures should lie flat and add as little bulk as possible, so pay attention to the way they lie when they are fastened. With men's trousers, there tends to be an extended inner tab at the waistband with an additional closure to keep the garment secure. If the trouser closures cannot fasten, assess whether there is sufficient extra fabric in the center back seam allowance to let the back crotch curve and waistline out.

If the trousers have a front fly area, avoid making an alteration which would require having to re-construct this area – better to choose another area on the trousers for the alteration or to pick another pair of trousers for the actor to try on.

If you are fitting jeans, it is common for the waistline to fit snugly and the closure to take a bit of effort to close because jeans are designed to fit snugly. The cotton or cotton-Spandex blend fabric the jeans are made of will relax enough to expand to fit smoothly within a few moments of putting them on. (However, a polyester-blend pair of jeans without any Spandex content will not relax at all, so check the fiber content of the garment before trying it on.) The wearer can often tell you whether the jeans are likely to relax enough to fit them, so it is worth having them put on the jeans as a first step during a fitting and letting the garment relax while you are fitting their shirt or blouse.

In any case where trousers are clearly too snug (Figure 14.3), the default option is to try a larger garment if it is available in order to have enough fabric to accommodate the wearer's body contours.

For a mockup, it may be easier for a beginner to fit a muslin mockup with the seams on the outside in order to have easy access to the stitch-lines. However, because the crotch seam allowance is being pulled against the concave shape it will take in the finished garment, when the garment is tried on inside-out, the crotch curve seam allowance must be clipped to release this tension. Clip the crotch curve seam allowance from the outer edges inward almost to the stitch-line, from the inseams upward to the center front and center back.

Trousers are traditionally fit with the center back seam open partway from the waistline toward the inseam, even if the finished garment is intended to have a center front fly closure. This is also true for trouser mockups.

Pin the trousers closed at the center back opening, starting at the base of the opening and working up toward the top of the garment as high as in comfortable on the wearer. Your goal is to get the seam pinned closed along the marked stitch-line, stopping at the desired waistline level.

If the trousers cannot be closed at the center back waistline, remove the waistband. Start at the center front, and clip into the waistline seam allowance, not quite cutting down to the marked stitch-line. Your clips will be about 1 ½" apart. Continue to clip carefully toward the marked stitch-line to release any tension caused by the seam allowance beyond the stitch-line. As you clip the waistline, continue to try to pin the center back stitch-line until it is completely closed. The wearer's posture may be such that the back waistline will not need to be clipped much if at all, and the finished waistline will be higher in the back and lower in the front than the original pattern. Or, the wearer may have a slight sway back, and the back waistline will need to be clipped past the drawn waistline in order to lift the trousers up to the wearer's waist.

If the garment will still not close, assess whether the side seams will need to be let out, darts reduced or eliminated, or whether you need to pin on additional fabric that will be incorporated later into the adjusted pattern.

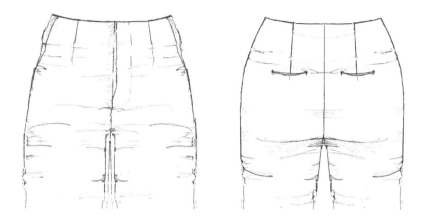

FIGURE 14.3 Trousers too snug: front (left) and back (right)

Have the wearer sit down to check that the garment is comfortable. The fabric should not bunch or stretch over the stomach, thighs, hips, and seat. After the wearer stands up, the trouser fabric should fall smoothly down the body without staying hitched up on the body, pulling open any pleats on the trousers, or creating vertical puddles of fabric. The area where these issues occur should be addressed first. If there are no clear fit issues, address the widest part of the body.

Once the trousers are closed, **fit the widest part of the body in the trousers first**. Adjust the widest area and then move on. Depending on the wearer's body shape, this may be the hips, seat, thighs, abdomen, or waistline. I have ordered the directions beginning with the hips, but it may make more sense to start with the seat and then **fit the other areas afterward in order of fullness**. Figure 14.3 shows an image on trousers that are too snug OVERALL. However, in most cases, there will be one to two areas that clearly need adjustment.

Check the Fit at the Hips

Look carefully at your research materials to evaluate the correct fit for the era and character that you are designing. The garment should sit level on the wearer at the widest part of the hips and not pull to one side or down in the back or front. The hip level line (as implied on an existing garment or actually drawn on a mockup) should sit parallel to the floor.

Trousers that are **too snug** will show **thin horizontal draw-line folds that radiate out from the area that is too small for the wearer** (Figure 14.4). This may occur because the trousers are too snug or because

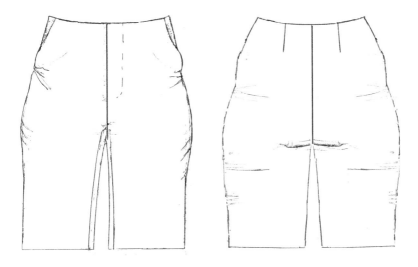

FIGURE 14.4 Trousers too snug at lower hips and upper thighs: front (left) and back (right)

they will need a half or full lining added to them to glide over the wearer's body.

Too tight trousers may crawl up the body when walking or sitting, creating a "wedgie" effect. They will also tend to bag at the seat once they have been worn a few times. In this situation, having a little more ease over the hips will allow the garment to fall smoothly.

For an existing garment, if the fabric has 2–5% Lycra/Spandex, allow the wearer to move and sit for a few minutes before determining whether the trousers will actually be too snug to use onstage. In fact, if the wearer is used to wearing jeans, which traditionally have a snugger fit than do trousers, there may need to be some careful negotiation in the fitting room with the wearer as to whether particular trousers actually do fit or not because the wearer will assume that a tight fit is always correct. In this situation, look carefully at your research materials to evaluate the correct fit for the era and character that you are designing.

It may make more sense to try on a larger size garment and take it in than to re-make an existing garment unless there are ample seam allowances available to adjust, particularly at the side seams. Also consider how a side seam alteration will affect the side seam pockets.

For a mockup, let out the side seams at the tight areas and taper the adjustments smoothly into the original seamline where the garment fits well, to allow more room over the hips. Redraw the position of any side seam pockets.

Consider the fabric that the finished trousers will be constructed from. If the fabric will have 2–5% Lycra/Spandex, the mockup can be fit closer to the body than if it will be built of non-stretch fabric. However, any draw-lines or twists in the garment should be corrected.

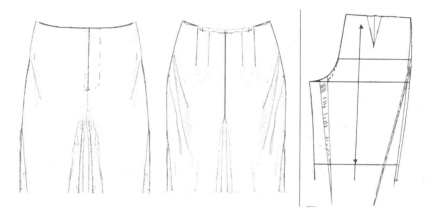

FIGURE 14.5 Trousers too loose: front (left), back (center), and areas in red to be folded out from the garment pattern to reduce the size of the back trouser panels (left)

Trousers that are loose will fall in **loose vertical folds** (Figure 14.5). Look carefully at your research materials to evaluate the correct fit for the era and character that you are designing. Determine whether the fullness around the hips is consistent with the design and with your research images. With trousers, loose vertical folds that fall from the waistline area can be taken out in the side seams first but may also need to be taken out at the inseams and even (slightly) through the back curved crotch seam.

For an existing garment, pin in the side seams in the areas that are too loose, very gradually tapering out to the original side seam at the upper and lower ends of this alteration. If there are side seam pockets, the excess fabric may need to be taken ONLY from the back part of the trousers at the side seams to avoid closing up the pockets, unless one is willing to move the pockets and re-sew them in the new side seam position.

If you are fitting jeans, which usually fit closer through the hips than do trousers, more fabric can be pinned out than would be taken for trousers. There should be ½–2" of ease at the hip level rather than the usual 2–4" for trousers. If there is a flat-felled seam on the outseams, you may need to put all of the alteration on the side seam into a vertical tuck that follows the edge of the flat-fell. If the outseams are sewn with a standard seam but you will not be able to re-construct this area by removing the waistband, you can take a tuck through **the entire side seam**, including the waistband, to take in the sides. I have used this method when I needed to take in borrowed trousers that could later be restored to their original condition, or for altering jeans.

For a mockup, pin in the side seams where they are too loose, very gradually tapering out to the original side seam at the upper and lower ends. If there will be side seam pockets, re-mark their position on the adjusted side seams.

If the trousers hang in loose folds, these areas can be pinned out of the pattern. This works as long as the pinned-out area has **straight edges** and **originates and ends at the outer edges of the pattern piece** (Figure 14.5, right). For example, a vertical tuck can be pinned out of the garment to bring in the side seams without adjusting the pocket placement. The pinned-out fabric is then folded out of the paper pattern to reduce the shape of the final pattern piece.

Look at the back view of the trousers to be sure that any hip alterations are not creating draw-lines over the seat because they are making the garment too snug. It is better to have the garment slightly loose than too tight. Ask the actor to sit and walk, to check that you have not made the trousers too snug with the alterations.

Check the Seat and Tops of the Inseams

The area where the curve crotch seams and the inseams converge is crucial for making trousers fit correctly over the body, beginning with the seat and the top of the inseams. **In addition to the crotch seam, the trouser seat is affected by the height of the inseams and the width of the thighs**. Check the back view to check that the top of the inseam and under-seat area are not **sagging** because there is too much fabric (i.e. because the inseam is too tall as compared to the wearer's seat and therefore the garment fabric is being pushed down below the base of the wearer's seat), or **pulling** because the crotch extension is too short and does not fit across the inner thighs. A wearer with a rounded seat may need more room let out at the back upper

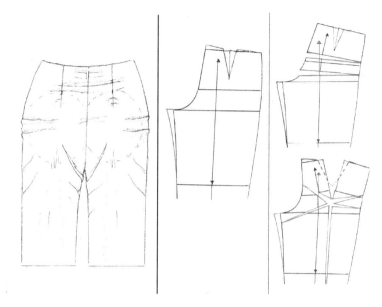

FIGURE 14.6 High round seat, and crotch curve too short, with possible pattern corrections shown in red.: trouser back (left); standard pattern adjustments which are similar to what may be attempted on an existing garment (center); and an advanced pattern correction (upper right) to increase the back curved seam through slashing. A pattern that is too flat for a curved part of the body may also be opened up to give more room over the fullest seat by pivoting in more room (lower right)

inseams so that the thighs do not bind (Figure 14.6). A wearer with a flat bottom or underslung seat may need to have the inner thighs taken in at the back inseams (Figure 14.7).

When fitting the seat, the width of the upper inseam area/crotch extension and the length of the curved crotch seam are your main adjustment points.

For a wearer with a round, high seat (Figure 14.6), **the back crotch curve may need to be lengthened** to accommodate the buttocks and to sit smoothly at the back waistline without pulling up in the back, binding at the inseams, and/or pulling across the stomach in front.

For an existing garment, the trousers should be un-stitched the inseams from the crotch curve to the knee and re-sewn with a narrower seam allowance down to the knee level, especially on the back trouser panel. This will create more length in the back crotch curve and more room in the back seat area. Check that at least ¾" inseam seam allowance fabric is available before trying trousers on a wearer with a high seat.

If you have matching or similar fabric available, add a gusset to the inseam of the trousers in order to lengthen the total crotch curve area by extending the inseam area. If the waistband can be un-stitched in the back, it may also be raised slightly to help lengthen the back crotch curve seam.

The side seams can be adjusted in the upper back to help fine-tune the seat area after adding the extra fabric in the inseam.

For a mockup, the trousers can be lengthened in the crotch curve by adding width at the back inseams from the top to the knee, adding more height at the center back of the crotch curve, or by slashing the pattern to pivot in more length through the back seam. The red outlines in Figure 14.6, center and right, show options of where the garment patterns could be adjusted to make these alterations; **not all of the adjustments will be needed for all garments**. (Please note that the grainline position will need to adjusted because of pattern adjustments.) Taper the added height at the center back crotch curve to meet the original position of the side seams, unless the side seams are also too short at the top. In that case, both the front and back side seams will need to be lengthened to match one another.

A more advanced alteration is to slash through the trunk area (Figure 14.6, lower right) to add more fullness over the highpoint of the seat, similar to what was discussed to accommodate a fuller bustline area in Chapter 8 (Figure 8.10, left). Because this alteration will result in a much larger back dart intake area (red dashed lines) than the original pattern, split the resulting intake dart into two darts. One may reduce some of the upper side seam area to create a smoother curve, and reduce the total back dart intake by the same amount as has been taken off the side seam.

If you have made these adjustments snd still have a wide back dart (over 1 3/4" total) split the dart into 2 darts for a smoother effect.

For trousers with a back seat area that is too long for the wearer's body, there will be too much fabric pooling over the buttocks and the back thighs, and the back crotch curve will need to be shortened (Figure 14.7).

For an existing garment, the inseams can be taken in by un-stitching the inseams to the knee level and re-stitching them to take more fabric out of the back leg (Figure 14.7). A temporary version of this adjustment is to take a long, thin dart parallel to the inseam on the back legs.

The waistband may also be removed from center back to the side seams and dropped slightly lower on the center back area. Increase the back dart intakes or slightly ease the upper back waistline edge before re-attaching the waistband. If a quicker adjustment is needed, a thin horizontal two-ended dart may be taken along the lower edge of the horizontal back waistband seam to shorten the back rise.

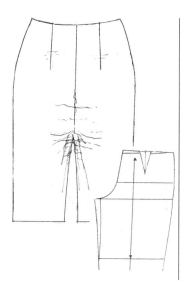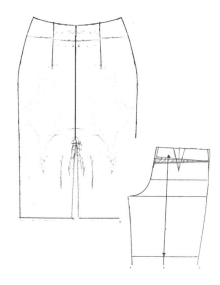

FIGURE 14.7 Crotch curves too long. Trouser crotch curve too long for the wearer (left), and flat trouser seat that has horizontal wedges of extra fabric (right). Pattern corrections are shown in red

---

For a mockup, pin out any extra horizontal wedges of fabric across the seat to reduce the crotch curve length. The wedge should taper to nothing at the side seams. The exact placement of the horizontal wedge may need to be tried in a few locations to find the best solution. Sometimes, you may need to take several narrow wedges in a few positions. The amount of fabric that is pinned out should be folded out of the pattern.

If pinning out a horizontal area of the seat does not solve the problem, try lowering the back waistline position, which will pull the seat upward and shorten the crotch seam. You will need to reduce the back waistline circumference at the lowered position to fit the wearer's waistline, either through increasing dart intakes, easing the upper edge of the fabric, or tapering in the center back and side seams.

Front Rise

Having dealt with the rear seat area, it is time to look at the front rise. The back seat and the front rise are actually two parts of the continuum of the curved crotch seam, and adjustments in one area of the seam will affect other areas of the seam. On trousers that have a front fly, the front rise will be difficult to adjust. Therefore, adjusting the front rise may involve altering the back crotch curve, the waistline level, and the width of the inseam/crotch extension area.

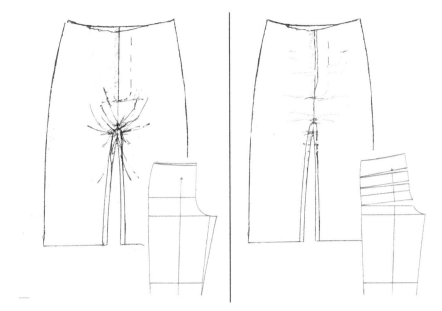

FIGURE 14.8 Front rise too short for the wearer (left and right), with adjustments in red on patterns

The front rise seam should be near to the body, without either pulling up uncomfortably or bagging far below the body. Have the wearer move and sit during the fitting. Check whether there is tension and binding over the lower front crotch (Figure 14.8), indicating a too short front rise, or if there an extra "pouch" of fabric at the lower front, indicating a too long front rise (Figure 14.9).

If the trousers are too short in the front rise, they will be uncomfortable to wear (Figure 14.8). In addition to the trousers themselves being too short, this situation can arise with a curvy wearer who is wearing the trousers over a rounded belly, which forces the inseam position to pull forward and the rear crotch area to bind over the buttocks.

Men often appreciate at least ½–¾" room between their bodies and the crossed seams at the base of the crotch level for dress and suit trousers; therefore, some extra length at the front rise may be welcomed by a male-identified actor for the trousers to fit comfortably and not bind over the crotch.

For existing garments, try on a variety of trousers to find a style with a sufficiently long front rise for the wearer to sit and walk comfortably. You may be able to add a little more room by letting the inseams out as much as possible at their upper ends, lengthening the crotch seam (Figure 14.8, pattern left). If matching fabric is available, a triangular gusset added to the inseam can help.

If there are any sort of seam allowances available on the front waistline and waistband, un-stitch this area from the center fronts to the side seams, and re-sew with a smaller seam allowance to slightly raise the waistband position. If needed, one may even use the self-facing found on the back of a waistband to make a taller waistband, and use a different fabric for the facing on the new, taller waistband.

Wearing trousers in a larger waistline size with suspenders can help place the trousers in the right alignment on a wearer with a curved stomach and/or buttocks area. The person may need to wear the larger sized garment in order to get enough length to fit their rise comfortably; the garment waist can more easily be taken in to fit than the front rise can be adjusted.

On a mockup, the inseams will need to be extended outward in the front. This will lengthen the front crotch curve to fit the measurement of the wearer's front rise (with added ease for comfort). Make the alteration with long stitches at first and have the wearer sit and move around before permanently stitching and clipping the alteration.

You may also raise the front waistline from the center front and taper out to zero at the side seams to add length to the center front rise, especially if you are fitting a person with a rounded tummy.

For an overall lengthening of the front rise, clip through the pattern horizontally from the center front to the side seams. Pivot the pattern pieces open to create more length (Figure 14.8, pattern left).

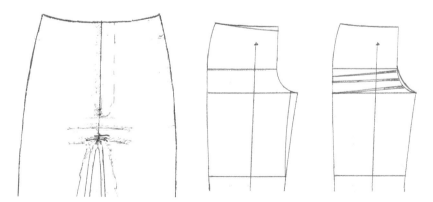

FIGURE 14.9 Front rise too long for the wearer (left), pattern adjustments in red lines(center) and pattern adjustments for a mockup (right)

If the trousers are too long in the front rise (Figure 14.9 right), they can be uncomfortable and look awkward. The too long point where the trouser legs meet will lie further down the legs than the point where the wearer's anatomical legs meet, and the too low placement of the crotch seam will restrict movement, particularly for stage combat or dancing. Have the wearer move and sit during the fitting to test comfort.

Women's trousers are often worn close up to the front crotch point on the body. However, if there is too much length in the trouser front rise, it will create a "pouch" effect when sitting, even if the back rise is too short through the seat, creating back snugness. This situation is more often seen on women if they are wearing trousers that are not cut for their curves. This issue is dealt with in more detail in the section on crotch curve shape, later in this chapter (Figures 14.11 and 14.12). The main areas of adjustment are available at the ends of the rise seam, at the waistline, and at the inseam.

For existing garments, too much length in the rise can be tricky to adjust. The trousers should be adjusted at the waistband and possibly also at the inseams. If the waistband can be slightly lowered in front and tapered back to the original position at the side seams, this will shorten the front rise from the top end. For a quicker adjustment, a narrow curved tuck can be taken just below the front waistband seam (Figure 14.9, center upper edge).

You may also remove a curved wedge of fabric by sewing right along the inseams on the front panels of the trousers, starting at the original seam line at knee level, tapering to take up ½–¾" total through the crotch point on the front panels. This will reduce front crotch seam length (Figure 14.9, center). This adjustment will raise the point where the front inseams interest the curve crotch seam. However, since the back inseam will not be adjusted, the back pant panel will need to be slightly stretched to fit the front at the new front inseam position. This is not ideal, but the alteration can work when the trousers are both too long in the front rise and loose at the inner legs.

For a mockup. the alterations suggested above for an existing garment will also work with a mockup. Lower the front waistline position and shorten the length of the front crotch extension at the inseam to shorten the overall front rise seam.

The best way of addressing a too long rise is during the patterning process. While patterning the trousers, use the wearer's front rise measurement plus ¼–½" ease to draw a **shallower-than-usual** curved line from the front inseam to the center front waistline. This curve will be shorter than a conventional front crotch curve. The center front of the crotch curve should remain a straight line above the point where a zipper would end, also known as the fly nick.

You may also **lower the front waistline at center front** and taper out to zero at the side seams. This will pull the seam upward and shorten it so that the front crotch curve measurement fits the wearer's body measurements. You will need to reduce the front waistline circumference at the lowered position to fit the wearer's waistline, either by increasing dart intakes or tapering in the side seams.

If you prefer to make the adjustment during a fitting rather than in patterning, pin out a horizontal wedge or wedges of fabric across the lower front crotch area to reduce the crotch curve length (Figure 14.9, right). The wedge may either taper to nothing at the side seams or continue into the back trousers area as long as it either intersects with, or tapers to nothing, at the center back seamline. The exact placement of the horizontal wedge(s) you are pinning out may need to be tried in a few locations to find the best solution. Sometimes, several narrow wedges need to be taken in different positions. **The amount of fabric that is pinned out on the mockup should be folded out of the pattern**. Be sure that the area that you pin out has straight-line edges – you cannot accurately adjust a pattern with a curved area pinned out.

Crotch Curve Shape

The **shape** of the crotch curve is as important as the **length** of the curved seam in helping trousers fit correctly through the seat. The curved crotch seam created when the inseams are joined should be a similar shape to the wearer's crotch curve (Figure 14.10).

Comparing the shape of a person's crotch curve (as well as their posture) reveals that the central crotch curve created when the inseams are joined may

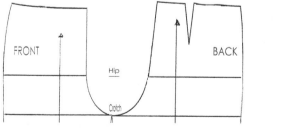

FIGURE 14.10 Shape of crotch curve created by joining front and back trousers at the inseams (left) and the assumed shape of a wearer's crotch curve

not fit the shape of the person wearing a pair of trousers (Figure 14.10). The greater the mismatch between these two shapes, the greater the fitting challenges. The crotch curve cannot be changed much for existing trousers but can be reshaped through pattern adjustments after a mockup fitting, or in the patterning process.

Figure 14.11 shows a sampling of some of the crotch curve shapes for different wearers. The common shape of a male-identified wearer (Figure 14.11, left and Figure 14.10, right), with body volume at the lower front crotch and somewhat flat seat, fits the standard drafted trouser pattern; the inseams meet at the lowest point of a smooth crotch curve. For a person with a high, rounded seat (Figure 14.11, center), the back crotch curve may need more length to accommodate the curvy seat, but the front inseams are still close to the lowest anatomical point on the wearer.

However, for a person with no body volume at the lower front crotch AND a seat that is lower than the point where the inseams meet (Figure 14.11, right),

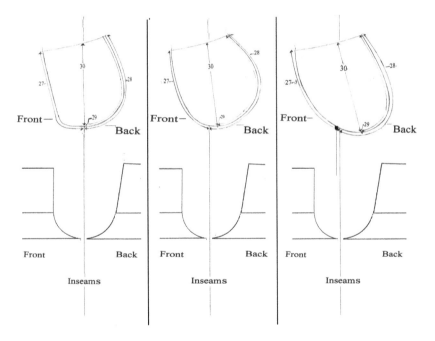

FIGURE 14.11 Comparison of the shapes of wearer's crotch curves and standard trouser crotch curve shapes: crotch curve shape for a male-identified wearer, and standard trouser crotch curve (left); crotch curve shape for a person with a high, round seat, as in Figure 14.6 (center), and standard trouser crotch curve; and crotch curve shape for a person with a low seat and a front crotch curve that is higher than the back, and standard trouser crotch curve, as in Figure 14.12

the shape of the trousers will fight against the wearer's shape. The inseam may also be positioned too far to the back for the wearer's figure; see red line for a suggested placement closer to the body front.

For a wearer with a low, round seat that sits lower than the front pubic bone level (Figure 14.12), the garment back crotch shape is **too shallow** AND the length of the back curve on the garment is **too short** for the back rise on the wearer's body. In this case, the back rise seam will ride up the body too tightly to create a "wedgie" effect, because the garment's back curve is not scooped out at much as is needed. This will result in fabric bunching below the seat and creating soft horizontal folds on the wearer's upper back thighs because the inseams of the trousers are being pushed downward by an ill-fitting seat area when the wearer's buttocks are lower than the trousers will accommodate. The back waistline level will also tend to pull too low when the wearer is sitting. The wearer's buttocks are pushing the fabric downward because the garment fabric is in the wrong place, even if the garment measurements should fit.

The front of the trousers may hang loose below the lower front point of the wearer's crotch seam because the **rise is too long for their body shape**. To check this on a garment, confirm that the horizontal lines below the fly zipper are **rounded folds**, indicating too much length where the garment fabric is hanging loose below the wearer's front crotch, rather than tight horizontal strain lines, indicating the garment is too snug. The extra trouser length is visible when the wearer sits, creating a loose pouch in front.

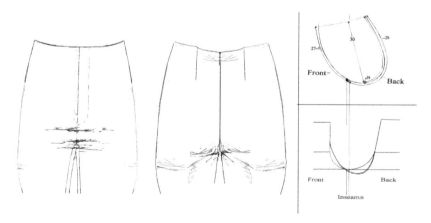

FIGURE 14.12 Low seat area combined with a high front rise: trouser front too low for the wearer (left) and trouser seat back too high for the wearer (center). Right hand images show the shape of the wearer's crotch curve (upper right) and some pattern adjustments to correct the mismatch in the trouser pattern (lower right)

For an existing garment, repeat the same alteration described above for a rounded seat.

If the waistband can be un-stitched in the back and you have matching or coordinating fabric, add a back yoke similar to a jeans-type yoke at the top of the existing back waistline level to lengthen the center back crotch curve. This will help alleviate the back waistline pulling down while sitting. To address the excess length on the garment front crotch area, you may remove a curved wedge of fabric by sewing right along the inseams on the front panels of the trousers, starting at the original seam line at knee level, tapering to take up ½–¾" total through the crotch point on the front panels. This will reduce front crotch seam length (Figure 14.9, center).

For a mockup, consider revising the shape of the back crotch curve on the pattern to match that of the wearer's body in profile. Use the back lowest crotch curve measurement (29) as the lowest point when drafting the crotch curve, along with the front rise (27) and back rise (28) measurements to establish the shape. I have found that the back crotch curve may need to dip down below the horizontal line that is generally used to create the crotch level, and the front crotch curve needs to curve upward to fill in the open space that a horizontal crotch curve will create – the loose "pouch" that occurs when the front rise is too long. The red lines in Figure 14.12, right, suggest how to adjust the crotch curves.

Thighs

There should not be discernable pulling on the fabric across the thighs. Any diagonal or horizontal folds tend to point toward the area of the trousers that do not fit over the body.

Have the actor walk toward and away from a full-length mirror and then sit, to check how the fabric moves over the thighs. If there are obvious horizontal stress folds through the thighs or the side pockets are pulling open, the pants do not fit. This may be a matter of garment size or the cut of the particular style of trousers.

For under-the-knee breeches, have the actor sit. The breeches should cover the knees while they are bent and should be wide enough to fit comfortably around the knees and thighs while the actor is seated.

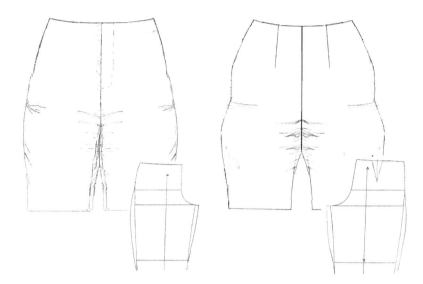

FIGURE 14.13 Thighs too snug: front (left) and back (right), with pattern adjustments

Horizontal draw-lines that radiate outward from the outer thighs and/or the inner thighs indicate that the garment thighs are **too snug** (Figure 14.13). The garment will need to be expanded in the area where it is too small for the wearer.

For an existing garment, it may mean choosing a larger sized garment to fit the thighs and taking in the waistline and lower legs to fit closer in those areas. Taper the seams smoothly back into the existing seams above and below the area that is too snug.

If the **outer thighs** of the garment are too snug, check the seam allowances and let them out at the upper thigh level. For most existing garments, you may be able to let out seams up to ¼" on each side of the seamline, which can gain up to 1" more room in total. If possible, keep the adjustment subtle on its upper edge to avoid disrupting any side seam pockets.

For the **inner thighs**, if there are sufficient seam allowances in a garment that otherwise fits, the inseams may need to be let out at the upper end, which will also slightly lengthen the crotch curve seam. In an extreme situation, one may choose to add a triangular gusset on the upper inner thighs if one has access to extra fabric to match the garment. This alteration is often used for dancers.

Jeans are usually fit with the thighs tighter than on trousers and are often patterned with a shorter crotch curve extension in the front than trousers to purposely create a snug fit at the inner thigh, seat, and crotch. If the thighs are simply too snug for comfort, they are difficult to let out at the jeans inseam because of the traditional flat-felled seam located there. In that case, try a different garment.

For a mockup, let out the seam allowances to accommodate the wearer's thigh shape.

I suggest starting with the **outer thighs** to start the process as it is easier to make the outseam than the inseam adjustment during a fitting appointment. The adjustment should begin and end several inches beyond the area that needs to be let out, in order that the altered seam can smoothly blend into the existing side seams without creating a noticeable "bump." The expanded seamlines may be curved, to reflect the shape of the wearer's body. Once the outseams are altered, adjust the placement of any side seam pockets.

Too snug **inner thighs** on trousers will require letting out the inseam to above the knee level or lower. If the mockup does not contain enough seam allowance, consider adding a "v" shaped gusset at the inseam to expand the thighs. Both adjustments will expand the crotch curve seam length, which may be helpful in fitting the wearer. However, if this is not ideal, the adjusted inner thigh seam may need to be curved or a long oval gusset may be added at the inseam to fit the shape of the wearer's thighs where they curve outward.

A wearer with developed front thighs, such as an athlete, will need more fabric added at the front inseam, whereas the back will not need additional fabric. A wearer with a flat bottom or underslung seat may even need to have the inner thighs taken in at the back inseams (Figure 14.14, right and left).

Check the Waistline and Abdomen

Once the widest areas of the hips, seat, and thighs fit, assess the garment at the support point of the waistline. Try on the shirt or blouse that will be worn with the trousers and tuck it in if this is how it will be worn onstage. If the garment is worn at the natural waistline, the fabric should fit smoothly without pulling across the stomach or the upper buttocks. If the garment is worn at a lower waistline level, it may be worn snugger at the waist in order that it

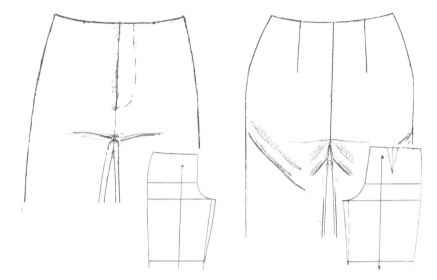

FIGURE 14.14 Wearer with more developed thighs in the front, and a flat seat, corrected by adding fabric to one inseam and reducing it from the other: front (left), back, (right), and pattern adjustments in red

does not slip down the body. The waistband should fit closely to the waist so that a shirt or top will stay tucked in, but not so tightly that it forces the body flesh into a so-called muffin-top over the top of the garment.

Letting out or taking in the center back seam at the waistline can help fit the trousers neatly through the waistline. The back waistline alteration will be successful if the adjustment is no more than 1 ½″ total in or out from the original seamline.

Whether the garment is too snug or too loose, moving the zipper placement should be the last resort only if there are no other possible options.

If there are horizontal draw-lines falling parallel to the waistline, the area is **too snug** (Figure 14.15 left).

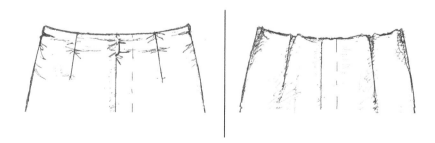

FIGURE 14.15 Waistlines: too snug (left) and too loose (right)

For an existing garment, a new pair of men's dress trousers may have the center back waistband and part of the back crotch curve left unsewn with a wide seam allowance in order to facilitate fitting. This seam can be pinned to fit the waistline and abdomen area correctly. If an old pair of trousers is snug at the waist, assess whether there is sufficient extra fabric in the center back seam allowance to let the back waistline out and taper the back crotch curve into the existing seamline, roughly at tailbone level. Be mindful that the center back alteration at the waistline and upper hips does not place the back pockets too far toward the side seams to look attractive in proportion to the garment's size, or that it does not pull the side seams too far toward the center front.

Women's trousers generally do not have the same amount of extra seam allowance available as men's trousers to allow for much expansion. In this case, it is best to try on a larger sized garment to accommodate the waistline and take in the outseams below the waistline area.

If you have no other option and need to re-make the trousers, remove the waistband and/or waistline facing, let out or remove any darts, and adjust the side seams and center back seams enough to create 1″ extra room for the necessary waistline ease. Make a new, larger waistband or facing to fit the adjusted area.

For a mockup, remove the waistband and/or waistline facing, let out or remove any darts, and adjust the side seams and center back seams to create extra room for the wearer's waistline measurements plus 1″ ease. Make a new, larger waistband or facing to fit the adjusted area.

If there are vertical soft folds where the trousers collapse, the waistline area is **too loose** (Figure 14.15, right).

For an existing garment, the center back seam at the waistline can be taken in approximately 1–1 ½″ total at the waist. Blend the waistline alteration back into the crotch curve at the tailbone level, where the curve begins to turn toward the underside of the buttocks. Be careful that the center back alteration at the waistline and upper hips does not bring the back pockets too close together to look attractive in proportion to the garment's size, or that it does not pull the side seams too far toward the center back.

If the waistband is the correct length but the back gaps on the wearer, you can take in up to ½″ total intake EACH for tiny darts in 2–4 spots through the back waistband. This results in a more curved shape to the back waistline that fits a wearer with a small waist and fuller hips (Figure 13.6). The sewn darts may extend into the upper back of the trousers if you need a little more shaping in this area. This is a reversable alteration that can quickly adjust rented or existing garments.

For a mockup, remove the waistband and/or waistline facing. Take in the garment at several locations rather than in one spot, in order to maintain balance in the legs. Add or increase the size of the darts, and adjust the side seams and center back seams, blending the center back alteration into the crotch curve at the tailbone level or above. Reduce the length of the waistband or facing to fit the adjusted area.

If the waistband fits at the lower edge but bows outward from the body at the upper edge, pin in up to ½" total intake each in 2–4 spots for tiny darts in the back waistband to make more curved shape to the back waistband (Figure 13.6). This helps fit a wearer with a small waist and fuller hips. Redraw the waistband pattern to reflect the curvier shape you have created with the pinned darts.

Check that the waistline falls at a flattering level and does not reveal too much when the wearer bends over or squats, or is so high-waisted that it visually shortens the torso length, draws too much focus to the tummy, or is uncomfortable when the wearer bends over. **On an existing garment**, it is difficult to change the waistline level. **On a mockup**, you can raise the waistline position by re-drawing the waistline higher on the seam allowances or adding fabric to the upper edge of the trousers, or lower it by pinning out a horizontal fold through the garment above the hip level.

Leg Shape and Width

These aspects will be determined by the pant style, fashion style or time period, and the fabric chosen for the trousers. Be sure to check with the design reference or the research materials when fitting the legs. Also consider all of the garments that will be worn with the trousers to check the overall proportions of the ensemble as a whole.

The specific leg style will be a matter of fashion, but generally, a straight leg style that does not markedly taper inward will be a good starting point.

Be careful of very tapered trousers, which can make the hips or feet look larger in contrast to the narrow hemline. Evaluate the trousers in profile to balance the shape of the seat. Contemporary men's trousers have a fairly straight taper from the hip level toward the hem without much of an indentation at the knee level – this indentation is more common in trousers of the early-to-mid-19th century, the 1970s, or women's trousers. For all wearers, especially those with a rounded derriere, evaluate the trousers in profile and choose a leg width that complements the shape of the seat. Step back and look at the totality of the actor's body shape and proportions, the shoe size and the width of the hips when evaluating trouser leg shapes and widths.

Flat-front or pleated trousers will be the prevailing fashion in various time periods, and whenever one style is considered "out," it is more difficult to use that style onstage for a contemporary play.

Flat-front trousers tend to give a sleeker effect than do pleated trousers, and body-conscious trousers will appear younger. This should be evaluated in term of whether the character is young or old, especially if the actor playing the character is much younger than is the character. Be aware that flat-front trousers should have enough room in front that a male-bodied actor has comfortable width and depth for the crotch. Very snug flat-front trousers may require a careful conversation with the actor about to which side he "dresses" or arranges his front crotch in the trousers.

Pleated trousers have a forgiving fit but may not automatically be more flattering to the heavier figure. The extra fabric from the pleats can either smooth over the figure or can add additional bulk if the pleats do not hang perfectly vertically on the body. The best practice here is to try on both styles if they are both under consideration, and to have the wearer move and sit during the fitting to see what is more flattering on their figure.

In the late 20th and early 21st century, the standard leg opening on men's trousers at the hemline is 17″. However, this may have to be adjusted to compliment the shoe size and the width of the hips. A slim wearer with a larger shoe size may benefit from a bit more width at the hem of the trouser leg to visually balance the shoes and to have room for the trousers to fall smoothly over the shoe tops. A wearer with wide hips may also be flattered by more width at the hem of the trouser leg, to avoid the contrasting a narrow hem and wide hips that will bring attention to the hips. At the same time, very wide-legged trousers can give a heavy, skirted effect to the bottom half of the figure.

Lengths

Try the trousers on with the intended footwear. Allow the wearer to relax into their natural posture. The trouser hem should be level or angle slightly toward the back when seen in profile. The narrower the pant hem opening, the flatter the angle possible on a hem.

Trouser hem lengths will be a matter of a time period's prevailing fashion as well as of wearer flattery. The back hem of a pair of trousers classically hits anywhere from the top of the shoe heel to halfway down the length of the heel of the shoe worn with the trousers. If the trousers are worn with very high shoes, one may choose to cover most of the heel height with the pants. The longer the trouser length, the more formal the effect.

A full "break" or bend in the front of the pants is created when the pants cover the top 1/3 of the shoe. A full break is appropriate for menswear of the 1970s to the early 2000s and is the classic choice for menswear. Because actors move vigorously around the stage, a full break is a good starting point for a trouser hem length, as it will be long enough when the actor sits that their shins will not be exposed.

A half or partial or medium break is a slight bend over the upper edge of the shoe. The half break is appropriate for the middle of the 20th century and seems to be a good visual compromise between extremes if pant-length research on the period is inconclusive.

If pants are hemmed high enough that they do not break, the effect is more appropriate for 19th and early 20th century trousers, or for the most fashion-forward styles of the early 21st century. Shorter trouser lengths work best with a narrow trouser leg.

Trousers that will be added to costume stock and are expected to be reused for future productions should retain 2 ½–3″ of hem fabric with enough extra fabric left in the seam allowances that they can be lengthened without changing the shape of the trouser leg. For cuffed trousers, three times the intended cuff height needs to be available BELOW the intended pant length to allow for the cuff fold and hem. For casual trousers, the hem is often 1 ½–2″ deep and is machine sewn in place. For jeans, the conventional hem is a turn-and-turn hem that takes up approximately ½″ on each turn and is sewn with heavy topstitching thread.

When adjusting the hem position on trousers, the placement of any shaping at the garment's knee level may also need to be adjusted to fit better with the wearer's knee level.

Pockets

After the body of the trousers is fit correctly, check the position and hang of pockets. Poorly placed or poorly sewn pockets can make the garment look shoddy.

Look at the front pockets to make sure that they fit flat against the body when the wearer is standing, sitting, and moving. For the back pockets, confirm that the spacing is such that the pockets are slightly closer to the center back crotch seam than to the side seams, and that the placement looks attractive.

If the wearer needs to use the pockets onstage, check that the pockets have enough room inside to allow the wearer to put their hands into the pockets and to carry intended items. If the pockets are too shallow, extra lining can be added to extend the depth of the existing pocket bag. If the pockets are not needed, they may be stitched closed. Pocket linings may be cut out and sewn closed if they are too bulky, or a thick lining may be replaced with a thinner fabric.

For an existing garment, the layers of fabric and linings in a usable pocket will add slight bulk to the garment. If vertical slant pockets stick out slightly from the body, this may be corrected by topstitching, or hand stitching, ¼" of the upper and/or lower ends through all layers to keep the pocket in place (topstitching that matches the garment fabric will not be noticeable). If the garment fits very close to the wearer's body, the pockets can gape because they are being pulled too tightly. Slightly let out the garment at the side seams in order for the pockets to lie more smoothly, or stitch the pockets closed if they are not needed.

On lower priced trousers and on some women's jeans, faux pockets may be sewn without any linings at all. These are for decoration rather than function. If the garment has enough room to allow for a pocket bag, the stitched-down faux pocket may be opened up and a pocket bag added. However, if the garment is intended to fit very snugly, pockets may be best left non-functional, so that they do not look lumpy when items are put into them.

For a mockup, if pockets are not included in the mockup garment, draw their placement onto the garment. The layers of fabric and linings needed to construct a usable pocket will add slight bulk to the garment. It may be necessary to slightly let the garment out at the upper side seams in order to have enough room for the intended pockets to lie smoothly.

At the end of the fitting, consider whether you will need to have an additional fitting with the actor to try on more options, or whether you need to construct a second mockup to correct numerous adjustments. Trousers are complex garments and may need several tries to perfect. However, once you are comfortable with fitting trousers on a variety of bodies, you will have mastered some of the most useful skills for creating correct fit in a garment.

BIBLIOGRAPHY

The best teacher is practice with repeated fittings on a variety of wearers over time. However, the following sources were especially helpful in developing this book:

Ingham, Rosemary and Covey, Elizabeth, *The Costume Technicians Handbook, 3rd edition*; Portsmouth, NH: Heinemann, 2003

Joseph-Armstrong, Helen, *Patterningmaking for Fashion Design, 5th edition*; Upper Saddle River, NJ: Pearson Prentice Hall, 2014.

Julian, Tom, *Nordstrom Guide To Men's Style, 1st edition*; San Francisco, CA: Chronicle Books, 2009.

Julian, Tom, *Nordstrom Guide to Men's Everyday Dressing, 1st edition*; San Francisco, CA: Chronicle Books, 2010

Liechty, Elizabeth L.G., Rasband, Judith A., et al., *Fitting and Pattern Alteration: A Multi-Method Approach to the Art of Style Selection, Fitting, and Alteration, 3rd edition*; New York, NY: Fairchild Publications, Inc., 2016.

Rasband, Judith A. and Liechty, Elizabeth L.G. *Fabulous Fit: Speed Fitting and Alteration, 2nd edition*; New York, NY: Fairchild Publications, Inc., 2006.

"Men's Suit Fit Guide & Size Chart." *Nordstrom Inc., 2022.* https://www.nordstrom.com/browse/style-guide/mens-tips/mens-suits-sportcoats-fit-guide

INDEX

Note: Page number in *Italics* for figures.

www.ingramcontent.com/pod-product-compliance
Ingram Content Group UK Ltd.
Pitfield, Milton Keynes, MK11 3LW, UK
UKHW020346010325
455677UK00019B/322